Washburn and Company

Washburn and Co.'s Amateur Cultivator's Guide to the Flower and Kitchen Gardens

Containing a Descriptive List of Two Thousand Varieties of Flower and Vegetable Seeds

Washburn and Company

Washburn and Co.'s Amateur Cultivator's Guide to the Flower and Kitchen Gardens
Containing a Descriptive List of Two Thousand Varieties of Flower and Vegetable Seeds

ISBN/EAN: 9783744681094

Printed in Europe, USA, Canada, Australia, Japan

Cover: Foto ©Lupo / pixelio.de

More available books at **www.hansebooks.com**

1869. ESTABLISHED 1845. 1869.

WASHBURN & CO.'S
AMATEUR CULTIVATOR'S GUIDE
TO THE

Flower and Kitchen Garden:

CONTAINING A DESCRIPTIVE LIST OF

TWO THOUSAND VARIETIES
OF

FLOWER AND VEGETABLE SEEDS;
ALSO A LIST OF
FRENCH HYBRID GLADIOLUS.

HORTICULTURAL HALL.

RAISED AND IMPORTED BY

WASHBURN AND COMPANY,
SEED MERCHANTS,
HORTICULTURAL HALL, No. 100, TREMONT STREET,
BOSTON, MASS.

CONTENTS.

	PAGE.		PAGE.
Agricultural Seeds, in quantity	126	Lilies, Japan	2d page of cover
Annuals, Sowing and Cultivation of	4	Lilium Auratum	see cut
Biennials and Perennials, Culture of	3	Mushroom Spawn	135
Collection of Flower-Seeds, by mail	12	Novelties for 1866-67	92
Collection of French and German Flower-Seeds	90	Novelties and Specialities for 1867-68	130
		Novelties for 1869	141
Cabbage, Marblehead Drumhead	131	Ornamental Tree-Seeds	129
Collection of Vegetable-Seeds, by mail	127	Rare Seeds and Novelties	136
Collection of Kitchen-garden Seeds	127	Seeds for Hedges	129
Clover-Seeds	129	Special Directions for Cultivators of Flowers	6
Culinary Roots, Plants, &c	129	Summer Flower-Garden	3
Facilities for forwarding Seeds by mail	12	Strawberry-Seeds	129
Flower-Seeds	13-89	To our Amateur Friends	11
Flower-Gardens, Plans of	8	Tree-Seeds	129
Fruit-Seeds	129	Tobacco-Seed	152
Great Inducements for forming Clubs	12	Tritomas	152
Grain and Grass Seeds	129	Tigridias	152
Gladiolus, French Hybrid	149	Tuberoses	152
Hotbeds, Preparation of	7	Vegetables Seeds, Select List of	103
Horticultural Books	2d page of cover	Vegetables Seeds, in quantity	126
Introductory	2	Zea, or Japanese Maize	102
Lawn-Grass	128		

BOOKS FOR FARMERS AND OTHERS.

FOR SALE BY WASHBURN & CO.

Any of these books will be forwarded by mail, post-paid, on receipt of price.

Allen's (L. F.) Rural Architecture	$1 50	Garden Vegetables, and how to raise them. By Fearing Burr	2 50
Allen's (R. L.) American Farm-Book	1 50	Garden Flowers, and how to cultivate them. By Edward S. Rand, Jr	3 00
Allen's (R. L.) Diseases of Domestic Animals	1 00	Gardening for Profit. By Peter Henderson	1 50
American Bird-Fancier	30	Gardening for the South. By the late William N. White	2 00
American Pomology, by Dr. J. A. Warder	3 00	Grasses and Forage-Plants. By Charles L. Flint	2 50
American Rose-Culturist	30	Gregory on Squashes, paper	30
American Weeds and Useful Plants	1 75	Harris's Insects Injurious to Vegetation, cloth $4.00: extra	6 00
Bement's Rabbit-Fancier	30	Hop-Culture	40
Bommer's Method of making Manures	25	Hunter and Trapper	1 00
Book of Evergreens (J. Hoopes)	3 00	Leuchar's how to build Hothouses	1 50
Breck's New Book of Flowers	1 75	My Vineyard at Lakeview	1 25
Bulbs: A Treatise on Hardy and Tender Bulbs and Tubers. By Edward Sprague Rand, Jr	3 00	Norton's Scientific Agriculture	75
Buist's Flower-garden Directory	1 50	Onion Culture	20
Buist's Family Kitchen-Gardener	1 00	Our Farm of Four Acres, paper, 30c. cloth	60
Chorlton's Grape-grower's Guide	75	Pardee on Strawberry-Culture	75
Cobbett's American Gardener	75	Peat and Its Uses. By Prof. S. W. Johnson	1 25
Cole's (S. W.) American Fruit-Book	75	Quinby's Mysteries of Bee-Keeping	1 50
Country Life. By R. M. Copeland	5 00	Randall's Sheep-Husbandry	1 50
Cultivation of Flowers for the Parlor and Garden. By Edward Sprague Rand, Esq	3 00	Richardson on the Dog, paper 30 c. cloth	60
Dadd's (Geo. H.) Modern Horse-Doctor	1 50	Rivers's Miniature Fruit-Garden	1 00
Dana's Muck Manual	1 25	Saunders's Domestic Poultry, paper 40 c. bound	75
Darwin's Variation of Animals and Plants 2 Volumes	6 00	Skilful Housewife	75
Dog and Gun (Hooper's) paper, 30 c. cloth	60	Stewart's (John) Stable-Book	1 50
Downing's Fruit and Fruit-Trees of America	3 00	The Book of Roses. By Francis Parkman	3 00
Draining for Profit and Health, by G. E. Waring, Jr	1 50	Tim Bunker Papers	1 50
Eastwood on Cranberry	75	The Culture of the Grape. By W. C. Strong	3 00
Elliott's Western Fruit-Grower's Guide	1 50	Tobacco-Culture	25
Field's (Thomas W.) Pear-Culture	1 25	The Field and Garden Vegetables of America. By Fearing Burr, Jr.	5 00
Flax-Culture	50	Warder's Hedges and Evergreens	1 50
French's Farm Drainage	1 50	Woodward's Country Homes	1 50
Fuller's Grape-Culturist	1 50	Woodward's Graperies, &c.	1 50
Fuller's Small-Fruit-Culturist	1 50		
Fuller's Strawberry-Culturist	20		

THE
SUMMER FLOWER-GARDEN;

CONTAINING

BRIEF DIRECTIONS FOR THE CULTIVATION OF ANNUAL, BIENNIAL, AND PERENNIAL FLOWER-SEEDS.

ANNUAL flowers are not only among the most beautiful ornaments of the summer flower-garden, but the ease with which they are cultivated, and the long time they remain in bloom, give them the highest claim to our attention and care. Without them, however much we may admire the various showy bedding plants, a continuous and uninterrupted display of flowers, from spring till frost, cannot well be obtained; and when we add the charm of novelty, and the still greater one of variety, we have only enumerated a few of the claims of these most desirable and effective ornaments of the gardens of "the million."

In consequence of their simple culture, and the small amount of trouble they give to the amateur, as well as their comparative inexpensiveness for their rich array of beauty, they are yearly becoming more generally grown. Bedding-plants are charming objects; but the yearly propagation required for geraniums, verbenas, &c., the labor of potting and watering, and the expense of wintering them, are not within every one's means; but a few dollars expended in seeds, and a little pleasant labor in the sunny days of early spring, will give an amount of real enjoyment beyond belief. The most desolate garden may be made a scene of beauty in scarcely more than a month's time. Annuals are not what they were in former days. The skill of the hybridizer in the production of new varieties, and the diligence of the enthusiastic florist in the selection of the finest plants, have entirely changed the character of many of these flowers; and, if to this we add the new acquisitions from Japan, how could we well make up a summer-garden without them? What should we do without the grand Pœony-flowered Asters, the brilliant double Zinnias, the boldly-marked and rich-colored Petunias, the Double Portulacas, — like miniature roses, — the Heddewiggi pink, the Tropæolum, &c.? These give an entire new feature to our annuals, to be cherished by every lover of beautiful flowers.

We therefore make no apology for giving a few brief hints on the cultivation of these, as well as some of the biennials and perennials, equally important in the decoration of the flower-border.

ANNUALS.

Among florists and gardeners, the term "annual" is given to those plants which are sown in the spring, bloom and seed in the summer, and soon afterwards perish. A few are included among annuals, like the Marvel of Peru, &c., because they flower the first year; but they are only annual as regards treatment. By cultivators they have been divided into three classes; viz., *Hardy, Half-hardy*, and *Tender Annuals*, — a very convenient classification; and as such we shall treat of them here.

HARDY ANNUALS.

These are so called because they do not require any artificial heat at any period of their growth, and are capable of enduring any ordinary weather from April to November; a frosty morning, not unusual in the former month, or even in May, doing them no injury, if advanced beyond the seed-leaf. Many of them may be sown in autumn; and the young plants will make their appearance early in spring, and flower stronger than when it is deferred till April.

THE SOIL AND ITS PREPARATION.

The best soil for annuals, and indeed for most flowering plants, whether biennials or perennials, is a light, rich loam, neither too sandy nor too stiff. In such they grow readily, and attain to great perfection of bloom, with but little care; but it is hardly necessary to say that few persons have just such a soil, nor is it possible often for the cultivator to have much choice. He must take such soil as he has, and make the most of it; and, by the application of proper manures, or sand or clay, he can bring it to such a condition as to answer all the purposes of a flower-garden. Moving large masses of soil is very expensive; and writers who advise the addition of rich loam seem not to be aware of the difficulty of procuring it, or the expense and labor attending the same. For the complete garden of the wealthy, this may and should be done; but the mass of cultivators need not fear of obtaining good results without it. Deep and thorough trenching in the autumn, if possible, and the application of very old decayed manure or leaf-mould, will give the amateur a well-prepared and suitable soil. If the situation of the garden is low or damp, first of all, it should be well drained; for, in addition to the injury from excessive moisture, such soils are cold, and the young plants are injured by early frosts, when they would escape damage in one of the opposite character: neither should the situation be too dry, as, in this case, the plants would suffer in summer, and present a meagre in place of a vigorous bloom. Where the soil is too light, a thin layer of clay, if to be had, spread over the surface in the autumn, and dug in, after being pulverized by the winter frosts, in the spring, is the best remedy. This, with the use of old manure, — that which has lain a year or more, and been frequently turned over till it becomes thoroughly decayed, — will keep the garden in good condition. No unvarying rules can be given: much must be left to the judgment of the amateur. He must understand that the soil of a good garden should be deep, well pulverized, friable, and rich; and if the opposite, to make it as near that as possible.

When the flower-garden is to be a speciality, — a piece of ground set apart for that object, and laid out in geometrical order, and all the beds edged with box or thrift, — then more pains ought to be taken; and those who are about to do this, if they have not the requisite information, will consult something more than a catalogue. Our hints are intended for the mass of the people who love flowers, — who have but little leisure, — and do not wish to incur great expense in the gratification of their taste.

PERIOD FOR SOWING.

This must depend much upon the season, as well as the locality. Our Northern springs are so variable, that no definite period can be named. As a general rule, the proper time to commence sowing is about the middle of April, though a few sorts may be planted as soon as the ground can be got ready; and, for a succession, the sowing should be continued until June. In the Southern States, of course, January, February, or March will be the time to sow, as they correspond with April, May, and June of the North. The Californian annuals, now so numerous and so ornamental, are very hardy, and should be sown early, as they get well established before the heat of summer. To avoid all danger of injury, the sowing may be deferred till the last of April; but, when a little labor is of no consideration, the sowing may be made earlier, and in case of failure to grow, or subsequent injury from frost or wet, another sowing may be made when the weather is more favorable. Because we recommend April, it is not to be understood the sowing must be made at that time. The only object is to obtain a vigorous growth and early bloom. If sown in any part of May, they will flower later but abundantly throughout the latter part of summer.

MODE OF SOWING.

This must be varied according to the style of the garden and the variety to be sown. Many of the most showy and beautiful annuals are very impatient of removal; and these must be sown where they are to remain and flower. Such are the Lupins, Sweet Pea, Eschscholtzia, Poppies, &c. Indeed, most of the tap-rooted annuals will not bear transplanting. Other annuals which may be transplanted, and some of which flower stronger for removal, may either be sown in the places where they are to bloom, or in prepared beds, from whence they are to be transplanted to the flower-garden. In small gardens, undoubtedly the best way is to sow where they are to remain, thinning out the superfluous plants; this gives the least trouble: but in larger gardens, or where there are beds of early spring bulbs to be filled, the safest and best plan is to sow in well-prepared beds, and, when the young plants are of proper size, to transplant to the flower-garden.

Never sow seeds when the ground is very wet, particularly early in the spring. Select a time when the soil is neither wet nor dry. The sowing must be left to the taste of the cultivator, and the extent of surface. If there are vacant beds, the seeds may be sown in rows across the bed; but if in the border, where there are only limited spaces among the perennials or bulbs, they may be planted in masses or groups, in which mode we think annuals produce the greatest effect. Our plan has always been to mark out a circle a foot or more in diameter, and level the ground evenly and nicely with the rake; then, with the back of a trowel, press the surface firmly down; around the circle make a slight drill of the proper depth, in which the seeds are thinly sown, covering them lightly, and again pressing the earth upon the seeds with the back of the trowel. If the soil should happen to be too wet, or stiff and adhesive, fill the drill with some light, sandy loam, and make firm, as before ordered.

And here we should remark that great care should be exercised in covering the seeds. It is the great error to cover too deep; and the cause of more than half of the complaints against seedmen of selling old and worthless seeds comes from inexperience or want of judgment in sowing. No rule can be given in this respect; but, as a general guide, all large seeds, such as Sweet Peas, Lupins, &c., may be sown half an inch deep, — smaller, less; and for the smallest, such as Clarkia, Pinks, &c., a covering of one-sixteenth of an inch suffices. If sown too deep, they are longer in germinating, and are liable to decay. Avoid the general error of sowing the seeds too thick, as it causes an elongated and feeble growth, which no subsequent thinning will entirely remedy.

If the weather should be warm, or the soil very dry, it will be advisable to give a slight watering with a watering-pot with a fine rose. It is not often that seeds planted in April need watering; but later in the season they frequently require it. Use water of the same temperature of the soil; or, if warmer, it will do no harm. The waterings should be given early in the afternoon, and repeated every few days, as, when the seeds begin to swell, they are more susceptible of injury from drought, and the young plants often perish when it is neglected. A good plan with very small seeds is to cover them with an inverted flower-pot, being careful to remove it before the young seedlings appear above the surface, otherwise they will be drawn up weakly, and are likely to be injured by the hot sun or a cool night. Seeds vary in their period of germination. Some will be above ground in a week, while others require two or three weeks.

As soon as the seedlings have made three or four leaves, and are an inch high, they should be thinned out. If they are kinds which will bear removal, they may be replanted in vacant spaces in the border. No rule can be given for thinning. Tall-growing plants with spreading branches will require more room than slender-growing dwarf kinds; and in this the cultivator must be guided by the Catalogue. Stir the soil around the plants from time to time; and, if they appear crowded, a

THE SUMMER FLOWER-GARDEN.

second thinning will be of great benefit to those that remain. If the growth is not strong, from the nature of the soil, apply occasionally a very small amount of guano or bone-dust.

TRANSPLANTING.

Presuming that many cultivators will sow their seeds in prepared beds, whence the plants are to be removed to the borders to bloom, it is necessary that the work should be carefully performed to insure success. Transplanting should, if possible, always be done in cloudy weather, and towards evening. If the soil is dry, the plants will require a light watering to settle the earth around the roots; and, if warm sunny days succeed the operation, they will root all the better to have a little shade for a day or two, which may be done by spreading an old newspaper over them, or covering with a mat, removing either at night. All large-growing plants should be transplanted singly; but many of the smaller may be removed in patches, without any trouble, if the soil is previously well watered. We have found very little difficulty in moving Zinnias, Asters, and smaller plants, after they have begun to bloom. After the plants are established, they will need no other care than to tie up the taller-growing sorts to stakes to prevent the wind and rains from beating them down to the ground, and injuring their blossoms.

HALF-HARDY ANNUALS.

We have already remarked that half-hardy annuals are those that require the aid of artificial heat to assist germination; but it should be remarked that this is not absolutely necessary if the sowing is deferred until the ground is warm, — say the last of May. This is exemplified in the Portulaca, which sows itself; but the plants never appear above ground till June; and those who do not wish the trouble of sowing seed early should plant in open ground in May. But to gain time, and insure an early and abundant bloom, it is best to plant early, and assist the growth by a gentle artificial heat. Some of the most magnificent annuals are embraced in this class, of which the Aster, Zinnia, and Balsam are examples. The cheapest, most convenient, and simplest mode of doing this is the ordinary hotbed of stable manure, which gives a gentle bottom-heat quite sufficient for any of this class. Its construction is simple, and generally understood by most owners of a garden; but, as there may be some of our readers who do not know how to make a good hotbed, we add the details at the close of our remarks, observing, however, that it is so valuable an aid in the forwarding of flowers as well as vegetables, that no one having a garden can well dispense with it.

Presuming that the bed is made and all ready for use, the seeds may be sown on the prepared soil, just the same as in the open ground, and afterwards transplanted to the borders; but, as this is often attended with many failures in inexperienced hands, it is the safest to sow the seeds in pots or pans; if in neither of these, in shallow boxes. The pots should be about four or five inches in diameter, and should be perfectly clean. The soil should consist of a uniform compost of light, sandy loam, enriched with some fine leaf-mould, avoiding any raw or crude manures, which are certain to injure the young plants. Put in a few crocks at the bottom of each pot for drainage, and fill to the brim with the compost, giving the pot one or two gentle knocks on the bottom to settle the earth, which should be within half an inch of the rim. Level the surface by gently pressing it with the bottom of a pot, or a circular piece of wood made for the purpose, as this will not only be beneficial to the seeds, but assist in distributing them more evenly and regularly over the soil. Observe the same rules in regard to covering that we have already named. Some kinds will need nothing more than a thin sprinkling of earth just to fairly cover the seeds; and each pot should have the surface again gently pressed down: a slight watering with a very fine rose will complete the operation of sowing.

When all the pots are filled and planted, and marked as they should be with the name of each, and date of sowing, upon a neat label, remove them at once to the hotbed or frame, and place them perfectly level, so that each pot may receive its proper proportion of water evenly over the surface. If there are but a few pots, and a greenhouse is at hand, they may have a place on a sunny shelf near the glass, shading them during the middle of the day. Shading will also be necessary in the hotbed. The temperature should not exceed 75° or 80°, or the seeds will germinate too quick, and be drawn up weakly. As the seedlings appear above ground, give air by tilting the sashes at the back. Give water as the pots require it (which is usually once a day), and always of the same temperature of the bed, and be careful in the operation not to wash away or destroy the young and slender seedlings. During cold nights, a mat may be thrown over the frame, which will prevent the loss of heat, and maintain a more even temperature. As some of the seeds will make their appearance before others, those that appear above ground should be placed together towards the back of the frame, where they can have a greater abundance of air and be more freely watered than the others. As the plants acquire a proper size, they should be thinned out so as not to injure those that remain; and then, when farther advanced, should be transplanted into four-inch pots, — one, three, or five plants in each, according to the variety, — using a compost similar to that in which they were sown, replacing the pots in the bed, and shading slightly till they are well established, and able to bear the full sun. Those that are later in vegetating should be treated in the same manner, until all are transplanted, unless it is such kinds as will not bear removal safely; and must be allowed to remain in the pot in which they were sown, thinning them out, so that not more than three or five plants are left. The Cypress-vine, Thunbergia, &c., are of this character.

By the middle of May, the seedlings will be ready for transferring to the beds or borders where they are to bloom; but, before this is done, the plants should be "hardened off," as it is termed, in order to prepare them for the change. This is effected by gradually giving the plants more air, and when the weather is favorable, both day and night, removing the sashes wholly during the day; or, if more convenient, removing them to a cold frame, where they can be fully exposed in the daytime, and protected at night, if cold, with a covering of mats. Much must be left to the judgment of the cultivator and the amount of available space, the object being to prevent the plants from being injured by a too sudden exposure to the open air. Proceed in transplanting as we have already recommended under that head for hardy annuals.

TENDER ANNUALS.

We have stated that the classification of hardy, half-hardy, and tender annuals, was a convenient one; but really there is scarcely an annual but will grow freely in our climate in the open ground in summer. The term *tender* has been applied by English gardeners because the plants do not attain full perfection unless grown in pots in the greenhouse. Such are the Globe Amaranth, Balsam, Egg-plant, &c. All the tender annuals, therefore, may be treated in the same manner as the half-hardy, and with equal success.

BIENNIALS AND PERENNIALS.

Biennial and perennial plants are almost indispensable additions to the flower-garden, displaying their blossoms both early and late, succeeding and even flowering with the spring bulbs, and continuing long after the frost has destroyed the hardiest annuals. They are also so easily cultivated, and require so little care for their great amount of beauty, that they must be ranked as the most permanent and showy objects of the flower-border. We only need name the Larkspur, Phlox, Lychnis, Coreopsis, Saxifrage, &c., as a few among the many imposing and elegant groups.

Biennials are those plants that generally do not flower until the second year, and, after blooming, die. These include, however, many splendid species, such as the Foxglove, Canterbury Bells, Sweet Williams, Hollyhocks, &c. Perennials are plants which generally do not bloom until the second year, but continue to bloom for years in succession, and may be propagated, after once obtained, by division of the roots, growing more vigorously and flowering better if divided and re-planted every three or four years.

The proper time for sowing the seeds of hardy kinds is in April or May, at the period of sowing the hardy annuals, in order to obtain a good strong growth the first year, and a greater abundance of flowers the second; but the sowings may be continued with success as late as August, after which the plants will not become strong enough to flower the following year. Whether the seeds are sown in beds or in the border, the young plants should be thinned out, and afterwards transplanted, just as we have directed for hardy annuals, only giving them more room, and encouraging a vigorous growth by hoeing, watering, &c. On the approach of severe frosty weather, protect the plants with a light covering of leaves or coarse manure, and the succeeding year they will blossom in great profusion.

SPECIAL DIRECTIONS TO AMATEUR CULTIVATORS.

In addition to the preceding remarks, which are given as the results of our own practice for many years, and which, we think, are adequate for all general purposes, the following special directions are added for the guidance of amateurs in the treatment of many of the more choice and new flowers enumerated in our Catalogue. If carefully followed, it is hoped they will remove all causes of failure in the attempt to cultivate many of the most beautiful plants.

FRENCH AND GERMAN ASTERS. — These now justly admired and most beautiful annuals should be sown in pots, pans, or boxes, in a well-prepared soil, and placed in an exhausted hotbed or cold frame, watering them gently till the plants are an inch high; when, after hardening off by gradual exposure to the air, they should be transplanted into the open ground in a light, rich soil, placing them in rows six inches apart, shading for a few hours in the middle of the day, until well rooted. In the course of two or three weeks, they will have become stout and stocky, and ready for replanting out where they are to flower. Before transplanting, give the bed a good watering; then with a trowel take each plant up separately and carefully, and remove it to the bed or border; finish with another liberal watering, which must be repeated if the weather is dry: they will soon take root, however, and will make a rapid growth. Before the flowers expand, tie each plant up to a neat stick, and, if the soil is not rich, apply a light sprinkling of guano. The first week of June is the best period for final planting.

ZINNIAS may be treated precisely like the Aster. The double varieties, in eight distinct colors, are superb ornaments of the garden.

EPACVISES, HEATHS, AZALEAS, and RHODODENDRONS should be planted in boxes or pans, well drained, and filled with light, very sandy loam, with a small quantity of peat. Make the earth firm, and give a thorough watering before sowing. Cover the surface with a little sand, upon which the seed should be thinly scattered, covering with the least possible quantity of fine sand. Place the pans or boxes in the greenhouse, where they can be wholly shaded from the mid-day sun, and lightly damp the surface when dry. The young plants will make their appearance in three or four weeks; and, when strong enough to handle easily, transplant into boxes an inch or two apart, and gradually harden them off, so as to remove to frames or the open air.

CALCEOLARIAS, CINERARIAS, and CHINESE PRIMROSE, require similar treatment. The seeds of the former are so minute, that they are liable to be destroyed by covering; and complaints are frequent of the failure to make the seed grow. If the following directions are carefully observed, an abundance of plants may be easily raised: —

The seed should be sown in pots prepared in the following manner: The pot to be half filled with drainage, over that rough siftings of the mould, and the surface covered with soil as fine as possible, half of which should be composed of silver sand. When prepared thus, it should be watered with a fine rose, immediately after which sow the seed carefully without any covering of soil. The pots should then be placed under a close frame or hand-glass, in a shady part of the garden (no artificial heat being required). In large establishments, of course, they may have propagating or other

THE SUMMER FLOWER-GARDEN.   7

houses that will do, where the same kind of moist temperature could be obtained; but any exposure to the sun must be carefully guarded against by mats or paper. If the situation is of the proper temperature, they will require watering but very seldom. Directly the seedings are strong enough, they must be pricked off in pots prepared as before, and placed in the same situation. From the store-pots they will require to be potted off singly; after this they will grow very rapidly. Through the winter, the plants will thrive well on the shelves near the glass, in the greenhouses; and, to obtain fine specimens, they must be shifted freely till the flower-stalks have started, and should always be smoked with tobacco directly the green-fly appears, as no plants in cultivation so readily suffer from this insect as the Calceolaria.

It is necessary to remark, that one of the most frequent causes of the appearance of these injurious insects is the plant becoming *root-bound;* to avoid which evil, it is important that it should frequently be repotted during the growing season.

ACACIAS of all kinds should have *scalding* water poured over the seeds, and be allowed to soak for twelve or twenty-four hours: they should then be planted in pots, in light, rich, sandy soil, covering one-fourth of an inch deep, and placed in the hotbed or greenhouse.

GLOBE AMARANTH, LINUM, and CYPRESS-VINE seeds should be soaked in tepid water for twelve hours to insure a quick germination. Rub the seeds with a little dry sand when ready for sowing.

LILIUMS of all kinds should have their seed planted immediately they are gathered, if possible, as they vegetate sooner. They remain good, however, for three or four years, but, when sown in spring, do not often vegetate until the second year.

CYCLAMENS should be sown in the greenhouse or hotbed, in pans of light rich soil, well drained. Transplant singly into pots, and keep them constantly growing the first year.

STOCKS of the winter-flowering varieties should be sown in July, and pricked off singly into small pots, shifting them as they require it, and keeping them in cold frames as long as it can be safely done.

CANNA-SEEDS have a hard, horny covering, and require to have the seed soaked in warm water for ten or twelve hours, planting them in hotbed while the heat is brisk and strong. Transfer to the open ground June 1st, and take up the roots before hard frosts.

GLOXINIAS and ACHIMENES require to be grown in pots in the greenhouse, or a warm frame. The soil should be light and rich,—leaf-mould, loam, and sand.

FERNS are easily raised from the spores (or seeds) with a little care. Sow in pots which should be half filled with a good drainage of crocks, and the remainder, to within a inch of the rim, with coarse sandy peat or leaf-mould; make the surface smooth, and cover with a thin layer of sand; on this sprinkle the spores. Set the pot in a pan of water in a warm, shady part of the greenhouse, and cover with a pane of glass. In a month or two, the plants will be ready to pot off singly in small pots.

THE CONSTRUCTION AND MANAGEMENT OF HOTBEDS.

We have already alluded to the importance of a hotbed for the successful growth of many of the half-hardy annuals and more delicate greenhouse plants. Though most or all kinds of seeds may be raised in a frame without bottom heat, yet this can only be done so late in the season, when the weather has become warm, that many of the annuals are late in blooming, and the greenhouse plants do not ripen and mature their wood, and are therefore ill adapted to winter well. It is to obviate this that the hotbed is recommended to all amateurs. It is so easily made, and at such slight expense, that it will well repay all who would secure an abundance of flowers early in the season.

SITUATION OF THE BED.—This should be in a warm position, fully exposed to the sun, facing the east or south, and sheltered by a fence or hedge on the west or north. The soil should, if possible, be light and dry, as in this case the bed can be sunk a foot or more in the ground; but, if damp or cold, it should be built upon the surface.

MAKING THE BED.—Manure fresh from the stable is best. This should be thrown over and thoroughly shaken up with the fork, making it into a conical heap. In this state it should be allowed to remain four or five days, at the end of which time it should be turned over, shaking it up as before. At the end of another three or four days, it will be ready to make up the bed. Lay out the ground six inches larger than the frame, and put down a stake at each corner. The frame may be of any size; but the most convenient is nine by three feet, which will take three lights three by six feet, the ordinary size, which can always be had ready made. Proceed to build up the bed to the height of two and a half or three feet, making it rather firm, and watering, if the manure is dry. When the bed is finished, put on the lights, and let it stand to settle and exhaust the violent heat. In a day or two add three or four inches of light sandy loam, spreading it evenly over the bed. If the seeds are to be sown in the soil of the bed, two or three more inches should be added; but if in pots, no addition will be necessary.

The pots being ready, and sown with the various seeds, should be put into the frame, shading them during the day, and regulating the temperature, by tilting the lights at the back, both night and day, and covering at night with mats. Plunge the pots in the soil, and, with proper care, the seeds will soon be above the soil. A thermometer placed in the bed will be the safest guide to the inexperienced. It should not rise above $85°$ in the day, nor sink below $60°$ at night. As the heat declines, linings of fresh manure should be applied around the outside of the bed; but, ordinarily, for seeds this is not necessary.

The length or number of the frames is immaterial; but they should be nine to twelve inches deep at the front, and fifteen to eighteen inches at the back. This will give a good slope to carry off the rain. Cold frames are simply the hotbed-frame set upon a warm spot of ground, covering it at night to keep in the warmth accumulated during the day.

THE FLOWER-GARDEN.

The arrangement of a flower-garden must depend so much upon the taste or fancy of the cultivator, that it is very difficult to lay down any rules applicable to general use. All we can do to aid the inexperienced is to give such plants as display correct principles in their general features, which will serve as a guide in grounds of smaller or larger extent. Of course, we have reference to flower-gardens, or spots of ground set apart for annuals, bedding-plants, or bulbs, as any thing more extensive would be beyond the scope of a catalogue.

Where the flower-garden already exists, and is laid out in beds or borders for miscellaneous plants, all the information necessary to the amateur will be found in our preceding remarks, except that, perhaps, in reference to the disposition of colors. If, however, the form is not a fanciful one, or one laid out in the true principles of the geometrical style, it may be remodelled upon some plan which will combine the merits of those we now annex.

Commencing with the simplest form of ground, where there is no pretension to artistic display, the two following will be found well adapted for annuals or bedding-plants, or the two combined.

In the first plan (No. 1), the ground may be arranged as follows: In the centre may be double Zinnias, if a grand display is desired; but if not, then Zinnias, Marigolds, Asters, and similar tall-growing annuals, placing the tallest in the centre. The eight small beds adjoining the centre one may be planted in alternate colors, or mixed, with Clintonia, Portulaca, Verbenas, Pansies, Agrostemma, Lobelias, &c. The four larger beds may be planted in four different colors, or mixed, or in the ribbon style; in the latter case using Perilla Nankinensis for the centre row, and other decided colors for the outer rows, which should be dwarf at the edge. The four corner-beds may be filled with Mignonette, Sweet Alyssum for the fragrance, or with other more showy plants.

No. 1.   No. 2.

The second plan (No. 2) admits of a greater display, and particularly if masses of one color are desired. The centre may be filled with any tall plants of one color; viz., Zinnias, Asters, Marigolds, or Balsams. Two of the four oval beds may be Portulaca, scarlet and white, or golden and scarlet; the other two with blue and white Lobelia, or crimson and white Candytuft. Two of the four large beds between the oval ones may be planted with Tropæolums in two colors, and the other two with crimson and variegated Petunias. The four small beds may be planted with Abronia umbellata, Nolana, Phlox Drummondii, and Linum Grandiflora. The four oval corner-beds may be planted with ornamental foliaged-plants, Perilla in two, and Coleus Verschaffeltii in the other two. Four of the small corner-beds may be filled with Mignonette and Alyssum, and four with Dianthus

THE SUMMER FLOWER-GARDEN.

Heddiwiggi. These may be varied to suit the fancy of the possessor with the newest annuals described in the Catalogue, selecting them according to colors, and height of growth. All the beds should be edged with box or thrift. The extent of ground is thirty-two feet square.

For more artistic and complete grounds, we add two plans from two of the most elegant flower-gardens of England.

The first plan (No. 3) is extensive and elaborate in design, and evinces artistic skill and arrangement of a high order. The length of the garden is a hundred and sixty feet, and the width seventy-two feet.' The walks are of gravel, and the beds are all edged with box. It may be filled with bedding-plants or with annuals; and, supposing the amateur to desire a mixture of the two, the following is an appropriate list, Scarlet Geraniums and Verbenas being the most effective of bedding-plants:

1. Verbena (blue).
2. Verbena (white).
3. Pansies, of the fine showy sorts.
4. Portulaca (white).
5. Tom Thumb Geranium.
6. Verbena (striped).
7. Portulaca (golden).
8. Campanula Carpatica, with Tree Rose in the centre.
9. The same.
10. Tom Thumb Geranium.
11. Portulaca (white).
12. Verbena (striped).
13. Portulaca (golden).
14. Pansies of the fine showy sorts.
15. Verbena (white).
16. Verbena (blue).
17. Ageratum.
18. Heliotrope.
19. Tom Thumb Geranium.
20. Verbena, Sunset (rose).
21. Portulaca (golden).
22. Portulaca (scarlet).
23. Same as No. 8.
24. Geranium, Lucia Rosea (pink).
25. Tom Thumb Geranium.
26. Tom Thumb Geranium.
27. Geranium, Lucia Rosea (pink).
28. Portulaca (scarlet).
29. Tom Thumb Geranium.
30. Heliotrope.
31. Verbena, Sunset.
32. Portulaca (golden).
33. Ageratum.
34. Same as No. 8.
35. Vase, or Statue. If a vase, to be filled with Verbenas, Petunias, &c. If a statue, to be surrounded with a circle of Oxalis Floribunda.

But, when it is intended to be filled with annuals, this may easily be done by substituting Candytuft, Alyssum, Eschscholtzia, Lobelia, Agrostemma, Petunias, Dwarf Convolvulus, Clarkias, &c.

The last plan which we give (No. 4) is a copy of the flower-garden of the Duchess of Bedford, at Camden Hill, near London. In harmony of arrangement, it stands very high ; and, offering as it does a great variety in the disposition of the beds, it contains, in an eminent degree, the two great elements of a select garden, — harmony and variety. "Two things," says a well-known writer, "are necessary to the beauty of a flower-garden, — harmony and variety. Harmony consists in agreeableness of form, likeness of size, and relation of color: variety is the indefinite diversity of vegetative existence. If there is variety merely, the garden is strange, extraordinary, fantastic; it is not fine. If harmony alone is displayed, then it is monotonous, dull, and wearisome. But in the happy combination of the two resides its power to awaken agreeable sensations, and impart delight. This union is well exemplified in this plan."

No scale is given; but we suppose the ground to contain a circle of one hundred feet, — about fifty feet to the inch. The plants employed, annuals and bedding-plants, would be as follows, according to the numbers:—

THE SUMMER FLOWER-GARDEN.

CENTRE.

1. Sweet Alyssum (white).
2. Lobelia (blue).
3. Verbenas (purple).
4. Portulaca (yellow).
5. Anagallis (blue).
6. Verbenas (scarlet).

FIRST CIRCLE.

7. Lobelia (blue).
8. Eschscholtzia (yellow).
9. Portulaca (scarlet).
10. Nierembergia Gracilis (white).
11. Verbena (deep purple).
12. Portulaca (yellow).
13. Lobelia (blue).
14. Verbena (scarlet).
16. Portulaca (yellow).
17. Linium Grandiflorum (crimson).
18. Sweet Alyssum (white).

SECOND CIRCLE.

19. Petunia (purple).
20. Cacalia Coccinea.
21. Convolvulus Minor (blue).
22. Anagallis (blue).
23. Sanvitalia Procumbens (yellow).
24. Verbena (lilac).
25. Verbena (scarlet).
26. Ageratum Albiflorum (white).
27. Nemophila Insignis.
28. Godetia Lepida (lilac).
29. Gilia Capitata.
30. Œnothera Drummondii.

No. 4.

THIRD CIRCLE.

31. Linum Grand. Rubrum (scarlet).
32. Clarkia Elegans (lilac).
33. Clintonia Elegans (blue).
34. Eschscholtzia (yellow).
35. Coreopsis Burridgii (yellow and brown).
36. Verbena (scarlet).
37. Candytuft (white).
38. Eutoca Viscida (blue).
39. Arctotis (yellow).
40. Phlox Drummondii Alba (white).
41. Geranium (scarlet).
42. Candytuft (crimson).

FOURTH CIRCLE.

43. Petunia (white).
44. Lobelia (blue).
45. Eschscholtzia (yellow).
46. Petunia (purple).
47. Geranium (scarlet).
48. Senecio or Jacobæa (purple).
49. Verbena (purple).
50. Portulaca (yellow).
51. Candytuft (white).
52. Verbena (scarlet).
53. Convolvulus Minor (blue).
54. Œnothera Drummondii (yellow).

FIFTH CIRCLE.

55. Phlox Drummondii (rose).
56. Bartonia Aurea (yellow).
57. Asters (white).
58. Salvia (scarlet).
59. Double Peony Aster (blue).
60. Double Zinnia (yellow).
61. Petunia (purple).
62. Candytuft (white).
63. Double Zinnia (scarlet).
64. Geranium (scarlet).
65. Double Asters (blue).
66. Double Zinnia (scarlet).

TO OUR AMATEUR FRIENDS AND CUSTOMERS.

AFTER the publication of our Catalogues for thirty years, during which period immense additions have been made to the list of Flowers and Vegetables, we now present our friends with a full and complete list of the accumulations of so long a time, with accurate descriptions of all that are really valuable, or worthy of cultivation. In doing this, we embrace the opportunity to offer a few friendly and familiar remarks.

From the small catalogue of a few hundred varieties, through the exertions of zealous florists, collectors, and skilful men, the number has been increased to thousands; while, during the same time, the cultivators of beautiful flowers have increased in a very much greater ratio. Hence the demand now of something more than a mere list of names to enable the inexperienced to obtain some knowledge of what they desire to plant, and the opportunity of making a judicious selection from the great number which are so well worthy a place in every garden. This has been almost impossible in the limits of an ordinary catalogue; and, to furnish the information really needed, it has now assumed the form of "The Cultivator's Guide to the Flower and Kitchen Garden."

Having enumerated in our Catalogues, from year to year, all these additions in a brief manner, we deem it quite unnecessary to say they have been heretofore, or that our present one is, without a rival, or is not surpassed by any one of the kind. This we leave to our amateur friends, who can carefully compare our Guide with others, either at home or abroad. Neither shall we speak of its truthfulness or beauty. Thirty years have, we trust, been quite sufficient to establish the former: the latter can easily be detected at a single glance. It is not the result of one or ten years' experience in the growth of numerous varieties, but of THIRTY YEARS devoted to the cultivation of every flower or vegetable embraced in these pages.

As regards the *freshness* of our seeds, or their *quality*, we have nothing to add. Our numerous customers throughout the country know us too well to ask any additional guaranty than that of the many years we have labored to place before them all the treasures of the flower-garden or conservatory, selected from the best sources in Europe and our own country, or grown or originated by us. Our long correspondence with the cultivators of England, France, Germany, and Prussia, has enabled us to be the *first* to possess every thing new, whenever introduced. The novelties described in our present Catalogue are nearly three times the number of those enumerated by any dealer in America.

We do not think it necessary to add that our stock is obtained without regard to price; for no really beautiful and first-class flower-seed can be had at a low rate. This is impossible. All who know any thing of the growth of seeds, know that the finest Double Asters, Zinnias, Petunias, Portulacas, &c., are so sparingly produced, that the supply is quite insufficient for the demand. Every lover of flowers cannot afford to procure the highest-priced seeds; and those who cannot are content with those of moderate excellence at a reasonable rate. Because they are cheap, it does not follow they should be rubbish, as is too often the case. It is often difficult to distinguish between those of moderate excellence and the so-called choice varieties.

Our seeds are put up in packages, with our name upon each, and a brief description of their quality, and the usual time of sowing. These are sent by mail, when desired, at the prices named, and postage paid, to any part of the United States or Canada; except peas, beans, corn, and potatoes, for which an additional remittance of 8 cents for every pound is required. When large orders are received, the seeds will be securely packed, and will be forwarded by express. All our orders are intended to be filled as soon as received; but, in the busiest season, it is impossible, with the very large quantity of orders, to prevent the delay of a few days.

COMMENDATIONS. — To attempt the publication of the numerous commendatory letters would fill several pages of our Catalogue. Gratifying as this would be to us, we are compelled to omit even the briefest extracts from the hundreds of letters expressing the satisfactory manner in which their orders have been executed, and the pleasure derived from the cultivation of our seeds.

COLLECTIONS OF FLOWER-SEEDS, BY MAIL, FREE OF POSTAGE TO PURCHASERS.

In order to more extensively disseminate our choice varieties of Flower-seeds throughout the country, giving those who reside at a distance the same facilities for procuring them as those who have the opportunity to make personal application, we put up select assortments expressly for sending by mail, giving particular attention to this department of our trade. The low rate of postage enables us to supply distant customers with all the choicest seeds upon the same terms as those who are near the market. Orders may be forwarded to us with the understanding that the seeds we furnish are of the very best quality, and the selection such as will gratify every purchaser. Our collections are made up with great care, and all the varieties, unless those entirely new, are such as we have seen and cultivated ourselves, and can confidently recommend; many of the superb double varieties being such as have been raised from the fine flowers, specimens of which have obtained the highest prizes of the Massachusetts Horticultural Society.

No. 1 contains twenty-four varieties of choice and beautiful Annuals $1.00
No. 2 contains twenty-four varieties of the finest hardy Biennials and Perennials . . 1.00
No. 3 contains ten varieties of extra fine Annuals and Perennials, including the beautiful French Asters, Double Camellia Balsams, Double German Stocks, and other choice flowers 1.00
No. 4 contains five varieties of very select flowers, including the best large English Pansies, Carnations, new Verbenas, new Double Zinnias, etc. 1.00
No. 5 contains one hundred varieties of Annuals, Biennials, and Perennials, including new and choice varieties 5.00
No. 6 contains fifty varieties of Annuals, Biennials, and Perennials 2.50
No. 7 contains twenty varieties of hardy Annuals, Biennials, and Perennials, for autumn sowing, in August and September 1.00
No. 8 contains fifteen different and choice kinds of greenhouse-plant seeds 3.00

The seeds in these assortments are all of our own selection. Purchasers who had rather make a selection from the Catalogue can do so, and a proportionate discount will be made.

FORMATION OF CLUBS.

The extensive distribution of our seeds is an especial object. Our Catalogue has been prepared with much labor; and it has been our constant aim to make it a complete and safe guide to the cultivator, both in the selection of varieties and their growth. As an additional inducement to individuals who desire to possess a large collection, or for the formation of clubs for the same object, we offer to send by mail, *free of postage*, to any address in the United States, on receipt of the amount of the order, seeds selected as follows:—

Purchasers remitting $1.00 may select seeds at Catalogue prices, amounting to $1.15
" " 2.00 " " " " 2.35
" " 3.00 " " " " 3.65
" " 4.00 " " " " 4.95
" " 5.00 " " " " 6.25
" " 10.00 " " " " 13.00
" " 20.00 " " " " 27.00
" " 30.00 " " " " 41.50

Persons desiring us to make their selections may rely upon our sending only those which are really showy and handsome, and easy to cultivate. We believe that our experience will enable us to make selections that cannot fail to give entire satisfaction to any lady or gentleman who may send us their orders.

In sending orders for seeds by mail, it will be only necessary to give the date of the Catalogue from which the selection is made, and the numbers, instead of the names, of the varieties. The name of the person to whom they are to be sent, and the names of the Town and State, should be so plainly written, that there may be no mistaking a single letter. We often receive letters containing money, the signatures of which are so indistinct as to make it almost impossible to decide where and to whom the seeds are ordered to be sent.

The above prices apply only to flower and garden seeds in packets; for prices by ounce and pound, see vegetable-seed department, in this Catalogue. Prices to dealers on application.

Address,   **WASHBURN & CO.,**
HORTICULTURAL HALL, BOSTON, MASS.

THE
AMATEUR CULTIVATOR'S GUIDE
TO THE FLOWER GARDEN.

To aid in making selections of seeds, the botanical name is given, and the popular name when there is such, together with the natural order to which it belongs, as indicative of the general character of the flower. These, with the full remarks, will enable the amateur to make a judicious selection.

In giving orders for seeds, it is preferable to mention the numbers; but, as the numbers are often changed, it is absolutely necessary to give the date of Catalogue.

FLOWER SEEDS.

ABRONIA UMBELLATA.

ABRONIA. Nat. Ord., *Nyctaginiaceæ.*

A charming plant, with verbena-like heads of sweet-scented flowers. Very effective in beds, rock-work, or in baskets suspended in a conservatory; growing freely in any light, rich soil, and flowering from August to October.

NO.		PRICE
1	Abronia Umbellata, rosy-lilac, half-hardy annual; from California. Half ft. high .	$0.10

ABUTILON. Nat. Ord., *Malvaceæ*.

These flowers are extremely beautiful for the conservatory; they are natives of Brazil, and half shrubby, with vine-like leaves and bell-shaped flowers, being richly veined and striped, of a wax-like appearance. Many of the varieties succeed well in the open ground during the summer. Half-hardy.

No.		Price
2	Abutilon Alphonse Karr. Orange, veined with crimson. Very fine. 5 feet.	$0.25
3	— Beranger. Yellow, striped with brown. 6 feet	.25
4	— Duc de Malakoff. Yellow, veined with maroon. Very fine. 6 feet	.25
5	— Esculentum. Very fine. 5 feet	.25
6	— Floribundum. Fine yellow. 5 feet	.25
7	— Hybridum. Lemon-color. 5 feet	.25
8	— Marmoratum. A beautiful variety, flowering in great profusion all winter; producing pure white flowers, veined and marbled with bright rose. One of the best. 6 feet	.25
9	— Mixed	.25

ABOBRA. Nat. Ord., *Cucurbitaceæ*.

A rare and extremely pretty tuberous perennial climbing Cucurbitaceæ, with elegant cut glossy dark-green foliage, and small oval vivid scarlet fruits. Suitable for planting out during summer, forming beautiful garlands.

10	Abobra Virdiflora	.25

ACACIA. Nat. Ord., *Leguminosæ*.

In praise of this class of ornamental shrubs, it is almost impossible to speak too highly: they are not only of invaluable use for greenhouse decoration, but also, during summer, they will be of equal service in the flower garden, where their beautiful foliage and neat habit alone cannot fail to render them very attractive.

They are all remarkably fine in foliage; but a lophantha and longiflora are pre-eminently so. Acacia Julibrissin is half-hardy and elegant, with tassel-like tufts of rosy flowers. Previous to sowing, soak the seed in water at 120° for six hours. Greenhouse shrubs.

11	Acacia Albicans. White, with beautiful silvery foliage; from Mexico. 5 feet	.25
12	— Armata. Golden ball-like flowers. 5 feet	.25
13	— Asparagoides. Yellow, very choice; from New Holland. 6 feet.	.25
14	— Argyrophylla. Superb; yellow, silvery foliage. 6 feet.	.25
15	— Cultriformis. Yellow; from New Holland. 5 feet	.25
16	— Cocoinea. The most novel of the Acacias; color, bright rose, fine foliage. 5 ft.	.25
17	— Capensis. Yellow. 5 feet	.25
18	— Dealbata. Canary-yellow foliage, very graceful; from Van Dieman's Land. 5 ft.	.25
19	— Douglassii. Yellow, graceful, and distinct; from North America. 5 feet	.25
20	— Grandis. Golden yellow, a most beautiful species; from New Holland. 6 feet	.25
21	— Ixiophylla. Golden yellow, a very graceful and handsome species; from Swan River. 6 feet	.25
22	— Julibrissin (silk-tree). A hardy and elegant shrub, with tassel-like tufts of beautiful rosy flowers; from Persia. 5 feet	.10
23	— Longifolia. Yellow, foliage long and slender; from New South Wales. 5 feet	.25
24	— Lophantha. Yellow, beautiful foliage; from New South Wales. 5 feet	.10
25	— Nematophyila. Bright yellow; a splendid acquisition, called one of the best of its class, flowering freely nearly the whole year; fine habit. 6 feet	.25
26	— Trinervata. Fine yellow; from New Holland. 5 feet	.25
27	— Xylophylloides. (New.) The most splendid of all the Acacias, producing rich clusters of golden blossoms, light-green lanceolated foliage; from New Holland. 6 feet	.25

ACANTHUS. Nat. Ord., *Acanthaceæ*.

These deserve a place in every collection, from their stately appearance, and the legend of their leaves having given the first idea of the capital of the Corinthian order of architecture. They require a good sandy loam, and plenty of room. Hardy perennials.

28	Acanthus Mollis. White; from Italy. 3 feet	.05
29	— Spinosus. White; from Europe. 3 feet	.05

ABOBRA VIRIDIFLORA. See page 14.

TO THE FLOWER GARDEN. 15

ACHILLEA. Nat. Ord., *Compositæ*.

Belonging to the genus known under their English name of Milfoil. Hardy perennial.

NO.		PRICE
30	Achillea Filipendula. Yellow; from Caspian Sea. 5 feet	$0.05

ACHIMENES. Nat. Ord., *Gesneraceæ*.

These are among the most beautiful plants for the decoration of a greenhouse or conservatory during the summer, being of dwarf, compact, branching habit, and flowering abundantly throughout the whole season. Grown in masses, in large pots or pans, they form superb objects for exhibition. Their culture is simple. After flowering, water should be gradually withheld, and allowed to remain in a dry state until they commence growing again.

| 31 | Achimenes. Mixed. Saved from one of the largest collections in Europe | .25 |

ACROCLINIUM. Nat. Ord., *Compositæ*.

An elegant new annual from Swan River, producing beautiful everlasting flowers resembling the Rhodanthe Manglesii, but much larger; should be grown in every collection; fine for winter bouquets, flowering in any garden soil. Hardy annuals.

32	Acrolinium Atroroseum. Deep rose-color. 1 foot	.10
33	—— Roseum. Light rose. 1 foot	.10
34	—— Album. Pure white. 1 foot	.10

ACONITUM (Monkshood). Nat. Ord., *Ranunculaceæ*.

A common border plant, commonly known as Monkshood, growing freely in any situation. Hardy perennial; from Europe.

| 35 | Aconitum Napellis. Mixed, blue and white. 2 feet | .05 |

ADIANTUM. Nat. Ord., *Cryptogamia*.

| 36 | Adiantum (Maiden Hair). Mixed. A beautiful species of fern | .50 |

AGERATUM. Nat. Ord., *Compositæ*.

Valuable plants for large beds or borders, and very useful for pot culture. Very good for bouquets. Hardy annuals.

37	Ageratum Mexicanum. Light-blue; from Mexico. 1½ feet	.10
38	—— Odoratum (fragrant). Much like the Mexicanum; from Mexico	.05
39	—— Alba. White	.10
40	—— Albiflorum Nanum. Dwarf, white; fine for pots	.10
41	—— Cœruleum Nanum. Dwarf-blue; fine for pots or open ground	.10
42	—— Conspicuum. New. Pure white	.10
43	—— Superbum. Dark-blue, fine	.10

AGAPANTHUS (African Lily). Nat. Ord., *Hemerocalidaceæ*.

A highly ornamental plant, with large, handsome heads of bloom; very effective for parterres, terraces, gravel-walks, or by the side of lakes and ponds; will not bear hard frost; may be kept in the cellar during the winter.

| 44 | Agapanthus Umbellatus. Blue; half-hardy bulb; from Africa. 2 feet | .25 |

AGROSTEMMA. Nat. Ord., *Caryophyllaceæ*.

Commonly called Rose Campion. Are perfectly hardy, very easily raised from seeds, and will well repay the little care they require. The flowers are produced on long stems, blooming freely throughout the season. Hardy perennial. For annual varieties, see Viscaria.

45	Agrostemma Coronaria. Deep crimson; from Russia. 2 feet	.05
46	—— Alba. White; from Russia. 2 feet	.05
47	—— Mixed. The above mixed	.05

AGROSTIS. Nat. Ord., *Gramineæ*.

These rank high among the ornamental grasses from their delicate and graceful growth, and are very useful for winter bouquets; will grow in any good garden soil. Hardy annuals.

16 AMATEUR CULTIVATOR'S GUIDE

NO.		PRICE
48	**Agrostis Dulcis.** Fine; from Greece	$0.10
49	—— **Effusus.** Fine; from Europe	.10
50	—— **Nebulosa.** One of the most graceful and elegant; from Europe	.10
51	—— **Plumosa.** Rare; from Europe	.10

ALONSOA. NAT. ORD., *Scrophularineæ.*

These plants are very ornamental, either in the greenhouse, or grown as annuals in the open border during the summer, flowering freely from June until frost. Tender perennials.

52	**Alonsoa Grandiflora** (large flowered). Deep scarlet. 2 feet	.10
53	—— **Incisifolia** (cut foliage). Orange scarlet. 2 feet	.10
54	—— **Warszewiczi.** Bright crimson; from Chili. 1½ feet	.10

ALSTRŒMERIA. NAT. ORD., *Amaryllidaceæ.*

This is a genus of tuberous-rooted plants, with beautiful flowers; requiring to be grown in a sheltered position to have them in perfection. Half-hardy perennials.

55	**Alstrœmeria Van Houtte.** Finest hybrids. 1½ feet	.25

ALYSSUM. NAT. ORD., *Cruciferæ.*

One of the most useful, free-flowering little plants either for growing in pots, on rockwork, or the open border, the annuals varieties blooming nearly the whole summer.

56	**Alyssum Argenteum.** Yellow, silvery foliage; from Switzerland. Hardy perennial. 1 ft.	.05
57	—— **Benthamii.** White, fine hardy annual. 1 foot	.05
58	—— **Saxatile.** Yellow, very showy, hardy perennial. 1 foot	.05
59	—— **Sweet (Maritima).** A well-known fragrant little annual, from England. 1 foot	.05
60	—— **Wiersbeck's.** White and yellow, half-hardy perennial	.10

AMARANTHUS. NAT. ORD., *Amarantaceæ.*

Ornamental foliaged plants, of an extremely graceful and interesting character, producing a striking effect, whether grown for the decoration of the conservatory or out-door flower-garden. If the seeds are sown early, and planted out the last of May or in June, in rich soil, they make exceedingly handsome specimens for the centre of beds, or mixed flower or shrubbery borders. Half-hardy annuals.

61	**Amaranthus Melancholicus.** New. A beautiful novelty, rivalling the Perrilla Nankinensis for groups and edgings; of dwarfer habit than the latter, and of a lively blood-red-colored foliage	.10
62	—— **Caudatus** (Love Lies Bleeding). Very pretty; from East Indies. 3 feet	.05
63	—— **Hypochondriacus** (Prince's Feather). Red; from East Indies. 3 feet	.05
64	—— **Monstrosus.** Very large and showy; from East Indies. 3 feet	.05
65	—— **Sanguineus.** A fine dark variety; from India. 3 feet	.10
66	—— **Tricolor** (Joseph's Coat). An old favorite, the chief beauty of which consists in its beautiful yellow, scarlet, and green variegated leaves. 2 feet	.05

AMMOBIUM. NAT. ORD., *Compositæ.*

A fine everlasting plant, valuable for making dried winter bouquets; pretty for the garden.

67	**Ammobium Alatum.** White; from New Holland. Hardy annual. 2 feet	.05

ANAGALLIS. NAT. ORD., *Primulaceæ.*

This is a class of beautiful trailing plants, that will be found highly ornamental for bedding purposes, as they bloom all the season. The Anagallis is also an old favorite for growing in greenhouses, presenting an extremely graceful appearance when cultivated in pots or vases. Hardy annuals.

68	**Anagallis India** (Indian Pimpernel). Blue, trailing; from Nepaul. Half foot	.05
69	—— —— **Carnea.** Flesh-color. Half foot	.10
70	—— —— **Coccinea.** Scarlet. Half foot	.10
71	—— —— **Grandiflora Cœrulea.** Splendid large flowers; blue. Half foot	.10
72	—— —— **Rubra.** Beautiful red. Half foot	.10
73	—— —— **Eugenie.** Beautiful light-blue, shaded from the centre to pure white. Half ft.	.10
74	—— —— **Garibaldii.** Rich vermilion; rare. Half foot	.10

AQUILEGIA GLANDULOSA. See page 93.

TO THE FLOWER GARDEN. 17

NO.		PRICE
75	Anagallis Grandiflora Memoria dell' Etna. New; large flowers, bright scarlet. Half ft.	$0.10
76	—— —— Napoleon III. Rich crimson maroon. Half foot	.10
78	—— —— Philippii. Large; blue. Half foot	.10
79	—— Mixed (India varieties). Good	.05
80	—— Mixed (Large-flowered varieties). Very fine	.10

ANCHUSA. Nat. Ord., *Boragineæ*.

Coarse growing plants, natives of the south of Europe, remarkable for their intensely blue flowers. Hardy perennials.

81	Anchusa Arvalis. Blue. 2 feet	.05
82	—— Italica. Delicate blue. 2 feet	.05

ANEMONE. Nat. Ord., *Ranunculaceæ*.

All the plants belonging to this genus are beautiful, and well deserving of cultivation; succeed well in any light soil. Hardy perennials.

83	Anemone Coronaria. Mixed from selected flowers. Half foot	.10
84	—— Pulsatilla (Pasque Flower). Violet.	.10

ANTHOXANTHUM. Nat. Ord., *Gramineæ*.

85	Anthoxanthum Gracile. A very pretty ornamental grass, from Sicily. Hardy annual. Half foot	.10

ANTIRRHINUM (Snapdragon). Nat. Ord., *Scrophulariaceæ*.

The Snapdragon, or Antirrhinum, is one of our most showy and useful border plants. Amongst the more recently improved varieties of this valuable genus are large, finely shaped flowers, of the most brilliant colors, with beautifully marked throats; will bloom the first season from seed, and are very effective in beds or mixed borders. Half-hardy perennials.

86	Antirrhinum Majus Album. Pure white. 2 feet	.10
87	—— —— Brilliant. Crimson and white. 2 feet	.10
88	—— —— Delila. Carmine, white throat. 2 feet	.10
89	—— —— Firefly. Orange, scarlet, and white. 2 feet	.10
90	—— —— Galathea. Crimson, yellow, and white. 2 feet	.10
91	—— —— Ghestia. Dark-crimson, rich foliage. 2 feet	.10
92	—— —— Henry IV. Bright cinnamon. 2 feet	.10
93	—— —— Papilionaceum. Bright scarlet and white; splendid. 2 feet	.10
94	—— —— Variegata. Beautiful, striped. 2 feet	.10
95	—— Nanum Album. Dwarf; pure white. 1 foot	.10
96	—— —— Aureum Striatum. Striped. 1 foot	.10
97	—— —— Kermesina Splendens. Crimson. 1 foot	.10
98	—— —— Delila. Carmine and yellow, with white throat. 1 foot	.10
99	—— —— Firefly. Orange, scarlet, and yellow. 1 foot	.10
100	—— Extra fine, mixed	.10
101	—— Good, mixed	.05

AQUILEGIA (Columbine). Nat. Ord., *Ranunculaceæ*.

This pretty and interestingly varied genus of plants scarcely meets with the amount of appreciation it deserves; it is an extremely showy and ornamental early summer flowering herbaceous plant, combining the most curious forms with the most beautiful and striking colors; succeeds in any garden soil. Hardy perennials.

102	Aquilegia Alba Pleno. New; double, white, fine	.25
103	—— Caryophylloides. White, variously striped with reddish crimson; a beautiful double variety. 1 foot	.25
104	—— Formosa. Double; crimson and orange. 1½ feet	.05
105	—— —— Rosea. Beautiful rose-color; double. 2 feet	.25
106	—— —— Rubro. Fine, crimson; double. 1½ feet	.25
107	—— Glandulosa. Blue and white. 1 foot	.10
108	—— Siberica. Violet; double. 1 foot	.25
109	—— Skinnerii. Scarlet and yellow; very beautiful; from Guatemala. 1½ feet	.10
111	—— Finest Mixed	.25
112	—— Good Mixed	.05

AMATEUR CULTIVATOR'S GUIDE

ARABIS. Nat. Ord., *Cruciferæ*.

An exceedingly early spring-flowering plant, contrasting beautifully in ribbons with the yellow Alyssum; valuable for rock-work, edging, &c., succeeding well in any good garden soil. Hardy perennial.

113 **Arabis Alpina.** Pure white; from Switzerland. Three-quarters foot . . . $0.10

ARBUTUS (Strawberry-Tree). Nat. Ord., *Ericaceæ*.

A handsome, nearly hardy, evergreen shrub, covered during October and November with pearl-like blossoms and strawberry fruit.

114 **Arbutus Unedo.** From Ireland. 10 feet 10

ARCTOCTIS. Nat. Ord., *Compositæ*.

Handsome, showy, free-flowering plants, of close, compact, dwarf habit, with large beautiful flowers in the style of Gazania Splendens; continuing in bloom the whole summer, and growing freely in any rich soil. Half-hardy perennials.

115 **Arctoctis Grandiflora.** Pale-yellow, dark-crimson centre; from Cape of Good Hope. Half foot 10

116 —— **Breviscarpa.** Deep-orange, with dark centre; from Cape of Good Hope. Half ft. .10

ARALIA. Nat. Ord., *Araliaceæ*.

117 **Aralia Papyrifera** (Chinese Rice-paper plant). Greenhouse shrub from China. 4 feet . .25

ARGEMONE. Nat. Ord., *Papaveraceæ*.

Exceedingly showy, free-flowering border plant, with large, poppy-like flowers; succeeding well in any common garden soil. Hardy annual.

118 **Argemone Grandiflora.** White. 2 feet 05
119 —— **Mexicanum.** Yellow. 2 feet 05

ASCLEPIAS TUBEROSA. (See next page.)

ARMERIA. Nat. Ord., *Plumbaginaceæ*.

Useful, hardy perennials; adapted for rock-work, edging, or culture in pots. Half-hardy perennials.

120 **Armeria Dianthoides.** Delicate rose. Half foot 10
121 —— **Formosa.** Rose and white. 1 foot 10

TO THE FLOWER GARDEN. 19

NO.		PRICE
122	Armeria Longiaristata. Blue. 1 foot	$0.10
123	—— Pinifolia. Fine foliage. 1 foot	.10
124	—— Splendens. Splendid variety, with large corymbs four to six inches in circumference, of brilliant rosy carmine flowers; good for bouquets. 1 foot	.25

ASCLEPIAS. NAT. ORD., *Asclepiadaceæ*.

Handsome plants, remarkable for the singularity and beauty of their flowers; requiring a light soil.

125	Asclepia Curassavica. Scarlet. Greenhouse perennial; from South America. 3 feet .	.10
126	—— Mexicanum. White greenhouse shrub; from Mexico. 5 feet	.10
126½	—— Tuberosa. (See engraving.) Orange. Hardy perennial	.10

ARUM. NAT. ORD., *Araceæ*.

Plants with singularly interesting and curious foliage; fine for mixed borders or front of shrubberies. Hardy perennials.

127	Arum Corsicum. Mottled, like a snake; from Corsica. 1 foot	.10

ASTER. NAT. ORD., *Compositæ*.

This splendid class of plants is not only one of the most popular, but also one of the most effective, of our garden favorites, producing in profusion flowers in which richness and variety of color are combined with the most perfect and beautiful form: it is indispensable in every garden or pleasure-ground where an autumnal display is desired. For flower-beds and mixed borders it stands unrivalled.

The Aster may be divided into two grand sections,—French and German. The French, as improved by Truffaut, has flat petals, either reflexed or incurved, the former resembling the Chrysanthemum; whilst the latter, by turning its petals towards the centre of the flower, forms, when well grown, a perfect ball, and is best described by its resemblance to the Peony. The German varieties are quilled; and the most perfect flowers are surrounded by a circle of flat or guard petals, as in the Hollyhock. The flowers of these are particularly admired for the exquisite symmetry of their form. The dwarf-bouquet varieties of this beautiful germ grow from nine to fifteen inches high, and are particularly adapted for small beds, edging, or for pot-culture. They often flower so profusely as entirely to hide their foliage. All the varieties delight in a rich light soil, and, in hot, dry weather, should be mulched with well-rotted manure, and frequently supplied with manure-water. This labor will be amply compensated by the increased size, beauty, and duration of the flowers. Half-hardy annuals.

128	Aster French Peony Perfection, representing the greatest perfection in form, size, and fulness of flower of the Peony class. In this variety the petals are turned towards the centre, and a flower not quite in full bloom: resembles a ball; but few side flowers; a beautiful variety of colors; mixed. A foot and a half	.10
128½	—— —— Truffaut's French Peony-flowered. Grown by Truffaut, the celebrated florist of Versailles, France. Acknowledged by all to be one of the best, in all respects. Twenty colors, mixed	.25
129	—— —— Dwarf Large-growing Peony. About half the size of the Peony Aster; habit, fine; pyramidal; flower, splendid, large and very double, in the way of the Peony, perfection. All colors, mixed	.10
130	—— —— Crown-flowered, or Cocardeau. The flowers of this variety have large white centres, surrounded by scarlet, carmine, violet, blue, and many other colors. Flower large and double; all colors, mixed	.10
131	—— Chinese. The variety most commonly grown. Mixed	.05
132	—— Original Chinese, with folded Petals. Two colors, mixed. The petals of this variety are folded in their length; the flowers are of an unusual size, from three to four inches in diameter; present the most striking colors of all Asters; plants tall; wide-spreading branches, and of a very curious and original aspect. New.	.10
133	—— German Dwarf. This is a fine variety, growing only three-quarters foot high; flowers similar to the double-quilled; good form; an abundant bloomer. All colors, mixed	.05
134	—— Dwarf Bouquet Pyramidal. The flower of this variety, when well grown, forms a complete bouquet of itself, the flowers completely hiding the foliage, and often numbering from a hundred and fifty to two hundred to a single plant. All colors, mixed	.10
135	—— Dwarf Chrysanthemum-flowered. This is a valuable late variety, coming in after many other varieties are gone. They grow very uniform in height. The flowers are from three to four inches in diameter, blooming so profusely as to completely hide the foliage; very good for pot-culture; splendid mixture	.10

NO.		PRICE
136	Aster Peony-Globe. A very early variety, of branching habit; color very distinct, and flower double. Mixed	$0.25
137	—— —— Pyramidal. This is a very popular variety of the Aster, growing very uniform in height and shape. The form of flower resembles an inverted pyramid. Some are quilled, others not; a fine mixture	.10
138	—— Globe-quilled. This is a fine old variety. The flowers are formed in the shape of a half-ball. Mixed	.10
139	—— Giant Emperor. This is a comparatively new variety. The flowers are very double, and of immense size. It does not flower so freely as many other varieties. In favorable cases it produces four to six flowers, of which the chief blossom is often four inches in diameter; a good variety of colors. Mixed	.25
139½	—— Imbricated Pompon. One of the most pleasing styles; of pyramidal growth, with medium-sized flowers of the most perfect form, very double and densely imbricated. Six colors mixed	.10
140	—— Porcupine, or Hedgehog. The flowers are composed of long, quilled, curious-looking petals: hence the name. Mixed	.10
141	—— Reid's Improved Quilled. One of the finest quilled varieties. Mixed . .	.10
142	—— Ranunculus-flowered. This is a small flowered variety, very double, imbricated, surrounded by a range of green leaves; not quite as showy as many other varieties, yet we consider it quite an acquisition; valuable for bouquets. Finest mixed	.10
143	—— Rose-flowered. A new class, of great merit, about two and a half feet high, of robust growth, fine habit, and profuse bloomers. The flowers are as large as Peony Asters, beautifully imbricated, of oval form, and very double. In habit, height of plant, and form of flower, intermediate between the Tall Chrysanthemum and Peony Perfection Asters, and which will become a favorite class. The colors are carmine, carmine and white, dark-blue, deep-lilac, deep-purple, deep purple-white, bright crimson tipped with white, white tinted blush, crimson, and crimson and white. Mixed	.25
144	—— Dwarf Turban, or Chessboard. Leaves of dark-brown tint, with flowers of a deep rose with white; an interesting species	.25
144½	—— Victoria. This beautiful kind forms a new class, allied to the Giant Emperor, but superior to that in habit of plant and form of flower. The plant is very robust, about one and three-quarters feet in height, bearing itself without assistance of a stick, forming a handsomely branched-compact bush, crowned with from ten to twenty large and smaller flowers, half of them of the size of the largest Giant Emperor Asters, which are of a beautiful globular form, regularly imbricated. It has, besides, the great superiority over the Giant Emperor Aster of being perfectly constant in height, and fulness of flower, and, in consequence, of great value for bedding	.25

Persons wishing any of the above Asters in separate colors are referred to the collections under the head of Assortments.

ASTRAGALUS. NAT. ORD., *Leguminosæ.*

A showy, beautiful, and useful herbaceous plant, succeeding in any common garden soil. Hardy perennial.

145	Astragalus purpureus; deep-red, a pretty trailer; from south of France	. . .10
146	—— Galegiformis; yellow, with pretty foliage; from Siberia. 3 feet	.10

ANTHANASIA. NAT. ORD., *Compositæ.*

147	Anthanasia Annua (African Daisy); yellow; from Barbary. Hardy annual. 1 foot	. .10

AUBERGINE (EGG-PLANT). NAT. ORD., *Solanaceæ.*

The varieties enumerated are the eatable fruited kinds so extensively grown about our cities. The white and scarlet are sometimes grown in pots, and are very interesting, being covered in autumn with beautiful egg-shaped fruit. The scarlet variety is a great novelty. They succeed in a warm southern location. Half-hardy annuals.

148	Aubergine, White-fruited. From France. 1½ feet	.05
149	—— Purple-fruited. Large; from France. 1½ feet	.05

NO.		PRICE
150	Aubergine, Scarlet-fruited. Very striking and handsome; from France. 1½ feet,	$0.10
151	—— Striped. New, very ornamental; from Guadeloupe. 1½ feet	.10

AURICULA. Nat. Ord., *Primulaceæ.*

A well-known garden favorite of great beauty, succeeding best in a northern aspect. Half-hardy perennial.

152	Auricula Alpine. This is the most hardy of all the Auricula. Mixed	.10
153	—— Extra German. Saved from German prize varieties. Mixed. Half foot	.25
154	—— English Prize. From named flowers. Half foot	.25

AZALEA. Nat. Ord., *Ericaceæ.*

Beautiful flowering plants, requiring very careful treatment. All the species should be grown in peat, leaf-mould, and a very sandy loam.

155	Azalea Indica. Saved from finest named collection; greenhouse shrubs. 4 feet	.25
156	—— Pontica. Saved from a fine collection. Hardy shrub. 4 feet	.25

BALSAM. Nat. Ord., *Balsaminaceæ.*

Magnificent conservatory or out-door plants, producing their gorgeous masses of beautiful brilliant colored flowers in the greatest profusion: when grown in pots, and large specimens are desired, they should be shifted into ten or twelve inch pots, using the richest and freest compost at command, and liberally supplied with manure-water; for out-door decoration, the soil should be of the richest possible character. Tender annuals.

158	Balsams, Camellia-flowered, or Blotched. A beautiful collection of ten colors, mixed; very double. 2 feet	.10
159	—— Double Tall. Twelve fine colors, mixed. 2 feet	.10
160	—— Double Dwarf. Twelve fine colors, mixed. 1 foot	.10
161	—— Improved Rose-flowered. A finely imbricated variety; flowers two inches in diameter; superb; twelve colors, mixed. 2 feet	.10
162	—— Rose-spotted. Six varieties, mixed. 2 feet	.10
163	—— —— Chamois. New and rare. 2 feet	.10
164	—— Aurora-colored. Very striking and beautiful. 2 feet	.10
165	—— Pale Yellow. Sweet-scented; fine. 2 feet	.10
166	—— Isabella. Pale rose, changing to yellow	.10
167	—— Smith's Prize. From a celebrated English collection; very fine	.25
168	—— Good Mixed	.05

The above Balsams may be relied upon as being first-class in all respects. For collections, see page of Assortments.

BARTONIA. Nat. Ord., *Loaseæ.*

169	Bartonia Aurea (golden). (See engraving.) Flowers yellow, about an inch and a half across, which have quite a metallic lustre when the sun shines upon them; very showy. 2 feet	.05
170	—— Nuda. This is a perfect gem. It grows two to three feet high, and is literally covered with its large white flowers, of the most delicate texture, surpassing even the finest lace-work. The flowers are two and a half inches in diameter, and produced in great abundance all the season; a perfectly hardy perennial, from North America.	.25

BALLOON VINE (Cardiospermum). Nat. Ord., *Sapindaceæ.*

A very pretty climbing plant, remarkable for an inflated membraneous capsule, from which it derives the name of Balloon Vine. It answers either for the greenhouse or open ground. Half-hardy annual.

171	Cardiospernum Halicacabum. White; from India. 5 feet	.10

BAPTISIA. Nat. Ord., *Leguminosæ.*

172	Baptisia Australis. A handsome border plant, of the easiest culture; flowers blue. Hardy perennial. 2 feet	.10

BELLIS (Double Daisy). Nat. Ord., *Compositæ.*

A well-known perennial. Many elegant varieties have been raised by saving the seeds from the handsomest kinds. They are admirable plants for making edgings, &c. Half-hardy perennial.

173	Bellis Perennis. Good. Mixed. one-quarter foot	.10
174	—— —— Extra Fine. Saved from named flowers	.25

AMATEUR CULTIVATOR'S GUIDE

BELVIDERE. Nat. Ord., *Chenopodiaceæ.*
A pretty, cypress-like plant, sometimes called summer-cypress; fine for a cemetery.
175 Belvidere. Hardy annual, from Egypt $0.05

BILLBERGIA. Nat. Ord., *Bromeliaceæ.*
A magnificent stove-plant, with long, graceful, delicate green foliage, beautiful zebra-striped flowers, extremely handsome and showy, succeeding best in sandy peat and loam.
176 Billbergia Zebrina. Scarlet and purple; beautiful; one and a half feet; from Rio Janeiro. 1½ feet 25

BEGONIA. Nat. Ord., *Begoniaceæ.*
A magnificent genus of ornamental greenhouse plants, as remarkable for the varied and beautiful foliage of many of its varieties as for the splendor and profusion of the flowers of others. Should be grown in sandy peat and loam.
177 Begonia, Mixed. Several of the most choice sorts mixed 25

BARTONIA AUREA. (See preceding page.)

BIGNONIA. Nat. Ord., *Bignoniaceæ.*
A highly ornamental greenhouse climber, producing its gorgeous flowers in panicles and in the greatest profusion.
178 Bignonia Tweedieana. Yellow, half-hardy shrub 25

BLUMENBACHIA. Nat. Ord., *Loaseæ.*
179 Blumenbachia Insignis. Quite handsome; flowers white; from Montevideo. Three-quarters foot 10

BOSSIÆA. Nat. Ord., *Leguminosæ.*
Handsome, free-flowering, and beautiful genus of greenhouse plants. Succeeds best in a compost of turf, loam, and peat.
180 Bossiæa Biloba. Three feet high; from New Holland 25
181 ——   Linophylla. Orange, three feet high 25

BOCCONIA FRUTESCENS.

BOCCONIA. Nat. Ord., *Papaveraceæ*.

A new and beautiful foliaged greenhouse plant, and one of the rarest plants yet introduced for the decoration of beds and lawns in summer.

182 Bocconia Frutescens. A splendid novelty; very rare $0.25

BRACHYCOME. Nat. Ord., *Compositæ*.

A beautiful free-flowering, dwarf-growing plant, covered, during the greater portion of the summer, with a profusion of pretty cineraria-like flowers, very effective in edgings, small beds, rustic baskets, or for pot-culture; succeeding in any light, rich soil. Half-hardy annuals.

183 Brachycome Iberidifolia (Swan-River Daisy). Blue; from Swan River. Half foot . .10
184 —— Albiflora. White; from Swan River. Half foot 10
185 —— Finest Mixed 10

BRIZA (Quaking-Grass). Nat. Ord., *Gramineæ*.

A very useful ornamental grass, fine for dried bouquets. Hardy annual.

186 Briza Maxima. Fine; from Cape of Good Hope 05
187 —— Gracilis (slender). From Cape of Good Hope 05

BRYZOPYRUM. Nat. Ord., *Gramineæ*.

A very pretty dwarf variety of the ornamental grasses; good for dried bouquets.

188 Bryzopyrum Siculum. Distinct and beautiful; hardy annual; from North America . .10

BROMUS. Nat. Ord., *Gramineæ*.

189 Bromus Bryzoporoides. A very pretty variety of ornamental grass; from south of Europe. Hardy annual 10

BROWALLIA. Nat. Ord., *Scrophulariaceæ*.

Very handsome profuse-blooming plants, covered with rich, strikingly beautiful flowers during the summer and autumn months; growing freely in any rich soil. Half-hardy annual.

190 Browallia Cerviskowskii. Blue, with white centre; beautiful. 1½ feet 10
191 —— Demissa. Light-blue and orange centre; from South America. 1½ feet . .10
192 —— Elata Cerulea. Upright; blue; from Peru. 1½ feet 10
193 —— —— Alba. White; from Peru. 1½ feet 10
194 —— —— Grandiflora. Sky-blue; large-flowered. 1½ feet 10

NO.		PRICE

CACALIA (Tassel-Flower). Nat. Ord., *Compositæ*.

A beautiful annual, with a profusion of scarlet tassel-shaped flowers from July to October.

195 **Cacalia Coccinea.** Orange, scarlet, flowering in clusters, very pretty; from South America. 1¼ feet $0.05
196 —— **Aurea.** Golden yellow variety of above 05

CALANDRINIA. Nat. Ord., *Portulaceæ*.

Very beautiful dwarf-growing plants, usually treated as tender annuals, though of perennial duration if protected in winter: they are a blaze of beauty wherever the sun shines upon them. They succeed well in a light, rich soil.

197 **Calandrinia Lindleyana.** Small red flowers, suitable for edging. Half foot 05
198 —— **Grandiflora.** Fine rosy-lilac flowers from July to October, very showy, and of easy culture. 2 feet 05
199 —— **Umbellata.** Very dwarf, with bright crimson flowers in clusters. Half foot . . .05

CACTUS. Nat. Ord., *Cactaceæ*.

An extremely curious and interesting genus, many of the varieties producing magnificent flowers of the most brilliant and striking colors; succeeds best in sandy loam, mixed with lime rubbish and a little peat or rotten dung. Greenhouse perennial.

200 **Cactus, Mixed.** A choice collection; from Africa 25

CALCEOLARIA. Nat. Ord.; *Scrophularineæ*.

Plants of a highly decorative character; an indispensable ornament for the drawing-room or conservatory. The shrubby variety is sometimes grown for in-door and sometimes for out-door decoration. They succeed in any light, rich soil. Half-hardy perennials.

201 **Calceolaria Hybrida.** Mixed. Saved from a named collection 25
202 —— —— **Superba Grandiflora.** Extra fine, spotted and striped, large-flowered; saved from the prize flowers from the London Exhibition of the past season; superb. 1 foot. 50
203 —— —— **Nana.** A new dwarf variety from Germany, beautifully marked, close, compact habit, free-bloomer; one of the best; mixed, saved from a prize collection. Three-quarters foot 50
204 —— **Rugosa.** A fine, shrubby variety for bedding 50
205 —— —— **Tigrini.** New; spotted and striped of the above; very fine 50
206 —— **Scabious-leaved (Scabiosæfolia).** Clear, sulphur-yellow flowers, in great profusion; fine. 2 feet 10

CALENDULA (Cape Marigold). Nat. Ord., *Compositæ*.

A very showy, free-flowering genus of plants, producing a pretty effect in beds or mixed borders, and growing freely in almost any soil. Hardy annuals.

207 **Calendula Hybrida.** White. 1 foot. 05
208 —— **Pluvialis.** White, large flowers. 1 foot 05
209 —— **Pongei, fl. pl.** Double white, fine. 1 foot 10
210 —— **Ranunculoides.** Ranunculus-flowered 05
211 —— **Officinalis Superba.** New variety of pot marigold, golden orange, with black eye, beautifully imbricated; fine 10
212 —— **Sulphurea.** New sulphur-colored pot marigold; very double and beautiful . . .10

CALLA. Nat. Ord., *Araceæ*.

A very handsome plant, either as an aquatic or for the ornamentation of the drawing-room or conservatory. Half-hardy perennial.

213 **Calla Æthiopica.** White; from Cape of Good Hope. 2 feet. 25

CALLIRHOE. Nat. Ord., *Malvaceæ*.

Too much cannot be said in praise of this beautiful summer-flowering annual; from two to three feet in height, with green sub-digitate leaves and leafy stems, terminating in large panicled racemes of rich violet or purple close-petalled flowers, with white centre, each from one to one and a half inches in width, and partially cupped; commences to bloom when about six inches high, and continues to yield a succession of its numerous attractive flowers throughout the summer and autumn till hard frost, forming an elegant object for groups, beds, or single specimens, of the easiest culture.

214 **Callirhoe Involucrata.** A trailing, hardy perennial, of great beauty; from Rocky Mountains; flowers are much like the Portulaca in form and color 10

NO.				PRICE
215	Callirhoe Pedata.	Rich violet-purple, with white eye, from North America. 2 feet		$0.10
216	—— —— Nana.	Like the above, only dwarf. 1 foot		.10
217	—— Verticillata.	A very pretty creeper; flowers similar to C. Pedata, but double the size		.10

CALLIOPSIS, or COREOPSIS. Nat. Ord., *Compositæ*.

This genus is amongst the most showy, free-flowering, and beautiful of hardy annuals. The tall varieties are very effective in mixed borders and fronts of shrubberies; and the dwarf kinds, from their close, compact habit of growth, make fine bedding plants, and are valuable for edgings; while the different varieties make very pretty ribbons. Hardy annuals.

218 Calliopsis Bicolor Tinctoria. A well-known favorite, the flowers having a dark-crimson, brown centre, with yellow rays. 2½ feet 05
219 —— —— Marmorata (marbled). Brown and yellow, that are inclined to be shaded. 2½ feet 05
220 —— —— Atropurpurea. Yellow centre, surrounded by a circle of dark-purple, beyond which, to the extremity of the petals, it is a fine red, scarlet color. 2 feet . .10
221 —— Cardaminifolia Hybrida. Brilliant yellow; growth, pyramidal; compact and free-flowering plant. 1½ feet 10
222 —— —— —— Atrosanguinea. Blood-red, flower very fine. 1½ feet 10
223 —— Coronata. Rich yellow; disk encircled with crimson spots; handsome; from Texas. 1½ feet 05
224 —— Drummondii. Yellow, with crimson centre; fine; from Texas. 1½ feet . .05
225 —— Filifolia (thread-leaved). Yellow, neat foliage 05
226 —— —— Burridge's. A new and exceedingly beautiful annual; flowers rich brown, tipped with bright orange; very showy. 2 feet 05

CALLICHROA. Nat. Ord., *Compositæ*.

227 Callichroa Platyglossa. Pretty light-yellow flowers in abundance; from California. 1 foot 05

CALAMPELIS SCABRA.

CALAMPELIS. Nat. Ord., *Bignoniaceæ*.

228 Calampelis Scabra. A very pretty climbing plant from Chili, with orange-colored flowers; very fine. 10 feet 10

CALLISTACHYS. Nat. Ord., *Leguminosæ*.

A handsome greenhouse evergreen shrub, with beautiful spikes of flowers. It is easy of culture, thriving in sandy peat and loam.

229 Callistachys Lanceolata. Yellow; beautiful; from New Holland. 6 feet 25

| NO. | | PRICE |

CAMELLIA. Nat. Ord., *Ternstromiaceæ*.

Favorite winter and spring-flowering plants of great beauty. The amateur, in sowing seed saved from the following choice sorts, has a fair chance of raising some valuable varieties; succeed in sandy peat and loam. Half-hardy shrubs.

230 **Camellia Japonica, Mixed.** From a choice named collection of double flowers . $0.50

CAMPANULA. Nat. Ord., *Campanulaceæ*.

The Campanulas are strictly biennial plants by pot-culture, and, without exception, some of the finest of all garden plants for decoration in conservatory, greenhouse, and flower-garden. By good culture in pots, the tall varieties assume a magnificent effect, attaining five to seven feet or more in height, with lateral flower racemes from the base, four to five feet in length. The beautiful white variety forms a most striking contrast. By good arrangement, a rich and imposing effect can be formed, altogether unequalled by any other plants.

231 **Campanula Loreii.** Fine, with large, expanded blue blossoms, which continue to be produced in succession through the summer; will grow in almost any situation; should be well thinned, so that the plants will be eight or ten inches apart; desirable for edging, or bedding, *en masse*. Half foot 05
232 —— —— **Alba.** Differing from the above only in color; white. Half foot . . .05
233 —— —— **Mixed.** The above two varieties mixed 05
234 —— **Pentagonia.** Blue; will bloom beautifully in open ground; requires the same treatment as C. Loreii. Three-quarters foot 05
235 —— —— **Alba.** White variety of preceding 05
236 —— **Carpatica.** Light, violet dwarf, and free; fine for beds and edging, &c. Half-hardy perennial 05
237 —— —— **Alba.** White variety of the preceding 05
238 —— **Persicifolia.** Large blue flowers, fine for borders. Hardy perennials. 3 feet . .05
239 —— —— **Alba.** White variety of preceding 05
240 —— **Grandis.** Deep-blue; from Italy. Hardy perennial. 3 feet 10
241 —— **Grandiflora.** A fine, free-blooming variety, with long, drooping, purple flowers. Hardy perennial 10
242 —— **Pyramidalis.** Very elegant, with fine blue flowers; may be trained to any form of growth; suitable for the border or pot-culture. Hardy perennial. 3 feet . .05
243 —— —— **Alba.** White variety of the above 05
244 —— **Trachelium, fl. pl.** A fine border-plant, with violet-blue flowers. Hardy perennial 05
245 —— —— **Alba.** White variety of the above 05
246 —— **Vidalis.** White, showy, half-hardy perennial. 1½ feet 10

CANARY-BIRD FLOWER.

CANARY-BIRD FLOWER. Nat. Ord., *Tropæolaceæ*.

The popular name of this pretty little annual alludes to the supposed resemblance of the flower to a bird with its wings expanded, the spur of calyx representing the head, and the two upper petals the wing; blooms from June to October; from Mexico.

247 **Canary-Bird Flower** (*Tropæolum Peregrinum*). Half-hardy annual. 20 feet . . .10

| NO. | | PRICE |

CANDYTUFT. Nat. Ord., *Cruciferæ.*

All the Candytufts are of the easiest culture, thriving in almost any soil or situation, and deserve to be cultivated more extensively in every flower-garden ; very good for pot-culture. Hardy annuals.

248 Candytuft Fragrans (*Iberis odorata*). Flower white, pinnated foliage ; from Crete. 1 foot $0.05
249 —— Crimson (*kermesina*). Bright and showy. 1 foot 05
250 —— Purple (*purpurea*). A favorite variety. 1 foot 05
251 —— Rocket (*coronaria*). Pure white ; fine. 1 foot 05
252 —— Rose (*rosea*). Rose-colored. 1 foot 05
253 —— White (*amara*). One of the best. 1 foot 05
254 —— Perennial (*sempervirens*). White. 1 foot 05

CANTERBURY BELLS. Nat. Ord., *Campanulaceæ.*

The Canterbury Bells have long been known among our most ornamental garden plants. Their large bell-shaped flowers, which are freely produced throughout the summer, render them strikingly effective. As they are strictly biennials, it will be necessary to sow the seed every year. Hardy biennials.

255 Canterbury Bells, Double White (*Campanula Medium*). From Germany. 2 feet . .05
256 —— —— —— Blue. From Germany. 2 feet 05
257 —— —— —— Lilac. From Germany. 2 feet 05
258 —— —— —— Mixed. All the above. 10
259 —— —— Single White. From Germany. 2 feet 05
260 —— —— —— Blue. From Germany. 2 feet 05
261 —— —— —— Lilac. From Germany. 2 feet 05
262 —— —— —— Mixed. Above single varieties 05

CANNABIS. Nat. Ord., *Articaceæ.*

263 Cannabis Gigantea (Giant Hemp). A very ornamental plant for shrubbery-borders. Hardy annual ; from India. 10 feet 05

CASSIA. Nat. Ord., *Leguminosæ.*

A genus of highly ornamental and exceedingly useful free-flowering shrubs, for conservatory or greenhouse decoration ; growing freely out of doors during the summer months ; succeeding best in a mixture of loam and peat. Greenhouse shrubs.

264 Cassia falcata superba. Yellow ; from Buenos Ayres. 3 feet 25
265 —— Grandiflora. Yellow, flowering profusely during autumn and winter ; from China. 4 feet 25
266 —— Lavigata. Sulphur-color, distinct ; from India. 4 feet 25
267 —— Marylandica. Yellow ; from North America. 4 feet 25

CANNA. (Indian Shot). Nat. Ord., *Marantaceæ.*

These stately species of plants are highly ornamental in flower-gardens, producing a rich and Oriental effect by their large, broad, massive foliage, and rich crimson and scarlet flowers. Though perennial, if sown early, they will make luxuriant growth, and bloom the first season. In late autumn, they should be carefully potted, and allowed to mature their bloom in the greenhouse or parlor, and afterwards preserved in a cool, dry cellar. In spring, again start them into growth, and replant them in the open air last of May or first of June. Before sowing, soak the seed in water at 125° for about twelve hours.

268 Canna Acharis. Dark-red ; from Mendoza 5 feet 10
269 —— Angustifolia Nana Pallida. Light-red ; a dwarf variety ; from South America. 1 foot 10
270 —— Anneii. Crimson ; very ornamental. 3 feet 20
271 —— Aurantica. Orange ; lively green foliage ; from Brazil. 3 feet 10
272 —— Aurea Vittata. Golden ; beautiful ; from New Holland. 4 feet . . .25
273 —— Bicolor of Java. Red and yellow ; from Java. 3 feet 10
274 —— Coccinea Vera. Scarlet ; very fine ; from South America. 2 feet . .05
275 —— Compacta Elegantissima. Large, reddish yellow ; from South America. 2 feet .10
276 —— Edulis. Red ; very fine ; from Peru. 3 feet 10
277 —— Gigantea Aurantica. Orange-red ; a beautiful large variety. 10 feet . .25
278 —— Indica. Red ; from Indica. 2 feet 05
279 —— Limbata. Intense scarlet, edged with yellow ; very striking ; from Brazil. 4 feet .10

CANNA.

No.		Price
280	Canna Leptophylla. Ruby; handsome foliage; from Laguna. 4 feet . . .	$0.25
281	—— Muelleri. Scarlet; flowers large and fine. 3 feet	.10
282	—— Mutabilis. Changeable; from Brazil. 5 feet	.10
283	—— Musæfolia Hybrida. Red foliage, resembling a small banana. 2 feet	.25
284	—— Napalensis. Clear yellow; large flowers; very pretty; from Nepaul. 3 feet	.25
285	—— Sanguinea Chatei. Deep red, dark foliage, and stems very large. 6 feet .	.25
286	—— Sellowii. Scarlet; from Africa. 5 feet	.10
287	—— Warczewiczii. Brilliant red, with variegated foliage; one of the best for masses; from Central America. 3 feet	.25
288	—— Zebrina. Beautiful, zebra-striped foliage. 3 feet	.25
289	—— Finest Mixed	.25

CARNATION (Dianthus). Nat. Ord., *Caryophyllaceæ*.

A magnificent class of popular favorites, most of them deliciously fragrant, and with colors extremely rich and beautiful. The seed we offer may be relied upon as being the finest, all having been selected expressly for us from some of the best collections of prize varieties in Europe, producing mostly all double flowers. Hardy perennial.

290	Carnation Pink. Good; mixed; for border-culture	.10
291	—— —— Fine German. A good selection from a named collection	.25
292	—— —— Sardinian. From choice double varieties	.25

TO THE FLOWER GARDEN. 29

NO.		PRICE
293	Carnation Pink. Choice Bizarres and Flakes. Saved from stage flowers; extra	$0.50
294	— — Perpetual, or Tree. Fine German; from selected flower. 1½ feet	.50
295	— — Extra Fine. Saved from prize-flowers; splendid	.50

CATANANCHE. Nat. Ord., *Compositæ*.

Exceedingly showy, free-flowering, hardy perennials, succeeding in any garden soil.

296	Catananche Bicolor. White; violet centre; from south of Europe. 2 feet.	.05
297	— Cærulea. Blue, with purple centre; from south of Europe. 2 feet	.05
298	— Lutea. Yellow; hardy annuals. 1 foot.	.05

CATCHFLY (Silene). Nat. Ord., *Caryophyllaceæ*.

A showy, free-flowering plant, for beds, borders, or ribbons; succeeds in any garden soil. Hardy annual.

299	Catchfly Lobels. Red; from England. 1½ feet	.05
300	— Alba. White; from England. 1½ feet.	.05
301	— Flesh. New; flesh-color; from England. 1½ feet	.05

CELOSIA AUREA PYRAMIDALIS.

CELOSIA. Nat. Ord., *Amarantaceæ*.

Magnificent, free-flowering, graceful-growing plants, producing in the greatest profusion spikes of the most beautiful feathery-looking flowers (*see engraving, which represents a*

NO.		PRICE

side-shoot of Aurea Pyramidalis). Celosia Argentea, however, produces its flowers in spikes, like a Gomphrena (*Globe Amaranthus*), but much longer; and, if gathered when young, they are valuable for winter bouquets. Plants of the Celosia flower freely if planted out in June in a warm, sheltered situation. Grown in pots, they are the most elegant of greenhouse and conservatory plants, where, with a little management, they may be had in flower the whole winter, growing freely in rich loamy soil. Half-hardy annuals.

302 Celosia Argentea. Silvery white, shaded with bright rose; very handsome. 3 feet $0.10
303 — Aurea Pyramidalis. Magnificent golden-feathered plant; can be most strongly recommended. 3 feet 25
304 — Coccinea Pyramidalis. Rich crimson, of the same elegant habit as the preceding, differing only in color. 3 feet 25

CENTRANTHUS. Nat. Ord., *Valerianaceæ*.

Very pretty, free-flowering, compact-growing plants; very effective in beds, ribbons, or as an edging; grows freely in any garden soil. Hardy annuals.

305 Centranthus Long-tubed (Macrosiphon). Rose-color, very pretty. 1 foot 05
306 — Alba. White variety of the above. 1 foot 05
307 — Nanus. A dwarf variety, pink flower. Half foot 10
308 — Carneus. Flesh-color. 1 foot 10

CENTAUREA. Nat. Ord., *Compositæ*.

Very showy, free-flowering border-plants, succeeding in any common garden soil. Hardy annuals.

309 Centaurea, American. A large-growing species; flower pink 05
310 — Depressa. Bright-blue, with deep-red centre; from Caucasus. 1 foot . . .05
311 — — Rosea. Rose; pink centre. 1 foot 10
312 — Cyanus (Bachelor's Button). Well-known, showy plants, in great variety of colors; of easiest culture 05
313 — Macrocephala. Orange-yellow flowers; hardy perennial. 3 feet 10
314 — Montana. Blue; hardy perennial. 1½ feet 10

CENIA. Nat. Ord., *Compositæ*.

315 Cenia Turbinata. Dwarf annual, with yellow, daisy-like flowers 05

CERASTIUM. Nat. Ord., *Caryophyllaceæ*.

316 Cerastium Tomentosum. Flower white, with silvery leaves; dwarf. Hardy perennial. Half foot. 25

CERINTHE. Nat. Ord., *Boragineæ*.

317 Cerinthe Gymnandra. Yellow and brown tubulous flower. Hardy annual. 1 foot . .10
318 — Lutesi. Yellow flower; tubes quite curious. Hardy annual 10

CENTAURIDUM. Nat. Ord., *Compositæ*.

319 Centauridum Drummond's. Very pretty free-growing plant; from Texas. 2 feet . .10

CESTRUM. Nat. Ord., *Solanaceæ*.

A genus of handsome plants for conservatory or greenhouse decoration; covered during the months of November and December with a profusion of beautiful tube-shaped blossoms; grows freely in rich loam and peat. Greenhouse shrub.

320 Cestrum Auranticum. Bright-orange; very pretty; from Guatemala. 3 feet . .25
321 — Parquii. Pale-yellow; from Chili. 3 feet 25

CHÆNOSTOMA. Nat. Ord., *Scrophulariaceæ*.

Neat, compact little plants; pretty for edgings, rustic or rock-work. Half-hardy annuals.

322 Chænostoma Fastigiatum. Rose-color; from Cape Good Hope. Three-quarters foot 05
323 — Polyanthum. Lilac; from Cape of Good Hope. Half foot 05

CHÆNESTES. Nat. Ord., *Solanaceæ*.

A beautiful greenhouse shrub, with handsome foliage and very showy tube-shaped flowers. It does well planted out against a wall in summer.

324 Chænestes Lanceolata. Bright-scarlet; from Quindiu. 5 feet 10

NO.		PRICE
	CHAMÆROPS. NAT. ORD., *Palmaceæ.*	
325	**Chamærops Humilis** (Fan Palm). A very ornamental palm, from six to ten feet high, and highly effective either for decorating the conservatory in winter, or the lawn in summer. It is so hardy it may be easily wintered in the cellar	$0.10
	CHENOPODIUM. NAT. ORD., *Chenopodiaceæ.*	
326	**Chenopodium Atriplicis.** Flowers small, clustered, covered, as well as the young leaves and shoots, with a glittering, purple meal, which renders the plant very ornamental. Hardy annual. 3 feet	.10
	CHELONE. NAT. ORD., *Scrophulariaceæ.*	
	An elegant summer-flowering, hardy herbaceous plant, adapted for a bed, group, or mass, with erect, slender, attenuated flower-stems rising two or three feet in height, having racemes of a bright-scarlet, Pentstemon-like flower-tubes, from one to two inches in length, forming a beautiful and effective object in borders, pleasure-grounds, &c. Hardy perennial.	
327	**Chelone Barbata.** Scarlet; from Mexico. 3 feet	.05
328	—— **Coccinea.** Brilliant-scarlet Pentstemon-like flowers; beautiful. 2 feet	.10
	CHLORA. NAT. ORD., *Gentianæ.*	
	A novelty of considerable promise, with glossy, oblong, handsome foliage, and a profusion of bright-yellow flowers. Half-hardy annual.	
329	**Chlora Grandiflora.** A new annual, highly recommended. 1½ feet	.10
	CHLORIS. NAT. ORD., *Gramineæ.*	
	A fine species: singularly elegant perennial grass, nine to twelve inches in height, with flower-scapes or stems, having slender flower-spikes or rachis radiating horizontally from the extremities of each scape like the concentric spokes of a wheel. Half-hardy annual.	
330	**Chloris Radiata.** From East India. 1 foot	.10
	CHRYSURUS. NAT. ORD., *Gramineæ.*	
	Very pretty ornamental grass, suitable for dried bouquets. Hardy annual.	
331	**Chrysurus Aureus.** From Levant. Half foot	.05
	CHINESE PRIMROSE (PRIMULA). NAT. ORD., *Primulaceæ.*	
	A charming, profuse-flowering plant, indispensable for winter and spring decoration, and a universal favorite. Our seeds are selected with great care from one of the finest collections in Europe. Greenhouse perennial.	
332	**Chinese Primrose, Purple.** Half foot	.25
333	—— **White.** Half foot	.25
334	—— **Fringed. Purple;** saved from only finest-fringed flowers	.25
335	—— —— **White.** Same as above	.25
336	—— —— **Rose-striped.** Bright rose-striped	.25
337	—— —— **Fringe-striped.** White, striped with red	.25
338	—— —— **Kermesina Splendens.** New and rare, flowers very large, bright velvet-like and crimson, with yellow eye. Half foot	.50
339	—— —— **Grandiflora.** This is one of the finest; flowers large, various colors, beautifully fringed; saved from prize flowers. Half foot	.50
340	—— —— **Erecta Superba.** A fine, new, erect-growing variety, with bright rose-colored flowers. Three-quarters foot	.50
341	—— —— **Macrophyilla.** Remarkable new variety, with long, massive foliage, and beautiful large flowers, of great substance, beautiful form, and finely fringed, of a rich purplish-carmine, with pentagonal, large yellow eye, surrounded by a brown zone; very conspicuous and splendid acquisition; comes true from seed	.50
342	—— —— **Good, Mixed**	.25
342½	—— —— **Extra, Mixed.** All the best varieties mixed	.50
	CHOROZEMA. NAT. ORD., *Leguminoseæ.*	
	A splendid profuse-flowering genus of shrubs, whose rich-colored blossoms and graceful habits render them remarkably effective objects for conservatory or greenhouse decoration; succeed best in sandy peat and loam. Greenhouse shrubs.	
343	**Chorozema, Mixed.** Including several fine varieties	.25

32 AMATEUR CULTIVATOR'S GUIDE

NO.   PRICE

CHRYSANTHEMUM POMPONE.

CHRYSANTHEMUM. Nat. Ord., *Compositæ*.

The following are the tall, double-flowered annual Chrysanthemums, which, when well grown, are amongst the most showy and effective of summer-flowering border-plants. They are also very effective in large pots for placing about terraces. The dwarf kinds make showy bedding-plants.

345   **Chrysanthemum, Double-white.**   Extra fine hardy annual; from Sicily. 2 feet . $0.05
346   —— —— Quilled. Extra fine 05
347   —— —— Yellow; extra fine hardy annual; from Sicily. 2 feet 05
348   —— Tricolor. Yellow and white; very showy; from Barbary. 1 foot 05
349   —— Burridgeanum. Crimson, with white centre; extra fine hardy annual; from Barbary. 1 foot 10
350   —— —— Venustum. White, with crimson centre; fine hardy annual; from Barbary .10
351   —— Mixed. The above varieties mixed 05

The Chrysanthemum Indicum and Indicum Nanum are well-known varieties, so extensively grown for late fall flowers. No garden should be without them. The seed we offer has been saved from the very finest new varieties, and will give a good proportion of double flowers.

352   **Chrysanthemum Indicum.** Tall, double, extra fine half-hardy perennial; from China. 3 feet 25
353   —— —— Nanum, Double-mixed (Dwarf Pompone). Half-hardy perennial; from China. 1 foot 25

CIMICIFUGA. Nat. Ord., *Ranunculaceæ*.

354   **Cimicifuga Americana.** Fine, hardy herbaceous plant, with elegant tall spikes of white flowers. 5 feet 10

CINERARIA. Nat. Ord., *Compositæ*.

A well-known favorite free-flowering plant, which may be had in splendid bloom through the greater portion of the year, and, from the richness and diversity of its colors, is one of the most valuable of our early spring flowers. Succeeds best in a light, rich, free, and open soil. Half-hardy perennial.

TO THE FLOWER GARDEN. 33

NO. PRICE

CINERARIA.

355	Cineraria, Fine-mixed. 1½ feet	$0.25
356	—— Extra Fine-mixed. Saved from the choicest named flowers. 1½ feet	.50
357	—— New Dwarf. Saved from the finest named flowers	.25
358	—— Maritima. Silvery foliage, beautifully cut; an admirable bedding-plant, and forms a fine contrast to Perilla nankinensis. 1½ feet	.10

CIRSIUM. NAT. ORD., *Compositæ*.

| 359 | Cirsium Pulcherrimum. Yellow, fine border; perennial. 3 feet | .10 |

CLEMATIS. NAT. ORD., *Ranunculaceæ*.

A handsome class of climbers, very desirable for growing against a wall or trellis. Seeds of this tribe require some time to germinate. Hardy perennials.

360	Clematis Flammula. White; very fragrant. 25 feet	.10
361	—— Paniculata. White. 10 feet	.10
362	—— Cirrhosa. A new variety, perfectly hardy; a very rapid climber, literally covering itself with large bunches of white sweet-scented flowers. 25 feet	.25
363	—— Crispa. Light-blue, well-shaped flowers	.10
364	—— Virginica (Traveller's Joy). White	.10

CLITORIA. NAT. ORD., *Leguminosæ*.

Splendid free-flowering greenhouse climbers, with large, elegant pea-shaped flowers, of great beauty, particularly adapted and very effective for training on trellis-work, wire globes, or any of the numerous contrivances on which plants of this character may be grown for greenhouse or conservatory decoration. Though perennials, they bloom the first year.

365	Clitoria Cœlestis. Sky-blue; from East Indies	.10
366	—— Gesnatia. Pale-blue, shaded with white; from East Indies	.25
367	—— —— Atro-cœrulea (new). Dark-blue; from East Indies	.25
368	—— Ternatea. Blue and white; from East Indies	.25
369	—— —— Alba. White; from East Indies	.25
370	—— —— Grandiflora. New large-flowered white	.50
371	—— —— Atro-cœrulea. Dark-blue; from East Indies	.25

AMATEUR CULTIVATOR'S GUIDE

NO.   **PRICE**

CLARKIA. Nat. Ord., *Onagraceæ.*

A beautiful tribe of favorite plants, with pretty, cheerful-looking flowers, growing freely and blooming profusely under almost any circumstances; and when planted in a rich soil, and properly attended to, they rank amongst the most effective of bedding-plants. Some of the new varieties are very good for pots, as well as the garden. Hardy annuals.

372	Clarkia Elegans. Rosy-purple. 1½ feet	$0.05
373	—— Rosea. A light rose-color. 1½ feet	.05
374	—— Rosea Plena. A fine double rose-flowering variety. 1½ feet	.05
375	—— Pulchella Grandiflora. Deep-rose. 1½ feet	.05
376	—— —— Alba. Pure white; fine	.05
377	—— —— Flore Pleno. Rich magenta flower; double; a very important addition to the many pretty varieties of the genus. 1½ feet	.10
378	—— —— Marginata. Rosy-crimson, edged with pure white. 1½ feet . . .	.10
379	—— —— Integripetala (whole-petaled). Rosy-crimson flowers; large and very handsome. 1½ feet	.10
380	—— —— Pulcherrima. Rose-violet; very beautiful color. 1½ feet . . .	.05
381	—— —— Tom Thumb. Rose-purple; dwarf, and of bushy habit; very fine for pots. Three-quarters foot	.10
382	—— —— Mixed. Good; mixed	.05

CLARY (Salvia). Nat. Ord., *Labiatæ.*

383   Clary, Mixed. Purple and red topped ornamental foliage; fine for mixed borders. Hardy annuals 05

CLEOME. Nat. Ord., *Capparidaceæ.*

384   Cleome Grandiflora Rosea. Purplish-rose flowers, in large spikes; very free-flowering. 3 feet 05

CLIANTHUS. Nat. Ord., *Leguminosæ.*

A genus of magnificent free-flowering greenhouse shrubs, with elegant foliage and brilliantly colored, singularly shaped flowers, which are produced in clusters, and have a splendid effect. Clianthus Magnificus and Clianthus Puniceus blossom freely out of doors in summer, against a trellis or south wall; Clianthus Dampierii succeeds best planted in the border of a greenhouse, and is one of the most magnificent plants of recent introduction; seeds sown in spring flower the first year; succeeds best in sandy peat or loam. Greenhouse shrubs.

384½ Clianthus Dampierii. Brilliant scarlet, with intense black spot in the centre of the flower. One of the most magnificent flowers in cultivation. Very rare . . .50
385 —— Magnificus (Glory-Pea). A beautiful scarlet-flowering shrub, with elegant foliage; from New Zealand. 4 feet 25

CLINTONIA. Nat. Ord., *Labeliaceæ.*

A pretty little plant, of neat, compact growth, with flowers resembling the Lobelia, and exceedingly beautiful; produces a fine effect in rustic baskets, rock-work, vases, boxes, or as an edging; succeeds best in light, rich soil. Half-hardy annual.

386 Clintonia Elegans. Light-blue; from Columbia. Half foot 05
387 —— Pulchella. Blue, yellow, and white; dwarf; and very pretty; from Columbia. Half foot .10
388 —— Atropurpurea Grandiflora. Violet-purple; centre yellow, margined with white; from Columbia. Quarter foot 10
389 —— Azurea Grandiflora. Azure, blue, yellow, and white centre. Half foot . . .25

COBÆA. Nat. Ord., *Polemniaceæ.*

390 Cobæa Scandens. A rapid-growing climbing plant, with large purple bell-shaped flowers, finely adapted for bedding out in summer; seeds should be sown early to secure well-established plants by the time the season arrives for planting out. Tender perennial. 20 feet 10

COCKSCOMB. Nat. Ord., *Amarantaceæ.*

Highly ornamental, curious-looking flowers, for decoration of the flower-house, drawing-room, and garden; all the varieties are remarkably attractive, producing a fine effect when grown in pots and mixed with other plants, either on the stage of a greenhouse, or planted in some warm situation out of doors. The following sorts have been saved from combs remarkable for their size and symmetry. Half-hardy annuals.

TO THE FLOWER GARDEN.

NO.		PRICE
391	Cockscombs, Mixed Varieties	$0.05
392	—— Dwarf Crimson. Brilliant and large; saved from a prize collection. Three-quarters foot	.10
393	—— —— Yellow. Same as above, except color	.10
394	—— New Giant. Very large, brilliant-red rose; beautiful rose-dwarf. Three-quarters foot	.10
395	—— Spicata Rosea. Silvery-white and rose. 1½ feet	.10

COLLINSIA. Nat. Ord., *Scrophulariaceæ.*

California annuals of great beauty, remarkably attractive in beds, mixed borders, or ribbons. Hardy annuals.

396	Collinsia Bicolor. Purple and white; beautiful; from Canada. 1 foot	.05
397	—— Alba. White; a charming variety. 1 foot	.05
398	—— Atrorubens. Red, purple, and white; pretty; from California. 1 foot	.05
399	—— Grandiflora. Blue, white, and lilac; beautiful; from Columbia	.05
400	—— Multicolor. Crimson, lilac, and white. 1 foot	.05
401	—— Marmorata. White and rose, marbled. 1 foot	.05

COLLOMIA. Nat. Ord., *Polemoniaceæ.*

402	Collomia Scarlet. Flowers in clusters; from Chili. 1½ feet	.05
403	—— Grandiflora. Saffron color; from North America. 1½ feet	.05

COMMELINA. Nat. Ord., *Commelinaceæ.*

Very pretty free-flowering tuberous-rooted plants, with rich blue flowers, succeeding in any rich soil. Half-hardy perennial, but flowering the first year.

404	Commelina Cœlestis. Sky-blue; Mexico. 1½ feet	.05
405	—— Alba. White; extremely beautiful; from Mexico. 1½ feet	.05
406	—— Variegata. Blue and white, striped	.10

CONOCLINIUM. Nat. Ord., *Compositæ.*

A greenhouse evergreen shrub, with beautiful, large clusters of Ageratum-like flowers; succeeds in a light, rich soil. Greenhouse shrubs.

407	Conoclinium Ianthinum. Pale-blue; very handsome; from Brazil. 2 feet	.25

CONVOLVULUS. Nat. Ord., *Convolvulaceæ.*

A beautiful, free-flowering, and remarkably showy class of plants, with exceedingly handsome, rich-colored flowers, producing in beds and mixed borders an unusually brilliant effect, either in distinct colors, ribboned or mixed beds. Half-hardy annuals.

408	Convolvulus Minor Tricolor. Rich violet-purple, with white centre; trailer	.05
409	—— Splendens. Rich violet; white centre	.05
410	—— Striped. Blue; beautifully striped with white; trailer	.05
411	—— Alba. White; beautiful trailer	.05
412	—— Good Mixed	.05
413	—— Flora Pleno. A new double variety; from France	.10
414	—— Monstrosus. Deep violet-purple; extremely large and handsome trailer	.10
415	—— Subcœruleus. Dove-color; trailer; very pretty; from Levant	.10
416	—— Cantabricus Stellatus. Flower of a beautiful pink, with pure white double star in the centre, and are produced in the greatest profusion. It forms a splendid bedding-plant, and is exceedingly elegant in hanging-baskets	.25
417	—— Mauritanicus. A beautiful creeper, with silvery foliage and lovely blue flowers; fine for hanging-baskets and rock-work	.25
418	—— Mixed. Good assortment of colors	.05
419	—— Extra Mixed. All the finest varieties	.25

CONVOLVULUS (Major). Nat. Ord., *Convolvulaceæ.*
(See Morning Glory.)

COLUMBINE. Nat. Ord., *Ranunculaceæ.*
Columbine in varieties. (See Aquilegia.)

COSMANTHUS. Nat. Ord., *Hydrophyllaceæ.*

A neat little plant, with prettily fringed flowers of a somewhat spreading habit.
420 **Cosmanthus Fimbriatus.** Lilac and white. Hardy annual; from North-America.
1 foot $0.05

COSMIDIUM. Nat. Ord., *Compositæ.*

421 **Cosmidium Burridgeanum.** An elegant annual; grows about two feet high, with beautiful Coreopsis-like flowers, with remarkable rich crimson, brown centre, and golden-orange, yellow border. Admirably adapted for brilliant-colored groups or marginal lines 10

COSMEA. Nat. Ord., *Compositæ.*

422 **Cosmea Grandiflora.** A hardy annual, with large lilac flowers of Dahlia form. 2 feet .05
423 —— **Atropurpurea.** Purplish-crimson. 2 feet 05

COIX. Nat. Ord., *Graminaceæ.*

424 **Coix Lachryma** (Job's Tears). A very curious ornamental grass, having seeds which have the appearance of large tears; from East Indies 05

COWSLIP. Nat. Ord., *Primulaceæ.*

Favorite, early, free-flowering plants, which should be extensively grown for filling the beds and borders of spring flower-gardens. Hardy perennial.
425 **Cowslip, New Giant.** Mixed; very large. Three-quarters foot 10
426 —— **Fine mixed.** From Britain. Three-quarters foot 05

CUCUMIS (Ornamental Cucumber). Nat. Ord., *Cucurbitaceæ.*

A most interesting tribe of plants, remarkable for luxuriance and rapidity of growth, which, if the soil be rich, is truly marvellous. Treat the same as the cucumber, and train against a wall or trellis, or in any way that may be desired. Cucumis Flexuosus, commonly known as the Snake Cucumber, is most singularly interesting in its fruit. Half-hardy annuals.
427 **Cucumis Acutangulus.** Curious forms 10
428 —— **Aradac.** Fruit small, growing in pairs; yellow 10
429 —— **Dipsacus.** Pale-yellow; Teasle-like; fine 10
430 —— **Flexuosus** (Snake Cucumber). Very peculiar, growing three feet long . . .10
431 —— **Melochito.** Variegated; brown and yellow 10
432 —— **Meduliferus.** Scarlet and thorny 10
433 —— **Mixed.** The above mixed 10

CUCURBITA (Ornamental Gourds). Nat. Ord., *Cucurbitaceæ.*

The tribe of Cucurbita or Gourds are well known as producing some of the most curiously shaped of all fruits, and being, like the Cucumis, of extremely rapid growth, are very desirable for covering trellis-work of arbors, &c., the varied and fantastic forms of the fruit adding a peculiar charm to the luxuriance of the foliage.
434 **Cucurbita Digitata.** A rapid grower, with fine-cut foliage marbled with white. The fruits are a beautiful dark-green striped with white. A splendid variety . .25
435 —— **Leucantha Longissima.** A curious variety, from four to six feet long . . .10
436 —— **Melopepo Variegata.** A small variety; green and yellow 10
437 —— —— **Maxima.** Green and yellow 10
438 —— **Powder-horn.** Powder-horn-shaped 10
439 —— **Mixed.** Above varieties mixed 10
(For other varieties, see Gourds.)

CUPHEA. Nat. Ord., *Lythraceæ.*

A highly ornamental and exceedingly beautiful genus of profuse-blooming plants, equally valuable for the ornamentation of the flower-house, drawing-room, and flower-garden. If sown early, they can be used for bedding-plants the first year.
440 **Cuphea Galcottiana.** A new species, with flowers nearly black; remarkable . .25
441 —— **Platycentra.** Well-known variety; flowers scarlet, black, and white; fine for pot-culture 10
442 —— **Strygulosa** (coarse-haired). Scarlet and yellow 10
443 —— **Silenoides.** Dark crimson-brown; a fine variety. Half-hardy annual . .10
444 —— **Zimpani.** A new variety, with large violet-red flowers 25

TO THE FLOWER GARDEN. 37

NO.   **PRICE**

CYCLANTHERA. Nat. Ord., *Cucurbitaceæ*.

Curious bird-shaped gourds, of a very ornamental character; rapid climbers; thrives in any rich soil in a warm situation. Very desirable for covering arbors, trellis-work, &c. Half-hardy annuals.

445 Cyclanthera Explodens. An elegant new climber, as hardy and as fast a grower as the Cyclanthera Pedata, with handsome foliage, and pretty oval-shaped fruits, exploding with a loud noise when ripe, and thus distributing their seeds . . $0.25
446 —— Pedata. Graceful slender-habited climbing-plants, with pendant branches of elegant balloon-like seed-pods; a novel plant, of easy culture. 15 feet 10

CYCLAMEN. Nat. Ord., *Primulaceæ*.

Few plants present a more gay appearance in the early spring months than the Cyclamen. From November to May, they enliven the greenhouse with their singularly shaped and various-colored flowers, often in such masses as to eclipse many more stately and conspicuous objects; yet, with such decorative qualities, they are but sparingly cultivated. Half-hardy perennial.

447 Cyclamen Africanum (Macrophyllum). White and rose; fine foliage; from Africa.
     Three-quarters foot 25
448 —— Hederæfolium. Exceedingly pretty; from Britain. Half foot 25
449 —— Persicum. White and pink; a charming sweet-scented variety; from Cyprus.
     Half foot 25
450 —— Vernum. A splendid variety 25
451 —— Mixed 25

CYTISUS. Nat. Ord., *Leguminosæ*.

An extremely useful free-flowering, ornamental tribe of shrubs, equally valuable for the decoration of the conservatory, drawing-room, and flower-garden; succeeding in any ordinary soil. Greenhouse shrubs.

452 Cytisus Attleyanus. A splendid shrub 25
453 —— Ramosissimus Superbus. Beautiful yellow; from Spain 25

CYPRESS VINE (Ipomea Quamoclit). Nat. Ord., *Convolvulaceæ*.

454 Cypress Vine, Scarlet. A tender, climbing annual, with graceful foliage and scarlet flowers; seed should not be planted in open ground before the last of
     May or first of June. 15 feet 05
455 —— White. Variety of the preceding 05
456 —— Roses. Rose-color 05

LILIPUTIAN OR BOUQUET DAHLIA. (See next page.)

DAHLIA. Nat. Ord., *Compositæ.*

A noble autumn-flowering plant. The seed offered by us has been saved from one of the best prize collections. Half-hardy perennial.

No.		Price
457	Dahlias, Good Mixed. A fine assortment of colors	$0.10
458	—— Extra Fine. Saved from a choice prize collection.	.25
459	—— Liliputian. Dwarf variety; beautiful	.25

DAISY. Nat. Ord., *Compositæ.*

(See Bellis Perennis.)

DAUBENTONIA. Nat. Ord., *Leguminosæ.*

Very handsome, free-flowering, elegant greenhouse shrubs, succeeding in sandy loam.

460	Daubentonia Punicea. Vermilion; from Spain. 4 feet	.25
461	—— Tripetiana. Scarlet; from Buenos Ayres. 3 feet	.25

DATURA WRIGHTII (one-fifth natural size).

DATURA. Nat. Ord., *Solanaceæ.*

A tribe of highly ornamental plants, producing large, sweet-scented, trumpet-shaped flowers of the most attractive character, and succeeding in most any rich soil. The roots may be preserved in and through the winter in a dry cellar. Half-hardy perennials.

TO THE FLOWER GARDEN. 39

NO.			PRICE
462	Datura, Wright's, or Meteloides (Datura Wrightii). A beautiful plant, producing flowers which are of extraordinary size, pure white at the centre, and passing imperceptibly to a lilac-blue at the border. The roots can be taken up in the autumn, and preserved through the winter, in the same manner as the Dahlia. 2 to 3 feet		$0.10
463	—— Carthageniensis. A new variety, comes highly recommended, and described as having very large flowers; white. 3 feet		.10
464	—— Humilis Flore Pleno. Double-yellow		.25
465	—— —— Chlorantha. A magnificent new variety, producing a profusion of deep golden-yellow flowers, very large, double, and sweet-scented; in bloom a long time. 2 feet		.25
466	—— Fastuosa Alba. Double-white. 2 feet		.10
467	—— —— Violacea. Violet-double. 2 feet		.10

DELPHINIUM. Nat. Ord., *Ranunculaceæ*.

A highly ornamental genus of splendid profuse-flowering plants, of an unusually high decorative character. When planted in large beds or groups, their gorgeous spikes of flowers, of almost endless shades, from pearl-white to the very richest and deepest blue, render them the most conspicuous and striking objects in the flower-garden or pleasure-ground. They delight in a deep, highly enriched soil. With the exception of Delphinium Cardiopetalum, they are all hardy perennials.

468	Delphinium, Chinese. Finest mixed; one of the most desirable of the tribe. 2½ ft.	.05
469	—— Cardiopetalum. Deep-blue; heart-shaped. Hardy annual; from Pyrenees. 1 foot	.05
470	—— Cœlestimum Grandiflorum. Celestial blue; long spikes; very handsome. 3 feet	.25
471	—— Elatum (Bee Larkspur). Blue. 3 feet	.05
472	—— Formosum. New flowers; large color; exquisite blue, with white; will flower the first season from seeds; finest of the tribe. 2 feet	.10
473	—— Grandiflorum. Dark-blue; fine	.10
474	—— Hybridum. Fine mixed. 3 feet	.10
475	—— Intermedia. Blue; a fine variety. 3 feet	.05
476	—— Iveryanum. Deep-blue; extra. 3 feet	.10
477	—— Perfecta Plena. Light-blue	.10
478	—— Punicea. Reddish-purple. 3 feet	.25
479	—— Wheelerii. Fine-blue. 3 feet	.10
480	—— Hendersonii. Splendid, large blue flowers; extra fine. 2½ feet	.10
481	—— Atroviolaceum. Dark-violet	.10

DIGITALIS (Foxglove). Nat. Ord., *Scrophulariaceæ*.

The Digitalis are too well known to need description. They are all useful and ornamental for general flower-garden purposes, and may be introduced into the shrubbery with fine effect, as their tall, spire-like spikes, crowned with their large thimble or bell-shaped flowers, will contrast finely with the green foliage of the shrubs. They are all hardy biennials, from three to four feet high.

482	Digitalis, Good Mixed. A fine assortment of colors	.05
483	—— Extra Mixed. All the newest kinds. 3 feet	.10
484	—— Grandiflora. Large-flowered; yellow. 3 feet	.10
485	—— Purpurea. Common purple variety. 3 feet	.05
486	—— Alba. Pure white. 3 feet	.05
487	—— Ferruginea. Brown. 2 feet	.10
488	—— Aurea. Golden. 3 feet	.05
489	—— Lutea. Yellow. 3 feet	.05
490	—— Gloxinioides. New and beautiful gloxinia-shaped flowers; extra spotted. 3 feet	.10
491	—— Cantua. White, tipped with black	.10
492	—— Hybrida. Pink; new and fine	.10

DIDYMOCARPUS. Nat. Ord., *Cyrtandaceæ*.

Exceedingly pretty greenhouse plant, flowering in bunches; succeeding best in light peaty soil.

493	Didymocarpus Humboldtianus. Blue; very pretty	.50

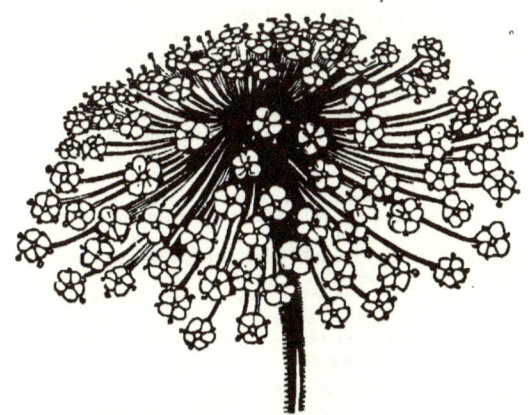

DIDISCUS CÆRULEA.

DIDISCUS. Nat. Ord., *Umbelliferæ*.

494 **Didiscus Cærulea.** Blue; a distinct and elegant plant; from Australia. Half-hardy annual. 1 foot $0.10

DIANTHUS. Nat. Ord., *Caryophyllaceæ*.

A magnificent genus, which embraces some of the most popular flowers in cultivation. The Carnation, Picotee, Pink, and Sweet William, all "household words," belong to this genus. The Chinese varieties may be considered the most beautiful and effective of our hardy annuals; the double and single varieties, with their rich and varied colors, in beds or masses, are remarkably attractive; while the recently introduced species, Dianthus Heddewigii and Dianthus Laciniatus, with their large and rich-colored flowers, three to four inches in diameter, close, compact habit, and profusion of bloom, are unsurpassed for effectiveness in beds and mixed borders.

495 Dianthus Caryophyllus. (See Carnation Pink) 05
496 —— Barbatus. (See Sweet William) 05
497 —— Atrorubens. Dark-red; handsome; hardy biennial; flowers first year from seed. 1 foot 10
498 —— Chinensis (Indian Pink). Mixed biennials of great beauty; blooms the first year from seed; perfectly hardy, and flowers strong the second year. The colors are exceedingly rich; crimson and darker shades of that color, approaching to black, are often combined in the same flower, with edgings of white, pink, and other colors; about one foot high, and of the easiest culture 05
499 —— —— Fine Double, Mixed. Same as above; selected from finest double flowers .10
500 —— —— Alba. Double-white; very fine 10
501 —— —— Marginata. White and rose-striped 10
502 —— —— Albus Pictus. White-marbled, with rose; beautifully fringed. Hardy annual 10
503 —— —— Heddewig's. A most beautiful new variety. The whole plant is scarcely one foot high, and very bushy; whilst always thirty or forty flowers are at once in blossom. The flowers are very large, from two to three inches in diameter, of a most beautiful shape, and of a variety and brilliancy of colors quite unsurpassed in pinks, from white mottled with rose, and purplish-red with dark centre, to velvety carmine-crimson, dark blood-red, and mottled and shaded with maroon and velvety-black. Hardy annual 10
504 —— —— Heddewig's, New Double. A new variety of this splendid new Pink, having beautiful double flowers, instead of the single. Hardy annual . . .25

NO.		PRICE

505 Dianthus Chinensis Laciniatus. A beautiful variety. The colors are pure white, flesh, rose, various shades of red, carmine, violet, purple, and rich maroon, some being selfs, others striped and spotted; all very delicately cut or fringed. Hardy ann. $0.10
506 —— —— Laciniatus, fl. pl. A double variety of the preceding; very fine . .25
507 —— Imperialis, fl. pl. Mixed; a fine double variety; annuals; from China . .10
508 —— Alba. White, hardy perennial; from Britain 10
509 —— Rubra. Pink; very fine; hardy perennial 10
510 —— Hispanicus. Finest mixed; from Spain. Hardy annual 05
511 —— Hybridus Corymbosus. A beautiful new hybrid; large double flower . .10
512 —— Moschatus (double garden-pink). Finest double-mixed; hardy perennial . .10
513 —— Plumarius (Pheasant-eye Pink). White or pink, with dark eye. The flowers are deeply fringed or feathered; very fragrant. Hardy perennial 05
514 —— Veitchii (Veitchs Hybrid). Beautiful cluster of flowers; pure white, with crimson centre. Hardy perennial 10
515 —— Dunnetti Superba. A beautiful hybrid variety, with corymbs of very rich dark-crimson flowers. 1 foot 10
516 —— Garnierianus (Garnier's Pink). A beautiful upright-growing variety, flowering freely through the summer; mixed colors. 1½ feet 10
517 —— Guttatus. Red and white; very dwarf; fine for edgings 10
518 —— Incarnatus. Rich crimson-scarlet 10

DODECATHEON (American Cowslip). Nat. Ord., *Primulaceæ*.

519 Dodecatheon Media. A pretty little border-plant, with flowers similar to the Cyclamen. Mixed; red and white. 1 foot 25

DOLICHOS (Hyacinth Bean). Nat. Ord., *Leguminosæ*.

Beautiful climbing-plants; flowers in clusters; treatment much the same as the common bean. Tender annuals.
520 Dolichos Lablab. Purple; from East Indies 05
521 —— —— Alba. White; from East Indies 05
522 —— —— Mixed. The above varieties mixed 05
523 —— Giganteus. A hardy ornamental climber; from East Indies 10

DICTAMNUS (Fraxinella). Nat. Ord., *Rutaceæ*.

A very fine hardy perennial. The leaves have a very pleasant smell, like lemon-peel, when rubbed. The seeds often remain in the ground several months before vegetating.
524 Dictamnus Alba. White; from south of Europe. 2 feet 05
525 —— Rubra. Crimson; from south of Europe. 2 feet 05

ECCREMOCARPUS. Nat. Ord., *Bignoniaceæ*.
(See Calampelis Scabra.)

EGG-PLANT. Nat. Ord., *Solanaceæ*.
(See Aubergine.)

ERYSIMUM. Nat. Ord., *Cruciferæ*.

Very showy, free-flowering, handsome hardy annuals; very effective in beds, mixed borders, or ribbons; succeed in any light, rich soil. Hardy annuals.
526 Erysimum Arkansanum. Sulphur-yellow; very handsome; from North America. 1½ feet 10
527 —— Barbarienum Variegatum. Yellow foliage; prettily variegated. 1½ feet . .10
528 —— Peroffskianum. Orange; very showy; from Palestine. 1½ feet . . .05

EUCALYPTUS (Gum-Tree). Nat. Ord., *Myrtaceæ*.

A tall and handsome fast-growing greenhouse shrub, suitable for conservatory decoration; thrives in peat and sandy loam.
529 Eucalyptus Floribunda. White; from Holland. 10 feet 25

EPACRIS. Nat. Ord., *Epacridaceæ*.

A well-known genus of extremely beautiful and interesting plants, flowering most profusely during the winter. Greenhouse shrub.
530 Epacris, Fine Mixed. Saved from a splendid collection 25

AMATEUR CULTIVATOR'S GUIDE

| NO. | | PRICE |

ERICA (Heath). Nat. Ord., *Ericaceæ*.

A well-known genus of extremely beautiful and interesting plants, flowering most profusely, and especially effective from their compact, close habit of growth. Both the hardy and greenhouse varieties require a sandy peat.

511 Ericas, Finest Mixed. A choice selection; from Cape of Good Hope. 2 feet . $0.25

ERYTHRINA. Nat. Ord., *Leguminosæ*.

A magnificent genus of half-hardy shrubs, with fine leaves, and beautiful, brilliant scarlet flowers, borne on spikes from one to one and a half feet long. They may be taken up in the fall, and kept in perfect preservation during the winter in a dry cellar, the roots covered with half dry earth: when taken up, the branches should be well cut back, say to within four inches of the previous year's growth. Plant them out in May, and they will flower beautifully three or four times in the course of the summer.

532 Erythrina Corallodendron (Coral-tree). Scarlet; from West Indies. 10 feet . . .25
533 — Hendersonii. Scarlet. 4 feet 25
534 — Laurifolia. Scarlet; from South America. 4 feet 25
535 — Crista Galli. Scarlet; from Brazil. 10 feet 25

ESCHSCHOLTZIA. Nat. Ord., *Papaveraceæ*.

Annual plants, with showy flowers; natives of California; on which account, the first species introduced was called the California Poppy; exceedingly profuse, blossoming from June until frost. Hardy annual.

536 Eschscholtzia California. Bright yellow, with rich orange centre; from California. 1 foot 05
537 — Compacta. Yellow and orange; from California. 1 foot 05
538 — Crocea. Deep orange; from California 05
539 — Alba. White; from California 05
540 — Tenuifolia. Primrose, with orange centre; very compact; from California. Half ft. .05

EUCHARIDIUM. Nat. Ord., *Onagraceæ*.

Exceedingly pretty, profuse-flowering, compact-growing plants, very effective for bedding, edging, or ribboning; succeeds in common garden soil. Hardy annuals.

541 Eucharidium Grandiflorum. Deep rose-shaded pink. 1 foot 10
542 — — Album. Pure white; beautiful 10
543 — — Roseum. Rose; very pretty 10

ERAGROSTIS. Nat. Ord., *Gramineæ*.

Ornamental grasses; suitable for winter bouquets.

544 Eragrostis Elegans (Love-grass). From south of Europe 05
545 — Cylindrifolia. From China 05

ERIANTHUS. Nat. Ord., *Gramineæ*.

546 Erianthus Ravennæ. This is a bold-looking, reed-like grass, from four to six feet high, with a fine foliage, resembling much in appearance the Pampas grass; rare. Half-hardy perennial; from south of Europe 25

ELEUSINE. Nat. Ord., *Gramineæ*.

Ornamental grasses; light and graceful.

547 Eleusine Coracana. From East Indies 10
548 — Indicum. From East Indies 10

EUTOCA. Nat. Ord., *Hydrophyllaceæ*.

Showy, free-flowering plants, suitable for beds or mixed borders; succeeds in any light, rich soil. Hardy annuals.

549 Eutoca Alba Stricta. White, striped with blue. 1 foot 10
550 — Multiflora. Lavender. 1 foot 05
551 — Ortgiesiana. Quite new; from Mexico; flower light, and dark-lilac with white . .25
552 — Wrangeliana. Lilac; pretty 05

EUCNIDE. Nat. Ord., *Loasaceæ*.

A charming golden-blossomed plant; alike effective and showy in mixed borders or grown in pots for conservatory decoration. Succeeds in a light, rich soil. Half-hardy annual.

564 Eucnide Bartonoides. Primrose; from Mexico 10

SILVER FERN. See page 43.

TO THE FLOWER GARDEN. 43

EUPATORIUM. Nat. Ord., *Compositæ.*

A pretty class of herbaceous plants, with bunches of showy flowers. Hardy perennials.

No.		Price
565	Eupatorium Argeratoides. White; fine for border	$0.10
566	—— Fraserii. White; from Carolina. 1½ feet	.10
567	—— Corymbosum. Blue; from Europe. 1 foot	.10
568	—— Aromatica. White; large heads. 2 feet	.10
569	—— Superbum. White; new species; fine. 2 feet	.10

ETERNAL FLOWERS. Nat. Ord., *Compositæ.*
(See Helichrysum and Xeranthemum.)

EUPHORBIA. Nat. Ord., *Euphorbiaceæ.*

| 571 | Euphorbia Variegata. A very pretty variegated foliaged plant. Tender annual | .05 |

FENZLIA. Nat. Ord., *Polemoniaceæ.*

A splendid, profuse-blooming, neat little plant of dwarf growth, very effective in small beds, vases, or rustic baskets or boxes for conservatory or window decoration; remains in flower the whole summer; thrives best in a light, rich soil, and requires to be well supplied with moisture.

| 572 | Fenzlia Dianthiflora. Rosy-lilac, crimson centre, with yellow anthers; hardy annual; from California. 1¼ feet | .25 |

FERNS. Nat. Ord., *Polypodiaceæ.*

This graceful and magnificent tribe is too well known and highly appreciated to need description. From the seeds we offer, the amateur has the certainty of raising many elegant and graceful varieties. Delights in peaty, sandy soil.

573	Ferns Adiantums. Fine mixed	.25
574	—— Pteris Argyrea. Beautifully variegated with silver	.25
575	—— —— Golden and Silver. Finest Mixed	.25
576	—— Mixed. Choicest greenhouse and stove varieties	.25

FABIANA. Nat. Ord., *Solanaceæ.*

A handsome Erica-like greenhouse shrub, a profuse bloomer, and of the easiest culture. Thrives best in sandy peat.

| 577 | Fabiania Imbricata. White; from Chili. 2 feet | .25 |

FEVERFEW (Pyrethrum). *Compositæ.*

Handsome, free-flowering, highly ornamental plants, producing a fine effect in the mixed flower and shrubbery borders. Succeeds in any rich soil.

| 578 | Feverfew, Double White. A beautiful bedding plant, blooming all the season; half-hardy. 1 foot | .10 |

FLOS ADONIS. Nat. Ord., *Ranunculaceæ.*

| 580 | Flos Adonis. Handsome foliage, with blood-red flowers; very pretty. Hardy annual | .05 |

FORGET-ME-NOT. Nat. Ord., *Boraginaceæ.*
(See Myosotis.)

FRAXINELLA. Nat. Ord., *Rutaceæ.*
(See Dictamnus.)

FOXGLOVE. Nat. Ord., *Scrophulariaceæ.*
(See Digitalis.)

FRENCH HONEYSUCKLE. Nat. Ord., *Leguminosæ.*

| 584 | French Honeysuckle (*Hedysarum*) Mixed. A fine border-plant; red and white mixed; from Italy. Hardy perennial. 3 feet | .05 |

FUCHSIA. Nat. Ord., *Onagraceæ.*

These beautiful plants are natives of South America, and have, until lately, been treated as greenhouse plants; but the greater number are now considered among the more ornamental of our hardy exotics; they grow freely in the open ground, and enliven our flower-gardens during the whole summer with their beautiful flowers. Half-hardy perennials.

| 585 | Fuchsia. From named varieties; superb | .50 |
| 586 | —— Good Mixed. Including many fine varieties | .25 |

NO.		PRICE

FUNKIA (Day Lily). Nat. Ord., *Liliaceæ*.

587	Funkia Cœrulea. Very showy hardy border-plant, with blue flower. 1½ feet	$0.10
588	—— Liliastrum. Lilac-variegated foliage. 1½ feet	.10
590	—— Sieboldii. Light-blue; fine. 1½ feet	.10

GAILLARDIA. Nat. Ord., *Compositæ*.

Showy and universally admired plants, and among the gayest ornaments of summer flowering annuals; of the easiest culture. Will thrive in almost any garden-soil or situation, and fine for masses. Hardy annual.

591	Gaillardia Picta (painted). Orange, red, and yellow; fine. 1 foot	.05
592	—— Alba Marginata. White-edged; fine	.05
593	—— Picta Coccinea. Scarlet; very showy	.10
594	—— Grandiflora Hybrida. Rich crimson and yellow flowers; very large	.10
595	—— Richardsonii. Orange, with brown centre; very fine. 1½ feet	.10
596	—— Wellsiana. Yellow and red; fine. 1½ feet	.10
597	—— Mixed. The above varieties mixed	.10

GAURA. Nat. Ord., *Onagrariæ*.

A plant of light and graceful habit, with spikes of white and red-tinted flowers; a profuse bloomer. Half-hardy annual.

| 600 | Gaura Lindheimerii. Very pretty. 2 feet | .10 |

GALEGA (Goat's Rue). Nat. Ord., *Leguminosæ*.

Very pretty pea-shaped flower; of easy culture. Hardy perennial.

601	Galega Lilacina. Fine lilac; 2 feet	.10
602	—— Orientalis. White. 2½	.10
603	—— Officinalis. White. 3 feet	.10

GARDOQUIA. Nat. Ord., *Labiatæ*.

A pretty dwarf-growing plant, continuing in bloom for several months; well worth cultivating on account of its large, showy flowers. Hardy perennial.

| 604 | Gardoquia Betonicoides. Pink; from Mexico. 3 feet | .10 |

GERANIUM (Pelarginium). Nat. Ord., *Geraniaceæ*.

There are few plants more easily grown, or that better repay the care of the cultivator, than geraniums, or, as they are more properly called, pelargoniums. The seeds we offer are selected with great care from some of the finest collections in Europe, and may be depended upon as being the finest in every respect. Half-hardy perennials.

605	Geranium, Good Mixed	.10
606	—— Finest Mixed. Saved from the finest fancy varieties	.25
607	—— French Hybrids (*Odiers*). New spotted varieties; very fine	.25
608	—— Scarlet. Very fine for bedding and pot-culture	.10
610	—— Mixed. Saved from a named collection of scarlet, salmon, rose, and white flowering varieties	.25

GESNERA. Nat. Ord., *Gesneraceæ*.

Showy hothouse plants, generally with scarlet flowers: they require a light, rich soil. Perennial bulbs.

| 611 | Gesnera, Finest Mixed. A fine collection, embracing an assortment of colors | .25 |

GEUM. Nat. Ord., *Rosaceæ*.

Very showy, long-blooming, hardy plants; succeed best in a sandy loam. Hardy perennial.

612	Geum Coccineum. Scarlet; from Chili. 2 feet	.10
613	—— —— Superbum. Scarlet; a fine variety; from Chili. 2 feet	.10
614	—— Grandiflora. A fine, large-flowered variety	.10
615	—— Macrophyllum. A fine new variety	.10

GENTIANA. Nat. Ord., *Gentianaceæ*.

Very useful perennials. Gentiana Acaulis, which has large, deep-blue gloxinia-shaped flowers, if grown in deep, rich loam, makes a splendid edging in early summer; all the small kinds make interesting rock-plants.

TO THE FLOWER GARDEN.   45

NO.		PRICE
616.	Gentiana Acaulis. Beautiful blue; from Wales. One-quarter foot	$0.05
617	—— Asclepiadea (*swallow-wort*). Blue; fine; from Australia. One-quarter foot	.05
618	—— Cruciata. Dark-blue; flowers in cluster	.05
619	—— Mixed. Above varieties mixed	.10

GAILLARDIA.

GAZANIA. NAT. ORD., *Compositæ*.

Amongst the most effective of bedding plants; its brilliantly colored and strikingly marked flowers are produced in great abundance, and are very effective for beds or ribboning; very beautiful. Half-hardy perennial.

620	Gazania Splendens. From Cape of Good Hope. 1 foot	.25

GILIA. NAT. ORD., *Polemoniaceæ*.

This is a very pleasing family of annuals; may be sown at any time, and will bloom in almost any situation. The flowers are disposed in panicles or clusters; and, from its neat growth, it is admirably adapted for culture either in masses or detached patches. The three-colored variety is the prettiest, and lasts the longest in bloom. Hardy annual.

620½	Gilia Achillæfolia. Lilac; from California. 1½ foot	.10
621	—— —— Alba. A very fine variety, with pure white flowers	.10
622	—— California. Pale-lilac. 1½ feet	.05

NO.			PRICE
623	Gilia Capitata. Sky-blue. Three-quarters foot		$0.05
624	— Laciniata. A distinct variety, blooming in the corymbose form; blue. Three-quarters foot		.25
625	— Tricolor. Yellow eye, surrounded by a purple ring bordered by pale-blue. 1 ft.		.05
626	— Rosea. Flowers, rosy-tinted. Three-quarters foot		.05

GLADIOLUS. Nat. Ord., *Iridaceæ*.

627 Gladiolus Gandavensis, Mixed. The seeds we offer of this beautiful summer-flowering bulb were saved from an amateur collection of prize varieties, and may be relied upon as being of superior quality. Half-hardy bulbs. We would also call attention to our list of Gladiolus and summer-flowering bulbs 25

GLOBE AMARANTHUS. Nat. Ord., *Amarantaceæ*.

The Globes are well known, and much admired for their ornamental effect in the garden, and are highly prized for their heads of flowers, which, if gathered before they are too far advanced, will retain their beauty for several years. The seeds are rather slow to vegetate in the open ground, the orange in particular, which seldom starts without bottom heat, and then very reluctantly. Tender annual.

628	Globe Amaranthus (*Gomphrena*). Crimson; fine. 2 feet	.05
630	— — Variegated. From India. 2 feet	.05
631	— — White. From India. 2 feet	.05
632	— — Orange (*Hoveyii*). From New Mexico. 2 feet.	.05
633	— — Flesh-color. From India. 2 feet	.05

GLOXINIA. Nat. Ord., *Gesneraceæ*.

A superb genus of stove-plants, producing in great profusion beautiful flowers of the richest and most beautiful. Thrives best in sandy peat and loam. Hothouse bulbs.

634	Gloxinia Erecta. Saved from a fine collection	.50
635	— Finest Hybrid. From finest-named flowers	.50
636	— Good Mixed	.25

GNAPHALIUM. Nat. Ord., *Compositæ*.

Fine everlasting flowers, useful for making dry bouquets; will grow in any common garden soil. Half-hardy annual.

637 Gnaphalium Fœtidum. Yellow. 2 feet 10

GODETIA. Nat. Ord., *Onagraceæ*.

All the varieties of Godetia are well worth growing, and indeed no garden can be said to be complete without them: their profuseness of bloom and delicate tints of color have long rendered them universal favorites.

638	Godetia Alba. Pure white. 1½ feet	.05
639	— Bifrons. Rose-lilac, blotched with carmine	.05
640	— Insignis. Red lilac-purple blotches	.05
641	— Lindleyana. Peach-lilac; carmine centre	.05
642	— Rubicunda. Rosy-lilac, with ruby centre	.05
643	— — Splendens. This is a very fine variety, differing from the preceding; larger, brighter color	.25
644	— — The Bride. Cup-shaped blossom of pure white, with a broad and brilliant crimson ring at base of corolla	.25
645	— Mixed. The above mixed; choice	.25
646	— Mixed. Fine mixed	.05

GOURDS. Nat. Ord., *Cucurbitaceæ*.

The tribe of Gourds is known as producing some of the most curiously shaped of all fruits, and, being of extremely rapid growth, are very desirable for covering the trellis-work of arbors, &c.; the varied and fantastic forms of the fruit adding a peculiar charm to the luxuriance of the foliage. Tender annual.

647	Gourds, Bottle. A very useful variety	.05
648	— Pear-shaped. Two-colored	.05
649	— Apple-striped. Very ornamental	.10
650	— Egg-shaped. Resembling an egg	.10
651	— Hercules' Club. Club-shaped; curious	.10
652	— Long-fruited. Some very fine ones	.10

TO THE FLOWER GARDEN. 47

NO.		PRICE
653	Gourds, Powder-horn	$0.10
654	— Orange. In the form of an orange	.10
655	— Mixed. The above mixed	.10

GRAMMANTHES. NAT. ORD., *Crassulaceæ*.

A charming, profuse-flowering class of miniature plants, with beautiful star-shaped flowers, delighting in warm, sunny situations, and especially effective in rock-work, rustic-baskets, or edging. Half-hardy annual.

656	Grammanthes Gentianoides. Rich orange-scarlet; from Cape of Good Hope. ½ ft. .	.25
657	— Cinnabarina. Crimson-scarlet. Quarter foot	.25
658	— Lutea. Yellow. Quarter foot.	.25

GYNERIUM (PAMPAS GRASS). NAT. ORD., *Graminaceæ*.

660 Gynerium Argenteum (Pampas Grass). This is, without exception, the most stately growing species of grass known. In stature it rivals the Bamboo, attaining, in its native plains (South America), from ten to fifteen feet in height. Splendid specimens, 10 feet high, with ten to twenty spikes of flowers, were exhibited last year at the exhibition of the Massachusetts Horticultural Society. In northern latitudes, it should be protected in winter by removing to the cellar or cold frame. South of Washington it will probably prove hardy. Half-hardy perennial. (See our engraving) 25

GRANGEA. NAT. ORD., *Graminaceæ*.

661	Grangea Maderaspatana. A beautiful variety of ornamental grass. 1 foot . . .	10

GYPSOPHILA. NAT. ORD., *Caryophyllaceæ*.

A pretty, free-flowering, elegant little plant, best adapted for rustic rock-work, and edging; succeeding in any garden soil.

662	Gypsophila Elegant (*Gypsophila Elegans*). Small, starry, purple and white flowers. Hardy annual. 1 foot	.05
663	— Rose-colored. A variety of the preceding, with rose-colored flowers. Hardy annual. 1 foot	.05
664	— Muralis. Beautiful dwarf plant, neat and pretty, with small flowers, which completely cover the plant. Hardy annual. Half foot	.10
665	— Paniculata. White, in large panicles. Hardy perennial	.10
666	— Rockyana. Hardy perennial. 1 foot	.10
667	— Saxifraga. Hardy perennial. Half foot	.10
668	— Steveni. White; in corymbs; fine for bouquets. Hardy perennial. 2 feet . .	.10

HABROTHAMNUS. NAT. ORD., *Solanaceæ*.

Exceedingly handsome greenhouse shrubs, with beautiful bunches of brilliant-colored flowers of a waxy appearance, especially useful for winter and spring decoration of the conservatory or drawing-room. Half-hardy shrubs.

669	Habrothamnus Elegans. Beautiful carmine; from Mexico. 6 feet	.25
670	— Fascicularis. Bright crimson; from Mexico. 6 feet	.25

HARDENBERGIA. NAT. ORD., *Leguminosæ*.

A very beautiful and ornamental greenhouse climber, producing a profusion of splendid pea-shaped flowers, especially suited for pillars, rafters, or wire globes. Succeeds best in peat and loam. Greenhouse shrub.

671	Hardenbergia Comptoniana. 20 feet	.25
672	— Lindleyana. Blue; from Swan River. 20 feet	.25
673	— Digitata. Purple; from Swan River. 20 feet	.25
674	— Lucida. Dark-violet. 20 feet	.25
675	— Makoyana. Blue; from Swan River. 20 feet	.25

HEARTSEASE. NAT. ORD., *Violaceæ*.
(See Pansy.)

HAWKWEED. NAT. ORD., *Compositæ*.

677 Hawkweed, Golden (*Crepis Barbata*). An old but beautiful annual, of the easiest culture; begins to bloom in July, and continues till frosts; covered with flowers, the rays of light yellow finely contrasted with the brilliant purple-brown centre. 1 ft. .05

NO.		PRICE
678	Hawkweed, White (*Crepis Alba*). A variety of the preceding, with white flowers, but of much less beauty. Hardy annual. 1 foot	$0.05
680	—— Red. From Italy. 1 foot	.05

HELIOPHILA. Nat. Ord., *Cruciferæ*.

Very useful, pretty little plants for small beds or edgings, flowering very profusely, and remaining a long time in beauty. Thrives in any light rich soil. Half-hardy annuals.

681	Heliophila Arabiodes. Bright-blue; very pretty for edging. Three-quarters foot	.05
682	—— Dissecta. Blue. Three-quarters foot	.05
683	—— Trifida. Purple. Half foot	.05
684	—— Cœrulea Stricta. Bright. 1 foot	.10
684½	—— Mixed	.10

HELIOTROPIUM. Nat. Ord., *Boraginaceæ*.

The Heliotrope is almost too well known to need recommendation. Its scent is delightful; well adapted for bedding or pot-culture. Seeds sown in spring make fine plants for summer decoration. Half-hardy perennial.

685	Heliotropium Anna Turrel. Violet	.10
686	—— Corymbosa. Light-blue	.10
687	—— Grandiflora. Large trusses; blue	.10
688	—— Roi des Noirs. Very dark purple	.10
690	—— Peruvianum. Bright-purple	.10
691	—— Triomph de Liege. Lavender	.10
692	—— Voltairianum. Dark-purple	.10
693	—— Fine Mixed	.10

HELIANTHUS (Sunflower). Nat. Ord., *Compositæ*.

A splendid genus of the most showy plants, remarkable for their stately growth and the brilliancy and size of their noble flowers. Hardy annuals.

694	Helianthus Argophyllus. Yellow foliage; silky-white; from South America. 5 feet	.10
695	—— —— Striatiflorus, Fl. Pl. Flowers double; yellow, striped with chocolate-brown; fine; compact in their growth, with beautiful silvery foliage	.10
696	—— Californicus, Fl, Pl. Very large and double; from California. 5 feet	.10
697	—— —— Nanus. Dwarf variety of preceding. 3 feet	.05
698	—— Green-centred. New; fine yellow; very double, with conspicuous green centre; one of the finest. 4 feet	.10
700	—— Macrophyllus Giganteus (Giant Sunflower). A very large-growing variety, with only one flower; from Africa. 10 feet	.15
701	—— Uniflorus. New; orange-color; said to be very fine	.10
702	—— —— Sulphurens. Sulphur-color	.10

HELICHRYSUM (Eternal Flowers). Nat. Ord., *Compositæ*.

The Helichrysum are very ornamental in the garden, and much admired on account of the beauty of the flower when dried, which, if gathered when they first open, and carefully dried, will retain their form and color for years. They are highly prized for winter mantle-bouquets and ornaments for vases. Hardy annuals; from New Holland.

703	Helichrysum Atrosanguineum Nanum. A new dwarf variety; deep-crimson; very free-flowering. 1½ feet	.25
704	—— Atrococcineum Nanum. Very dwarf; dark-scarlet; very fine. 1½ feet	.10
705	—— Borussorum Rex. New; white variety; very free-flowering	.25
706	—— Brachyrhynchum. Yellow; fine. 4 feet	.10
707	—— Bracteatum. Yellow	.05
708	—— —— Album. White	.05
709	—— —— Nanum. Yellow dwarf	.10
710	—— Compositum Maximum. One of the finest of the class; flowers very double, and a large variety of colors mixed	.10
711	—— Monstrosum Alba, Fl. Pl. White; large and handsome	.10
712	—— —— Brunenun, Fl. Pl. Fine orange-scarlet and dark reddish-brown	.10
713	—— —— Luteum, Fl. Pl. Double, yellow	.10
714	—— —— Roseum. Double, rose	.10
715	—— —— Purpureum. Double, purple	.10

NO.			PRICE
716	Helichrysum Monstrosum, Mixed		$0.10
717	—— —— Nanum. Good mixture . . .		.10
718	—— Leucocephalum: A pretty white-flowered variety, forming a dwarf bush covered with silvery-white flowers; from Australia		.10
720	—— Argenteum. A greenhouse variety		.25
721	—— Maritimum. A greenhouse variety		.25
722	—— Proliferum. A greenhouse variety		.25
723	—— Stahelina. White; a greenhouse variety		.25

HERACLEUM. Nat. Ord., *Umbelliferæ*.

724 **Heracleum Giganteum.** A gigantic-growing biennial plant, with large umbelliferous flower; adapted for wide border. 8 feet 10

HELIPTERUM. Nat. Ord., *Compositæ*.

725 **Helipterum Sanfordi.** Pretty dwarf-tufted everlasting, with small neat foliage, and large globular clusters of bright golden-yellow flowers. As it grows luxuriantly in the open border, and the flowers are excellent for winter bouquets, it is a very valuable acquisition; from Australia 10

HEMEROCALLIS (Day-Lily). Nat. Ord., *Liliaceæ*.

726 **Hemerocallis Cœruleus.** Blue; a fine border-plant 10

HIBISCUS. Nat. Ord., *Malvaceæ*.

One of the most ornamental, beautiful, and showy tribe of plants cultivated. Whether the hardy sorts be planted in mixed or shrubbery border, or the more tender varieties be grown for in-doors decoration, they are all alike characterized by the size and varied beautiful colors of their flowers.

727	Hibiscus Africanus. Cream-color; rich-brown centre. Hardy annual. 1½ feet .	.05
728	—— Cameronii. Striped rose; from Madagascar. Greenhouse shrub. 4 feet .	.25
730	—— Coccineus Speciosus. Scarlet; superb. Greenhouse shrub. 3 feet .	.25
731	—— Harrisonii. Yellow. 3 feet	.10
732	—— Liliflorus. Scarlet; lily-flowered. 3 feet	.10
733	—— Tricolor. Fine shrubby species; from Japan. 6 feet	.10
734	—— Trionium. Straw-color; dark-brown centre. Hardy annual. 1 foot .	.05
735	—— Palustris. Hardy perennial, with large pink flowers. 3 feet . . .	.10

HONESTY (Satin-Flower). Nat. Ord., *Cruciferæ*.

736 **Honesty** (*Lunaria Biennis*). An old plant, but singularly interesting from the transparent, silvery-like tissue or coats of the seed-vessels in their dry, matured state, through which the fruit is conspicuously seen, and retaining the same picturesque effect for any length of time; well adapted, in a cut state, for grouping with everlasting flowers, &c. 2 feet 05

HORDEUM. Nat. Ord., *Gramineæ*.

737 **Hordeum Jubatum.** A fine new ornamental grass. 10

HUMEA. Nat. Ord., *Compositæ*.

738 **Humea Elegans.** One of the most beautiful of all plants for decorations in gardens and pleasure-grounds; in appearance resembling a light, graceful, drooping pyramid of innumerable ruby-red, grass-like florets, rising at first in erect panicles from four to eight feet in height, and gradually assuming its exquisitely beautiful outline of growth. Blooms the second season through the summer and autumn months. Half-hardy biennial 10

HUNNEMANNIA. Nat. Ord., *Papaveraceæ*.

An exceedingly beautiful herbaceous plant, with very pretty Tulip-shaped flowers. Grows in a light, rich soil. Half-hardy perennial.

739 **Hunnemannia Fumariæfolia.** Fine yellow; from Mexico. 2 feet 10

HYACINTH-BEANS. Nat. Ord., *Leguminosæ*.

(See Dolichos.)

7

DOUBLE HOLLYHOCK.

HOLLYHOCK. Nat. Ord., *Malvaceæ*.

The great improvement that has been made in this fine old flower within a few years has now placed it among the most popular flowers of the day; its stately growth and magnificent spikes of flowers being among the most attractive objects of the garden. It flowers the second and third year after sowing, and then dies, unless it is kept up by cuttings, or divisions of root. Seeds sown in January will produce plants which will flower the same year. Hardy perennial.

740 **Hollyhock, Chinese, Annual.** Fine double; several beautiful colors; mixed. 2½ ft. $0.10
741 — Mixed (*Althea Rosea*). Fine varieties. Seventy-five per cent of the plants may be expected to be double 05
742 — **Extra Fine Mixed.** Saved from the finest new English and Scottish named sorts .25
743 — **Splendid Collections.** See page of assortments.

HYDROLEA. Nat. Ord., *Hydrolaceæ*.

An exceedingly handsome greenhouse herbaceous plant, producing its pretty flowers in bunches; succeeds well in loam and peat.
745 **Hydrolea Azurea.** Dark-blue; from South America. 1 foot 25

HYPERICUM. Nat. Ord., *Hypericaceæ*.

Very interesting and ornamental greenhouse shrubs, requiring only the usual greenhouse treatment.
746 **Hypericum Involutum.** Yellow; from New South Wales. 3 feet 25
747 — **Webbii.** A splendid new variety, with beautiful large foliage. 3 feet . . .25

INCARVILLEA. Nat. Ord., *Bignoniaceæ*.

Elegant free-flowering climbers, of graceful habit; succeeds best in loam and peat. Greenhouse climber.
748 **Incarvillea Sinensis.** White trumpet-flowers, shaded with rose; from China. 20 feet . .25
749 — **Grandiflora.** New. A very distinct and pretty dark-colored species 50

ICE-PLANT. Nat. Ord., *Ficoidiaceæ*.

A most singular, trailing plant, with thick fleshy leaves that have the appearance of being covered with crystals of ice; very ornamental for rock-work, or mixing with other plants in conservatory or flower-garden.
750 **Ice-Plant.** From Greece. Half-hardy annual. 05

IMPATIENS. Nat. Ord., *Balsaminaceæ*.

Handsome, showy border-plants; succeeds in light, rich soil. Half-hardy annual.
751 **Impatiens Glanduligera.** Yellow and crimson; from East Indies 10

TO THE FLOWER GARDEN. 51

NO.   PRICE

IBERIS TENOREANA.

IBERIS. Nat. Ord., *Cruciferæ*.

Profuse-blooming, pretty little plants, especially adapted for rookeries, old stumps, or rustic baskets. They come into flower amongst our earliest spring plants, and, for a long time, continue a dense mass of beauty; succeed in any garden-soil. Hardy perennials.

752	Iberis Candidissima. New; beautiful; pure white. Half foot	$0.05
753	—— Semperflorens. Fine, white; from Sicily. Half foot	.05
754	—— Umbellata. Very fine. Half foot	.05
755	—— —— Carnea. Light-pink. Half foot	.05
756	—— Tenoreana. Blush. Half foot	.05

INDIGOFERA. Nat. Ord., *Leguminosæ*.

A genus of elegant free-flowering greenhouse shrubs, of easy culture, thriving in sandy loam and peat.

757	Indigofera Australis. Pink; from New South Wales. 3 feet	.25
758	—— Cytisoides. Red; from China. 3 feet	.25
759	—— Sylvatica. Rose and lilac. 3 feet	.25
760	—— Tinctoria. Indigo of commerce	.25
761	—— Mixed	.25

IRIS. Nat. Ord., *Iridaceæ*.

762	Iris Anglica. Fine mixed	.25

IPOMEA (Convolvulus). Nat. Ord., *Convolvulaceæ*.

A genus of beautiful climbing plants, which, for the adornment of the conservatory and greenhouse, or for warm, sheltered situations out of doors, are pre-eminently beautiful, many of them combining marvellously brilliant colors with pure white margins, and varying in shade from the most intense violet-blue to the most delicate cerulean. All the varieties are splendid, and should be extensively cultivated. The perennial species are invaluable for greenhouse decoration. Tender annual.

52 AMATEUR CULTIVATOR'S GUIDE

NO.		PRICE
763	Ipomea, Bona Nox (*Good-night*). White; from West Indies. from 10 to 15 feet	$0.10
764	—— Coccinea (*Star Ipomea*). Fine scarlet	.05
765	—— Burridge's (*Morning Glory*). Fine variety, with large, bright crimson flowers. 15 feet	.05
766	—— 'Dickson's. A splendid Morning Glory, with large blue flowers	.05
767	—— Hederacea Superba Grandiflora. A large sky-blue flower, elegantly bordered with pure white; exceedingly beautiful. 12 feet	.25
768	—— —— Lilacina. Delicate lilac, beautifully bordered with white. 12 feet . .	.25
769	—— —— Atroviolacea. Violet, bordered with pure white; superb. 10 feet . .	.25
770	—— Limbata. Rosy-violet, elegantly blotched with white. 10 to 15 feet . .	.10
771	—— —— Elegantissima. One of the finest of all the Ipomea; blue, with intense purple centre in the form of a star, with pure white margin	.25
772	—— Purpurea (*Morning Glory*). Mixed	.05
773	—— Nil. Light-blue; fine. 10 feet	.05
774	—— Rubro Cærulea. Produces a profusion of very large azure-blue flowers, which, in its maturity, is one of the most lovely objects imaginable. 10 to 15 feet . .	.25
775	—— Learii. Magnificent mazarine-blue, shading to red. Greenhouse perennial. 10 to 12 feet	.25
776	—— Tuberosa. Pale-yellow; from West Indies. Greenhouse perennial. . .	.25
777	—— Wildenovii. Purple; from East Indies	.25
778	—— Quamoclit. (See Cypress-Vine)	.05

IPOMOPSIS. NAT. ORD., *Polemoniaceæ*.

Remarkably handsome free-flowering plants, with long spikes of dazzling orange and scarlet flowers; very effective for conservatory and out-door decoration; succeeds in light rich soil. Half-hardy biennial.

780	Ipomopsis Aurantiaca. Orange; from Carolina. 3 feet	.10
781	—— Beyrichi. Scarlet and orange; from Carolina	.10
782	—— Elegans. Scarlet; from Carolina	.10
783	—— Picta. Scarlet and gold	.10
784	—— —— Superba. Scarlet.	.10

ISOTOMA. NAT. ORD., *Lobeliaceæ*.

A neat, erect, slender-branched plant, from six to twelve inches in height, with starry, light porcelain-blue Lobelia-like flowers, which, producing a continuation of bloom throughout the summer, renders them very effective for bedding, edging, &c.

785	Isotoma Longiflora. White. 1 foot	.10
786	—— Petræa. Cream-colored	.10
787	—— Axillaris. Blue	.10

JACOBEA (SENECIO). NAT. ORD., *Compositæ*.

A useful and exceedingly showy class of gay-colored profuse-blooming plants, of the easiest culture; remarkably effective in beds or ribbons; delights in a light, rich soil. Hardy annual.

788	Jacobea. Double, Purple. 1 foot	.10
790	—— —— Dark-Crimson. 1 foot	.10
791	—— —— Flesh-color. 1 foot	.10
792	—— —— Dwarf-Blue. Silvery grayish-blue. 1 foot	.10
793	—— —— Lilac. Fine. 1 foot	.10
794	—— —— Magenta-color. Fine. 1 foot	.10
795	—— —— White. 1 foot	.10
796	—— —— Finest, Mixed	.10

NEW DWARF VARIETIES.

The following are of a very dwarf and compact habit, and fine for pots or beds.

798	Jacobea Dwarf, White. Double. Half foot	.25
799	—— —— Crimson. Double. Half foot	.25
800	—— —— Carmine. Double. Half foot	.25
801	—— —— Copper-color. Double. Half foot	.25
802	—— —— Dark-Blue. Double. Half foot	.25
803	—— —— Mixed. The above varieties	.25

| NO. | | | PRICE |

KAULFUSSIA. Nat. Ord., *Compositæ*.

A beautiful little annual, resembling an Aster, the ray florets of which curl curiously back after it has been expanded a short time. Half-hardy annual.

804	Kaulfussia Amelloides. Blue; from Cape of Good Hope. Half foot	$0.05
805	—— —— Alba. White. Half foot	.10
806	—— Atroviolacea. A beautiful, showy, intense violet-colored variety. Superb	.10

KENNEDYA. Nat. Ord., *Leguminosæ*.

These climbers are among the most striking of greenhouse ornaments, and deserve more extensive cultivation than has hitherto been extended to them, as few plants are more serviceable for greenhouse decoration. Their bright colors impart a most cheerful appearance during the early part of the season; and, if trained round fanciful wire shapes, a peculiarly interesting effect is produced. Steep the seed in warm water for six hours before sowing. Greenhouse shrub.

807	Kennedya Comptoniana. Blue; from New Holland. 12 feet	.25
808	—— Longiracema. Pink and scarlet; from New South Wales. 3 feet	.25
809	—— Marryattea. Scarlet; from Australia. 4 feet	.25
810	—— Ovata. Purple; from New Holland. 6 feet	.25
811	—— —— Alba. White; from New Holland. 6 feet	.25
812	—— Rotundifolia. Scarlet; from New South Wales. 5 feet	.25
813	—— Mixed	.25

KOLREUTERIA. Nat. Ord., *Sapindaceæ*.

A middle-sized deciduous tree; a native of China; very ornamental from its large variously divided foliage, and its conspicuous terminal compound spikes of rich yellow flower.

| 814 | Kolreuteria Paniculata. Yellow. 7 feet | .10 |

KALMIA. Nat. Ord., *Ericaceæ*.

| 815 | Kalmia Latifolia. A beautiful hardy shrub. White and pink. 4 feet | .10 |

LANTANA. Nat. Ord., *Verbenaceæ*.

A remarkably handsome free-flowering genus of plants, with brilliantly colored flowers constantly changing in hue; very effective either for pot-culture, or for bedding purposes when planted out, except in dry soil. The plants will bloom more profusely, if retained in their pots, and plunged where intended to flower.

| 816 | Lantanas, Mixed varieties. Saved from a named collection | .25 |

LARKSPUR (Delphinum). Nat. Ord., *Ranunculaceæ*.

One of the generally cultivated and ornamental genus of plants, combining unusual richness with an endless variety of colors, all of which are extremely beautiful and pleasing. The flowers are produced in the greatest profusion; and the plants, in beds, masses, or ribbons, are strikingly effective: indeed, few plants are so generally useful and valuable for their decorative qualities, either in the garden or when cut for vases. The great difficulty has hitherto been the procuring of seeds which would yield double flowers. To this object we have given special attention, and now offer seed saved only from such varieties as are really to be depended upon, and worthy of a place in every garden. For the guidance of amateurs, we may simply notice that the stock-flowered Larkspur is of the same habit as the old Dwarf Rocket, but has longer spikes, and much larger and more double flowers; the tall stock-flowered variety is the same style as the branching, but with more compact spikes, and larger and more double flowers. The tall-growing varieties scattered in shrubbery-borders produce a charming effect when backed by green foliage of the shrubs. Hardy annuals.

817	Larkspur Dwarf Rocket. A fine mixture; saved from a fine collection. 1 foot	.05
818	—— Tall Rocket. Same as preceding, except being taller. 2½ feet	.05
819	—— Hyacinth-flowered. Finest mixed	.05
820	—— Dwarf Stock-flowered. A very desirable variety; saved from a beautiful collection	.05
821	—— Tall Stock-flowered. Mixed; very fine	.05
822	—— Pyramidal. Mixed; a splendid mixture	.05
823	—— New Mauve-color. Very fine	.10
824	—— Tricolor Elegans. Beautifully striped	.10
825	—— German Branching. A good variety colors	.05

| NO. | | PRICE |

LATHYRUS (Perennial Pea). Nat. Ord., *Leguminosæ*.

Showy, free-flowering plants, growing in any common soil; very ornamental on trellis-work, old stumps, or for covering fences or walls. Hardy perennials.

- 826 Lathyrus Latifolius. Red; from England. 5 feet. $0.05
- 827 —— —— Albus. White. 5 feet 05
- 828 —— —— Grandiflorus. Large-flowered. 5 feet 05

LAVENDULA (Lavender). Nat. Ord., *Labiatæ*.

A genus of plants chiefly cultivated on account of the delicious fragrance of their flowers. They succeed in any garden soil. Hardy perennial.

- 830 Lavendula Spica. Lilac; from Europe. 2 feet 05

LAVATERA. Nat. Ord., *Malvaceæ*.

Very showy, profuse-blooming, handsome plants; exceedingly effective when used as a background to other plants. Hardy annuals.

- 831 Lavatera Rosea. Rose-color; fine. 2 feet 05
- 832 —— Alba. White; fine. 2 feet 05

LAGERSTRŒMIA. Nat. Ord., *Lythraceæ*.

A splendid greenhouse shrub, with exceedingly handsome flowers, sometimes called the Bride of India.

- 833 Lagerstrœmia Indica. Lilac; from East Indies. 5 feet 25
- 834 —— Barclayana 25
- 835 —— Rosea 25

LEPTOSIPHON. Nat. Ord., *Polemoniaceæ*.

A charming tribe of the most beautiful of our hardy annuals. Nearly allied to the Gilia, and requiring the same treatment.

- 836 Leptosiphon Androsaceus. Mixed; from California 05
- 837 —— Aureus. Golden-yellow; from California. Half foot 10
- 838 —— Luteus. Primrose; orange centre. Half foot 10
- 839 —— Densiflora. Rosy-lilac; from California. ' Half foot 05
- 840 —— —— Alba. White; from California. Half foot 10
- 841 —— Hybridus. New French Hybrids. This we consider the finest of them all, embracing all the colors from dark-maroon, orange, lilac, purple, crimson, violet, golden-yellow, and white; of compact growth. One-third foot 25

LIATRIS. Nat. Ord., *Compositæ*.

A hardy perennial, found in many parts of the United States, growing in meadows and moist places.

- 842 Liatris Spicata. Flowers bright-purple, on stems from three to five feet 10
- 843 —— Scariosa (Gay Feather). A showy variety, with purple flowers 10
- 844 —— Pumila. Purple; large-flowered 10
- 845 —— Graminifolia. Pink; in heads 10

LILIUM. Nat. Ord., *Lilaceæ*.

The Lily stands pre-eminent among all flowering bulbs. Stately in habit, varied in color, highly fragrant, perfectly hardy, easily cultivated, and blooming from June until frost, they can claim, as they fully deserve, a prominent place in the largest or smallest garden. The seeds often lie dormant several months before vegetating. Succeeds well in a mixture of loam, peat, and silver-sand.

- 846 Lilium Giganteum. The tallest and most magnificent of the lilies, growing ten feet high, with spikes of white trumpet-shaped flowers, with carmine streaks 25
- 847 —— Lancifolium Hybridium (Japan Lily). Finest mixed 25
- 848 —— Auratum. The new golden-banded Lily. This superb Lily has flowers twelve inches in diameter; pure white, with a yellowish band through the centre of each petal, and covered with brownish dots. It is deliciously fragrant; one stem often produces six to ten of its immense blossoms. We have a few well-ripened seeds of the above, which we offer. Ten seeds 50

LIMNANTHES. Nat. Ord., *Tropæolaceæ*.

Very beautiful, showy, profuse-blooming, dwarf-growing plants; slightly fragrant; particularly effective and valuable as edgings, succeeding in any soil or situation, but delighting most in a moist soil; from California. Hardy annuals.

TO THE FLOWER GARDEN.   55

NO.		PRICE
849	Limnanthes Douglassii. Pale-yellow, bordered with white. Half foot	$0.05
850	—— Alba. White variety; fine. Half foot	.05
851	—— Rosea. Rose-color. Half foot	.05
852	—— Sulphurea odorata. Sulphur-color; fragrant. 1 foot	.10

LINARIA. Nat. Ord., *Scrophulariaceæ.*

A handsome, free-flowering genus of snapdragon-like plants, remarkable for the beauty and variety of their colors; well adapted for and very effective in beds, or ribbons, rockwork, woodland-walks, &c. Succeeding in any garden soil. Hardy annual.

853	Linaria Macroura (Long-horned). Yellow; resembling, when in full bloom, a small compact bush of blossoms. 1 foot	.05
854	—— Purpurea. Purple dwarf. Half foot	.05
855	—— Carnea. Flesh-color. Half foot	.10
856	—— Triornithophora. Red, purple, and yellow; one of the finest. 1 foot	.05
857	—— Speciosa. Very showy; purple flowers. Half foot	.10
858	—— Bipartita Splendida. New; rich-purple; beautiful	.10
859	—— —— Lutea. New; brilliant-yellow	.10
860	—— Finest Mixed	.10

LINDHEIMERIA. Nat. Ord., *Compositæ.*

861 Lindheimeria Texana. A very pretty little plant, having a vanilla-like odor. Yellow; fine. Hardy annual. 2 feet 10

LISIANTHUS. Nat. Ord., *Gentianeæ.*

When well grown, this is a splendid plant for greenhouse or conservatory decoration. Its flowers are extremely handsome, and of rich dark-blue, which few greenhouse plants possess. Succeeds best in a sandy peat, with a very little loam. Winter in a warm greenhouse, and re-pot in spring.

862 Lisianthus Russellianus. Rich-blue, shaded with purple; from Mexico. 2 feet . . .25

LINUM. Nat. Ord., *Linaceæ.*

A genus of the most beautiful, free-flowering plants, amongst which stands, distinguished for its brilliant-colored flowers, Linum Grandiflorum Coccineum, being one of the handsomest, most effective, and showy bedding-plants we have; for, whilst its habit of growth is slender and delicate, it produces a profusion of beautiful, saucer-shaped flowers, of a rich scarlet-crimson, with crimson-black centre. Linum Flavum is a well-known favorite, while Linum Luteum Corymbiflorum is distinguished for its bunches of beautiful straw-colored blossoms, and contrasts beautifully with Linum Grandiflorum Coccineum. The whole genus deserves general cultivation. Most of the varieties make nice pot-plants.

863	Linum Grandiflorum Coccineum. Brilliant-scarlet, with crimson centre; from Algiers. 1 foot	.10
864	—— —— Album. Beautiful white variety. 1 foot	.10
865	—— —— Purpureum. A new variety, with rich purple flowers, similar to the above	.10
866	—— Flavum. Yellow; from Crimea. 1 foot	.10
867	—— Lewisii. Blue and white stripes; from North America. 2 feet	.10
868	—— Variegatum. Striped, lilac and white; new. 2 feet	.10
869	—— Perenne. Blue; handsome. Hardy perennial. 1½ feet	.05
870	—— Album. White-flowered. 1½ feet	.05
871	—— Candidissimum. White. Hardy perennial	.25
872	—— Usitatissimum Grandiflorum. Large, blue. Hardy annual. 2 feet	.05

LOASA. Nat. Ord., *Loasaceæ.*

The Loasa are beautiful, tender, climbing annuals, suitable for covering a trellis or ornamental wire-work.

873	Loasa Aurantica. Orange-color. 6 feet	.10
874	—— Herbertii. Scarlet. 6 feet	.10
875	—— Tricolor. Shaded, yellow. 6 feet	.10

LOBELIA. Nat. Ord., *Lobeliaceæ.*

A most elegant and useful genus of dwarf plants, of easy culture; well adapted for bedding, edging, pots, or rockeries. Lobelias, in fact, are employed as universally in the general summer-garden as scarlet geraniums, to beds of which they form a neat and effective edging. The varieties of Lobelia Erinus are generally used for this purpose, yet by some the

56   AMATEUR CULTIVATOR'S GUIDE

NO.   PRICE

varieties of Lobelia Ramosa are preferred, which, though larger in bloom, are neither so elegant nor compact. Lobelia Speciosa is the finest of all, from its intense dark-blue color, with a clear white spot, and its dark-colored foliage. The varieties of Lobelia Gracilis are the best adapted for rock-work, pots, or suspended baskets, to droop over. The seeds of Lobelias, being very small, cover very slightly when sown. A light rich soil is suitable for all the varieties.

876 **Lobelia Cardinalis** (Cardinal Flower). A well-known native variety, with scarlet flowers; one of the finest. Hardy perennial. 2 feet $0.10
877 —— **Hybridia Grandiflora.** A new hybrid variety; very fine. Hardy perennial . .25
878 —— **Erinus.** Flower deep-blue; a fine bedder. Half-hardy perennial. Half foot . .25
879 —— —— **Alba.** White; pretty. Half foot 10
880 —— —— **Compacta.** Dark-blue, with white centre; compact growth. Half-hardy annual. Half foot 10
881 —— —— **Grandiflora.** Large-flowered variety; dark-blue. Half-hardy annual . .10
882 —— —— **Marmorata.** Marble, blue and white. Half foot 10
883 —— —— —— **Superba.** A new variety, with large blue flowers; very fine. Half-hardy annual. Half foot 10
884 —— —— **Rosea.** Pretty rose-colored flowers. Half foot 10
885 —— —— **Ramosoides.** Dark-blue; dwarf-branching. Half foot 10
886 —— —— **Speciosa.** New. The most effective of all the varieties, yielding a long succession of its extremely rich and beautiful intense azure-blue flowers; fine for pots. Half-hardy annual. Quarter foot 10
887 —— —— **Paxtoniana.** A beautiful variety of the species; fine habit, with profuse bloom of pure white, with sky-blue belt; the largest flower and best habit in the tribe; a beautiful bedding-plant. Half-hardy annual. Half foot 25
888 —— **Formosa.** Beautiful; dark-blue. Half foot 10
889 —— **Gracilis.** A delicate-growing variety; dark-blue. Half-hardy annual. Half ft. .10
890 —— —— **Alba.** White. Half-hardy annual. Half foot 10
891 —— —— **Compacta.** Blue and white; fine. Half foot 10
892 —— **Ramosus.** Branching; fine dark-blue. Half foot 10
893 —— —— **Alba.** White; branching. Half foot 10
894 —— —— **Nana Nona.** A dwarf variety; fine. Half foot 10
895 —— —— **Rubra.** Red; fine. Half foot 10
896 —— **Trigonicaulis.** A new very fine variety; light-blue flowers. Half-hardy annual .25

LOPEZIA. NAT. ORD., *Onagraceæ*.

A superb greenhouse plant, flowering in beautiful bunches during the winter.

897 **Lopezia Miniata.** Deep-peach; from Mexico. 2 feet 25

LOVE-LIES-BLEEDING. NAT. ORD., *Amarantaceæ*.

898 **Love-lies-bleeding** (*Amaranthus Caudatus*). An old and well-known annual, with blood-red flowers, which hang in pendant spikes, and at a little distance look like streams of blood. 3 to 4 feet 05

LOVE-IN-A-MIST. NAT. ORD., *Ranunculaceæ*.

(See Nigella.)

LOTUS. NAT. ORD., *Leguminosa*.

An exceedingly ornamental genus of plants, with pea-shaped flowers. Half-hardy annuals.

899 **Lotus Jacobæus.** Dark-brown; fine for pot-culture; from Cape Verde Islands. 2 feet .10
900 —— **Luteus.** Yellow; from Cape Verde Islands. 2 feet 10

LOPHOSPERMUM. NAT. ORD., *Scrophulariaceæ*.

An elegant and highly ornamental genus of climbers, with handsome and showy foxglove-like flowers; very effective for conservatory, greenhouse, or garden decoration, and may be used with advantage for hanging baskets; will bloom the first season from seed. Half-hardy perennials.

901 **Lophospermum Coccineum.** Red 25
902 —— **Hendersonii.** Rose 25

TO THE FLOWER GARDEN. 57

NO. PRICE

LOPHOSPERMUM SCANDENS.

903	Lophospermum Scandens. Purple	$0.10
904	—— —— Cliftoni. Dark rose	.25
906	—— Punctatum. A splendid new spotted variety	.10
907	—— Mixed. The above varieties	.25

LUPINS. Nat. Ord., *Leguminosæ.*

A splendid genus of the most ornamental, beautiful, and free-flowering of garden plants, with long, graceful spikes of bloom; colors, rich and varied. Many of the varieties are of stately, robust growth, which makes them exceedingly valuable for mixed flower and shrubbery borders, while the dwarf varieties make neat, trim bedding-plants. Among the most distinguished, we may mention Lupinus Hartwegii and varieties; Lupinus Hybridus and varieties, L. Menziesii, L. Magnificus, L. Pubescens Elegans, and L. Subcarnosus.

908	Lupins, Garden. Large, blue. 1½ feet	.05
909	—— —— Yellow. 1½ feet	.05
910	—— —— Rose-colored.	.05
911	—— —— White. 1½ feet	.05
912	—— —— Mixed	.05
913	—— Affinis. Blue, white, and purple; very pretty; from California. Hardy annual. 1½ feet	.05
914	—— Alba-coccineus. New; rosy-red half way of the spike, from thence to the apex pure white. Showy	.25
915	—— Dunnetti Atroviolacea. A rich party-colored variety; violet, brown, and yellow	.10
916	—— Cruickshankii. Blue, white, and yellow; from Peru. 3 feet	.05
917	—— Hartwegii, Albus. Pure white. 2 feet	.05
918	—— —— Cœlestinus. Sky-blue. 1½ feet	.10
919	—— —— Rosea. Rose-color. 1½ feet	.10
920	—— Hybridus Insignis. Purple, white, and yellow, changing to purple-lilac. Hardy annual. 2 feet	.10
921	—— —— Superbus. Lilac, white, red, and yellow. Hardy annual	.10
922	—— Magnificus. Violet and white; from North America. Hardy perennial. 2½ feet	.10
923	—— Menziesii. Sulphur-yellow	.10

NO.			PRICE
924	Lupins Moritzianus. Fine blue. Half foot		$0.05
925	—— Mutabilis Varie-color. Colors various and handsome. Hardy annual		.05
926	—— Nanus. Dwarf, blue and white; very pretty. Hardy annual. Half foot		.05
927	—— —— Albus. Pure white. Half foot		.05
928	—— Polyphyllus. Blue. Hardy perennial. 2½ feet		.05
929	—— —— Alba. White. Hardy perennial		.05
930	—— —— Subcarnosus. Blue and white, the latter changing to crimson; from Texas. Hardy annual. 1 foot		.10

LYCHNIS. NAT. ORD., *Caryophyllaceæ*.

A genus of handsome and highly ornamental plants, of easy culture. Lychnis Chalcedonica is strikingly effective in mixed flowers and shrubbery borders. Lychnis Viscaria Splendens and Lychnis Haageana are extremely beautiful. They succeed in any good rich soil. Hardy perennials.

931	Lychnis Chalcedonica. Scarlet; from Russia. 2 feet	.05
932	—— —— Alba. White; from Russia. 2 feet	.05
933	—— —— Mutabilis. Rose-white; from Russia. 2 feet	.05
934	—— Flos Jovis (Jove's Flower). Bright-red; from Germany. 1½ feet	.05
935	—— Fulgens. Bright-scarlet; from Siberia. 1½ feet	.05
936	—— Haageana. Beautiful bright-scarlet. 1½ feet	.10
937	—— Sieboldi. White, fine. 1½ feet	.25
938	—— Presslii Multiflora. New	.25
939	—— Lapponica. New. Hardy perennial	.10

LYTHRUM. NAT. ORD., *Lythraceæ*.

940	Lythrum Roseum Superbum. Deep rose, in long spikes; a fine border-plant. Hardy perennial. 2 feet	.05

MAGYDARIS. NAT. ORD., *Umbelliferæ*.

A beautiful ornamental-foliaged plant, with immense heads of showy yellow flowers.

941	Magydaris Tomentosa. Yellow; from Algeria	.10

MADARIA. NAT. ORD., *Compositæ*.

942	Madaria Corymbosa. Pale-yellow; fine for borders; from California. 1½ feet	.05

MALOPE. NAT. ORD., *Malvaceæ*.

Handsome plants of branching habit, producing their large flower in great profusion; very effective in mixed borders.

943	Malope Grandiflora. Dark crimson; from Barbary. 2 feet	.05
944	—— Alba. White; from Barbary. 2 feet	.05

MARIGOLD. NAT. ORD., *Compositæ*.

All features considered, it is questionable whether any genus of plants amongst annuals can vie with either the French or African Marigolds in their glowing colors and their elegantly lobed leaves, of the richest green tint, and, above all, in their almost unequalled and sole adaption for summer and late autumn decoration in the flower-garden, retaining their verdant beauty and gorgeous colors undimmed and undiminished to the very verge of winter. No feature in their habit of growth is in excess either in leaf or flower, but admirably balanced for effect; neat, compact, and beautiful; of the easiest culture; should always be thinned or transplanted so as to stand single, at least eighteen inches distance from each other.

945	Marigold African (*Tagetes erecta*). Lemon-color. 2 feet	.05
946	—— —— Orange-color. 2 feet	.05
947	—— French (*T. patula*). New, orange. 1 foot	.05
948	—— —— Superb Striped. 1 foot	.10
949	—— —— New Dwarf. Fine. Three-quarters foot	.05
950	—— —— Miniature. A small-flowered variety. Three-quarters foot	.05
951	—— —— Good Mixed	.05
952	—— —— Superb Mixed. Saved only from selected double flowers	.10
953	—— Garden Superb. Large double orange flowers; very double	.05
954	—— Cape (*Calendula Pluvialis*). Purple and white. 1½ feet	.05
955	—— Ranunculus. Orange, double; fine	.05
956	—— Dunnetts. New, orange	.10

TO THE FLOWER GARDEN.

NO.   PRICE

MARVEL OF PERU. Nat. Ord., *Nyctaginiaceæ*.

957   **Marvel of Peru.** Splendid varieties mixed, including all the finest sorts; very picturesque and diversified colors, finely contrasted with its dark-green, glossy foliage, and densely branching habit; blooming throughout the summer and autumn months. 2 feet $0.05

958   —— **Assortments, Splendid.** Colors in separate packages (see collection).

MALVA OR MALLOWS. Nat. Ord., *Malvaceæ*.

Showy free-flowering border-plants; succeeding in any garden-soil. Hardy annuals.

959   **Malva Capensis.** Red and white; from Cape of Good Hope. 2 feet 05
960   —— **Coccinea.** Purple; from south of Europe. 2 feet 05
961   —— **Zebrina.** White and purple, striped 05
962   —— **Moschata.** Rose-foliage; musk-scented 05

MACHÆRANTHERA TANACETIFOLIA (one-fifth natural size).

MACHÆRANTHERA. Nat. Ord., *Compositæ*.

A pretty little dwarf free-flowering plant; flowers resembling Michaelmas Daisy. Hardy annual.

963   **Machæranthera Tanacetifolia.** Blush-purple, with golden-yellow centre. 1 foot

MARTYNIA (Unicorn Plant). Nat. Ord., *Pedaliaceæ*.

Handsome tropical annuals, remarkable for the size of their flower compared with the leaves; requires a light rich soil and a warm situation. The young fruit, or seed-pods, are considered fine for pickling. Tender annual.

964   **Martynia Angularis.** Purple; from Brazil. 2 feet 05
965   —— **Cramiolaria.** White; from Brazil. 2 feet 05
966   —— **Fragrans** (sweet-scented). Purple; from Mexico. 2 feet 05
967   —— **Lutea.** Yellow; from Brazil. 2 feet 05

MATRICARIA. Nat. Ord., *Compositæ*.

A beautiful dwarf-growing plant, well adapted for beds or edging. Half-hardy perennial.

968   **Matricaria Eximia.** Double, quilled. 1½ foot 10
969   —— **Capensis.** Double. White; very fine. Three-quarters foot 10

MAURANDYA. Nat. Ord., *Scrophulariaceæ*.

The most graceful and free-flowering of soft-wooded climbers, whether for the ornamentation of the conservatory and greenhouse, or for pillars, trellis-work, and verandas in the flower-garden. The effect produced by the profusion of elegant and varied-colored flowers is strikingly beautiful. Blooms the first season from seed. Half-hardy perennial.

MAURANDYA BARCLAYANA.

NO.				PRICE
971	Maurandya Antirrhinum. Pale-violet, 10 feet			$0.10
972	—— Barclayana. Rich violet. 10 feet			.10
973	—— —— Alba. White. 10 feet			.10
974	—— —— Coccinea. Scarlet. 10 feet			.10
975	—— —— Rosea. Rose. 10 feet			.10
976	—— —— Lilacina. Lilac. 10 feet			.10
977	—— Purpurea Grandiflora. Purple. 10 feet			.10
978	—— Semperflorens, Alba. White. 10 feet			.10
979	—— —— Rosea. Rose. 10 feet			.10
980	—— Mixed. Above mixed			.10

MELAMPODIUM. Nat. Ord., *Compositæ*.

982 Melampodium Macranthum. A pretty border-plant. Yellow. 2 feet 10

MESEMBRYANTHEMUM. Nat. Ord., *Ficoideæ*.

A brilliant and profuse-flowering tribe of extremely pretty dwarf-growing plants; strikingly effective in beds, edging, rock-work, rustic baskets, or vases, in warm, sunny situations; also for indoor decoration if grown in pots, boxes, or pans. Succeeds best in dry loamy soil. Half-hardy annual.

983	Mesembryanthemum Capitatum. Yellow. 1 foot	.05
984	—— Crystallium (Ice-plant). White. Half foot	.05
985	—— Glabrum. Smooth yellow. Three-quarters foot	.05
986	—— Pinnatifidum. Yellow. 1 foot	.05
987	—— Pomeridianum. Bright yellow, large-flowered	.05
988	—— Tricolor. Rosy-pink, purple centre	.05
989	—— —— Album. White, with purple centre	.10
990	—— Mixed. Above, mixed	.10

MELALEUCA. Nat. Ord., *Myrtaceæ*.

A genus of very desirable greenhouse or conservatory plants, remarkable for the neatness of their foliage, and the beauty of their flowers, which are produced on gracefully drooping branches.

991	Melaleuca Hypericifolia. Scarlet; from New South Wales	.25
992	—— Myrtifolia	.25

TO THE FLOWER GARDEN. 61

MANDEVILLEA SUAVEOLENS (one-fifth natural size).

MANDEVILLEA. Nat. Ord., *Apocynaceæ.*

Well known as a most elegant and beautiful pure white, large, open, highly fragrant, trumpet-shaped flower, freely produced in a profusion of racemes, which renders it extremely attractive either in greenhouse or garden. From Buenos Ayres.

993   Mandevillea Suaveolens.   White.   Greenhouse shrub.   10 feet $0.25

MELIA. Nat. Ord., *Meliaceæ.*

A very ornamental tree, continuing in bloom the whole summer; thrives best in peat, loam, and sand.

993½ Melia Azederach.   Blue; from Syria.   30 feet 25

METROSIDEROS. Nat. Ord., *Myrtaceæ.*

A splendid greeehouse shrub, with beautiful bottle brush-like flowers; succeeds in peat and loam.

994   Metrosideros Lanceolata.   Red; from New Holland.   10 feet 25

MICROPUS. Nat. Ord., *Compositæ.*

A new everlasting flower, of much promise. Half-hardy annual.

995   Micropus Supinus.   An interesting novelty 10

MIMOSA (Sensitive-Plant).   Nat. Ord., *Leguminosæ.*

996   Mimosa Pudica.   Grown as a curiosity, being so sensitive that the leaves close up by being slightly touched. Suitable for growing in pots, or the open border. 1 ft. .05

MIMULUS (Monkey-Flower).   Nat. Ord., *Scrophulariaceæ.*

A genus of extremely handsome, profuse-flowering plants, with singularly shaped and brilliantly colored flowers, which are distinguished by their rich and strikingly beautiful markings. Seeds sown in spring make fine bedding-plants for summer blooming, while seed sown in autumn produces very effective early-flowering greenhouse plants. Half-hardy perennials.

997   Mimulus Cardinalis (Monkey-Flower).   Very showy, with brilliant scarlet flowers; blooms readily the first year from seed.   Fine for bedding.   Three-quarters ft. . .10

62   AMATEUR CULTIVATOR'S GUIDE

| NO. | | PRICE |

998 **Mimulus Musk** (*Mimulus Moschatus*). The well-known musk-plant . . . $0.10
999 —— **Cupreus.** A new species, six or eight inches high, with handsome, glossy foliage, and large, finely-formed, orange-scarlet flowers; very free-flowering. Valuable for borders and beds 25
1000 —— **Hybrida Grandiflora.** White ground, with crimson spots. Superb. Half ft . .25
1001 —— —— Yellow ground, crimson blotches 25
1002 —— **Finest Mixed.** All the above mixed 25
1003 —— **Pardina** (*Tigrinoides*). An extremely beautiful new blotched and spotted hybrid, of Mimulus Cupreus and Luteus, having the dwarf-spreading habit and glossy foliage of the former, with large finely-shaped flower of a rich golden-yellow ground-color, blotched and spotted in a most striking manner with coppery maroon; a splendid mixture 25

MIGNONETTE. NAT. ORD., *Resedaceæ*.

A well-known fragrant favorite, which produces a pleasing contrast to the more showy occupants of the parterre. If well thinned out immediately the plants are large enough, they will grow stronger, and produce larger spikes of bloom. The seeds should be scattered about shrubbery and mixed flower-borders, where it grows readily. Hardy annuals.

1004 **Mignonette** (*Roseda Odorata*). The well-known sweet-scented variety. Half foot.
(25 per ounce) 05
1005 —— **Grandiflora.** Large-flowered variety; from Barbary. Half foot 05
1006 —— **Mycrophylla.** Thousand-leaved 10
1007 —— **Arborea** (Tree). Fine foliage. 2 feet 10

MONKSHOOD. NAT. ORD., *Ranunculaceæ*.
(See Aconitum.)

MORNING GLORY. NAT. ORD., *Convolvulaceæ*.

1009 **Morning Glory, Mixed.** The finest varieties. 20 feet 05
(For other varieties, see Convolvulus.)

MOURNING BRIDE. NAT. ORD., *Dipsaceæ*.
(See Scabious.)

MOMORDICA. NAT. ORD., *Cucurbitaceæ*.

The Squirting Cucumber; an annual gourd-like plant with woolly leaves and golden-yellow flowers, the fruit of which resembles a small cucumber, and, when ripe, bursts the moment it is touched, scattering its seeds, and the half-liquid pulpy matter in which they are contained, to a considerable distance. Half-hardy annual.

1011 **Momordica Balsamina** (Balsam Apple). From East Indies. 10 feet 05
1012 —— **Charantia** (Balsam Pear). From East Indies. 10 feet 05

MORNA. NAT. ORD., *Compositæ*.

1013 **Morna Elegans.** An everlasting flower; fine for dry bouquets; from Swan River.
1½ feet 05

MYOSOTIS (FORGET-ME-NOT). NAT. ORD., *Boraginaceæ*.

These beautiful little flowers are too well known to need recommendation; will grow around fountains, over damp rock-work, or in any moist situation. Hardy perennial.

1014 **Myosotis Alpestris.** A variety with blue flowers. Half foot 05
1015 —— —— **Alba.** White. Half foot 10
1016 —— **Palustris.** A well-known favorite, with clusters of delicate blue flowers appearing all summer; blooms the first year from seed. Half foot 05
1017 —— **Palustris Azurea Major.** A beautiful variety, with large blue flowers. Half foot 10
1018 —— **Azorica.** Blue, shaded with purple; a fine large-flowered variety 10

MUSK-PLANT. NAT. ORD., *Scrophulariaceæ*.
(See Mimulus Moschatus.)

TO THE FLOWER GARDEN.

NASTURTIUM (Tropæolum Majus). Nat. Ord., *Tropæolaceæ*.

This is a well-known ornamental annual, of easy cultivation. It flowers best in a light soil. It looks well, trained to a trellis or over a wall. The flowers are rich orange, shaded with crimson and various colors. The variety with crimson or blood-colored flowers makes a fine contrast with orange. The seeds are used as a substitute for capers, and the flowers sometimes eaten as salads. Half-hardy annuals.

NO.		PRICE
1020	Nasturtium Carneum. Flesh-color. 10 feet	$0 05
1021	—— Majus. Bright-orange. 10 feet	05
1022	—— Atrosanguineum. Dark-crimson. 10 feet	25
1023	—— Shillingii. Spotted-yellow, with dark spots on each petal. 10 feet	10
1024	—— Schenermanni. Straw-color, striped with brown; fine	05

(The above are all tall varieties.)

NASTURTIUM (Tropæolum Minor). Nat. Ord., *Tropæolaceæ*.

The dwarf-improved varieties of the Nasturtium are among the most useful and beautiful of garden favorites for bedding, massing, or ribboning, and rank with the Geranium, Verbena, and Calceolaria. Their close compact growth, rich-colored flowers, and the freedom with which they bloom, all combine to place them in the category of first-class bedding-plants. The Tom Thumb varieties are distinguished favorites, as are also the old crimson and the new Crystal-palace Gem. Half-hardy annuals.

1025	Nasturtium Dwarf Crimson. Very fine for groups. 1 foot	.05
1026	—— Scarlet. Brilliant. 1 foot	.05
1027	—— —— Spotted. Yellow, with dark spots. 1 foot	.05
1028	—— Tom Thumb, Scarlet. A beautiful variety, dwarf and compact; quite as rich in color and as effective as the Tom Thumb Geraniums; fine for pots or vases. 1 foot	.10
1029	—— —— —— Yellow. A variety similar to the last mentioned, with yellow flowers. 1 foot	.10
1030	—— —— —— Beauty. Yellow, blotched with crimson; fine. 1½ feet	.10
1031	—— —— —— Crystal-palace Gem. A new sulphur-color, spotted with maroon; a splendid bedding variety. 1 foot	.10
1032	—— —— —— Pearl. Creamy-white; a fine variety	.10
1033	—— —— —— New Hybrid. Saved from the finest-named varieties, producing flowers of various shades, — buff, yellow, crimson, maroon, in great profusion; beautifully blotched and marbled	.25

NEMESIA. Nat. Ord., *Scrophulariaceæ*.

Exceedingly pretty and profuse-blooming plants. Nemesia Compacta and Alba should be grown in every garden. Half-hardy annual.

1034	Nemesia Floribunda. White and yellow; sweet-scented	.05
1035	—— Versicolor Compacta. Blue and white. 3 feet	.10
1036	—— —— —— Alba. Pure white. Three-quarters foot	.10
1037	—— —— —— Insignis. New; light-blue. Three-quarters foot	.25
1038	—— —— —— La Superbe. Light-rose; fine. Three-quarters foot	.25

NERIUM (Oleander). Nat. Ord., *Apocynaceæ*.

A class of splendid double-flowering evergreen shrubs, of a highly ornamental character; fine for conservatory decoration, or placing on lawns and terraces during the summer; growing in any light, rich soil. Half-hardy shrubs.

1039	Nerium Oleander. Rosy-pink; double; from Italy. 6 feet	.10
1040	—— Variegata. Scarlet and white; from Italy. 6 feet	.10

NICOTIANA (Tobacco-Plant). Nat. Ord., *Solanaceæ*.

These are strong-growing, fine-foliaged plants. They are very effective for large shrubbery borders, and the leaves of some varieties are valuable for fumigating purposes. Tender annuals.

1041	Nicotiana Glauca. Yellow; native of America	.10
1042	—— Glutinosa. Scarlet; from Peru. 3 feet	.10
1043	—— Vincæflora. White; very pretty; from South America. 2 feet	.10

NIGELLA (Love-in-a-Mist). Nat. Ord., *Ranunculaceæ*.

A genus of very interesting, compact-growing, free-flowering plants, with curious-looking flowers and seed-pods. From the extraordinary motion manifested by the stamens, this

64 AMATEUR CULTIVATOR'S GUIDE

NO.		PRICE

genus has received the above singular names. Grows freely in any garden soil. From Spain. Hardy annual.

1044	Nigella Damascena. Blue; fine	$0.05
1045	—— —— Nana. A dwarf variety; flowers blue and white; double	.05
1046	—— —— Hispanica. Blue; very showy	.05
1047	—— —— Alba. Pure white	.05

NEMOPHILA MACULATA.

NEMOPHILA. NAT. ORD., *Hydrophyllaceæ*.

This is, perhaps, the most charming and generally useful genus of dwarf-growing hardy annuals. All the varieties have a neat, compact, and uniform habit of growth, with shades and colors the most strikingly beautiful, so that ribboned, sown in circles, or arranged in any style which the fancy may suggest, the effect is pleasing and very striking. They are also very useful for pot-culture. Hardy annual.

1048	Nemophila Atomaria. White, with blue spots. 1 foot	.05
1049	—— —— Oculata. Light-blue, blotched with black; fine. 1 foot	.10
1050	—— —— Discoidalis. Black, with white edge	.05
1051	—— —— Marmorata. Black-marbled, with white. 1 foot	.05
1052	—— Insignis. Bright-blue	.05
1053	—— —— Alba. White. 1 foot	.05
1054	—— —— Marginata. Sky-blue, edged with white	.05
1055	—— —— Grandiflora. Bright-blue, with white centre. 1 foot	.05
1056	—— —— Striata. Blue and white. 1 foot	.05
1057	—— Maculata. White; large purple spots. 1 foot	.05
1058	—— —— Variegata. White, veined with lilac, and blotched with violet; foliage finely variegated; very effective. 1 foot	.10
1059	—— —— Good Mixed	.05

GROUP OF PANSIES. See page 67.

TO THE FLOWER GARDEN. 65

NIEREMBERGIA. Nat. Ord., *Solanaceæ*.

Profuse-blooming, elegant, and charming little plants, exceedingly valuable for small beds, edging and rustic baskets or vases. Half-hardy perennials.

1060 **Nierembergia Gracilis.** White, veined with lilac; from Uraguay. Half-foot . $0.25
1061 —— **Intermedia.** Deep-crimson. Half foot 25

NOLANA. Nat. Ord., *Nolanaceæ*.

Very pretty trailing-plants, after the character of the Convolvulus Minor; fine for rockwork, hanging-baskets, old stumps, &c.; succeeds best in a light rich soil. Hardy annuals.

1062 **Nolana Atriplicifolia.** Blue, violet, and yellow; from Peru. Half foot 05
1063 —— —— **Alba.** White; yellow centre 05
1064 —— —— **Subcœrulea.** A fine variety, with mauve-colored flowers 10
1065 —— **Prostata.** Fine blue, streaked with black; from Peru 05

NYMPHÆA. Nat. Ord., *Nymphaceæ*.

Beautiful hardy aquatics, thriving in rich loamy soil at the bottom of ponds or lakes.

1066 **Nymphæa Alba.** White; a magnificent variety; from England. 3 feet 25

NYCTERINIA. Nat. Ord., *Scrophulariaceæ*.

Neat compact little plants, covered with pretty, sweet-scented, star-shaped flowers; valuable for edgings, rock-work, stumps, or small beds; succeeds in a light rich soil. From Cape of Good Hope. Half-hardy perennials.

1067 **Nycterinia Capensis.** White; yellow centre. Half foot 10
1068 —— **Selaginoides.** Pink; yellow centre. Half foot 10
1069 —— —— **Alba.** Pure white 10

OBELISCARIA. Nat. Ord., *Compositæ*.

Bold, showy plants, with rich-colored flowers and curious acorn-like centres; succeeds in any common garden-soil. From Texas. Half-hardy perennial.

1070 **Obeliscaria Pulcherrima.** Rich velvety-crimson, edged and tipped with yellow. Half-foot 05
1071 —— **Aurantiaca.** Yellow. 2 feet 10

ŒNOTHERA. Nat. Ord., *Onagraceæ*.

A magnificent genus; one of the most useful and beautiful either for beds, borders, edgings, or rock-work. All the varieties are free-flowering, and most of them perennials. The most remarkable of the perennial kinds are Œnothera Grandiflora Lamarckiana, with superb spikes of large flowers; Œnothera Macrocarpa, splendid for beds or edging, flowers six inches in diameter; Œnothera Acaulis, flowers silvery-white; and Œnothera Missouriensis. Of the annual varieties, Œnothera Drummondii Nana and Œnothera Bistorta Veitchii succeed in any good soil.

1072 **Œnothera Acaulis.** A large-flowered variety, with silvery-white blossoms; from Chili .10
1073 —— **Biennis Hirsutissima.** Crimson-orange; from California. Half-hardy annual. 2 feet 05
1074 —— **Bistorta Veitchii Grandiflora.** Pure yellow; crimson-spotted; from California. Half-hardy annual. 1 foot 10
1075 —— **Campylocarpa Grandiflora.** Crimson-orange; large-flowered; beautiful variety; from Peru. Half-hardy perennial. 1 foot 10
1076 —— **Cinnabarina.** Rich-orange; yellow throat, stained with rich salmon. Half-hardy perennial 10
1077 —— **Drummondii Nana Nova.** Dwarf; bright-yellow variety; from Texas. Half-hardy annual. 1 foot 10
1078 —— **Grandiflora Lamarckiana.** Bright-yellow; the most effective and strikingly beautiful of this splendid genus; flowers three to four inches in diameter, and produced in the greatest profusion; an exceedingly ornamental plant for mixed borders. 3 feet 10
1079 —— **Jarmesii.** Bright-yellow flowers; large, and produced in great profusion. 2 feet .10
1080 —— **Macrocarpa.** Rich yellow. Hardy perennial 10
1081 —— **Taraxacifolia.** Pure white. Hardy perennial. 1 foot 10
1082 —— —— **Lutea.** Yellow. Hardy perennial. 1 foot 05
1083 —— **Tetraptera.** Silvery-white; very handsome 05

9

ŒNOTHERA LAMARCKIA (one-tenth natural size).

1084 Œnothera Undulata. Primrose; from Peru. Hardy perennial. 1½ feet . . $0.05
1085 —— Fruticosa. A very fine perennial species; rich yellow flowers; numerous; open in sunshine (diurnal). 2 feet 10
1086 —— Glauca. Flowers deep, rich yellow; very free-flowering. Hardy perennial . .10

ONOPORDON. Nat. Ord., *Compositæ*.

1087 Onopordon Tauricum. A noble thistle-like plant, of very ornamental character; thrives well in any soil; flower purple. Hardy perennial. 6 feet 10

OXALIS. Nat. Ord., *Oxalidaceæ*.

Elegant flowering-plants, particularly adapted for the greenhouse or parlor, where they bloom in mid-winter.

1089 Oxalis Rosea. A very neat, erect-growing plant, six to nine or twelve inches high, with small, medium-sized leaves, and numerous conspicuous clusters of bright rose-colored, salver-shaped flowers 10
1090 —— Tropæoloides. Yellow. Tender annual. Quarter foot 10

OATS (Avena Sensitiva). Nat. Ord., *Gramineæ*.

A very curious genus of ornamental grasses; fine for dried bouquets; suitable for mixed borders. Hardy annual.

1091 Oats Animated. Curious. 2 feet 05

TO THE FLOWER GARDEN. 67

| NO. | | PRICE |

OXYURA. NAT. ORD., *Compositæ.*

1092 Oxyura Chrysanthemoides. A showy, free-flowering plant, with beautiful fringed
flowers; golden-yellow; from California $0.05

ENGLISH PANSIES.—PRIZE VARIETIES.

PANSY (HEARTSEASE OR VIOLA TRICOLOR). NAT. ORD., *Violaceæ.*

The Pansy, or Heartsease, is a general favorite and old acquaintance with every one who has any thing to do with a flower-garden. It begins to open its modest but lively flowers as soon as the snow clears off in the spring, and continues to enliven the garden till snow comes again. The flowers are in the greatest perfection in May and June: the burning sun of summer is unfavorable for their greatest beauty, but in autumn they are fine again. The Pansy is properly a biennial, but can be perpetuated by cuttings or division of the roots. Seeds sown in August, in the open borders, will come up readily in a few weeks. The seeds should be slightly covered with fine soil, if covered at all, as half the seeds sown rot in the ground from being covered too deep. As soon as they expand the second set of leaves, they should be planted out into beds; if planted in the spring, they should not be allowed to flower until late in the fall; the buds should be picked off during the summer, which will make the plants bushy and compact. They require to be covered during the winter with evergreen boughs or a cold frame. The following seeds were selected by some of the most celebrated European florists from prize collections, and we can recommend them as first-class in every respect.

1093 Pansy, Good Mixed 05
1094 —— Fine Mixed 10
1095 —— Extra Mixed. Saved from named flowers, from English prize collection; the
finest in habit of plant, size, form, and substance of flower. Superb 50

68   AMATEUR CULTIVATOR'S GUIDE

NO.			PRICE
1096	Pansy, Extra German.	These were selected by a celebrated German florist, and may be depended upon as very fine	$0.25
1097	—	New. Large-flowered, margined; fancy	.25
1098	—	Auriculaflora. Brown, rose-margined; fine	.25
1099	—	Atropurpurea. Pure, dark, velvety-crimson	.25
1100	— —	Marginata Alba. Velvety-crimson, with white eye, and margined	.25
1101	— —	Aurea. Velvety-crimson, with golden ground, and margined	.25
1102	—	Pelargonæflora. Each petal having a large maroon blotch on white ground; yellow eye	.50
1103	—	Picturata. Dark-maroon, marbled with bronze	.25
1104	—	Mixed. Above six varieties mixed. These varieties form a new class of 'FANCY Pansies, with unusually large flowers, conspicuous by their brilliancy and novelty of colors. They have the valuable property of resisting almost the greatest summer heat, and flowering most profusely. We offer the above as a superior strain obtained by careful selection	.50
1105	—	Pure White. Constant and fine	.25
1106	—	Golden-Yellow. Constant and fine	.20
1107	—	Dark-Blue. Constant and fine	.25
1108	—	Light-Blue. Constant and fine	.20
1109	—	Bronze-colored. Constant and fine	.20
1110	—	Fancy Striped. Constant and fine	.25
1111	—	Rose Marbled. Constant and fine	.25
1112	—	Violet. White margined. Constant and fine	.25
1113	—	Mixed. Above varieties mixed	.25
1114	—	Faust, or King of the Blacks. Flower, black; fine bedding variety	.20

PAMPAS-GRASS. Nat. Ord., *Graminaceæ.*
(See Gynerium.)

PAPAVER (Perennial Poppy). Nat. Ord., *Papaveraceæ.*

A highly ornamental and strikingly effective genus of plants, with brilliant colored flowers of an immense size, which, in select plantation and shrubbery borders, are unusually effective. Papaver Nudicaule is a dwarf-growing variety, and is especially adapted for rock-work. Hardy perennial.

1116	Papaver Bracteatum. Bright orange-crimson; large and handsome. 2 feet	.05
1117	— Involucratum Maximum. Brilliant orange-scarlet; from Levant. 3 feet	.10
1118	— Nudicaule. Bright-yellow; from Siberia. 1 foot	.10
1119	— Orientale. Deep scarlet, with large black blotches; from Levant. 2½ feet	.05

PASSION-FLOWER. Nat. Ord., *Passifloraceæ.*

A splendid class of climbers, with curious flowers produced in great profusion; fine for conservatory, or will answer for the garden, flowering freely during the autumn months.

1120	Passiflora Cœrulea. Light-blue; fine	.10
1121	— Gracilis. White, pretty	.10
1122	— Princeps. Splendid racemes of vermilion flowers; very fine	.25

PANCRATIUM. Nat. Ord., *Amaryllidaceæ.*

An exceedingly ornamental genus of hardy bulbs, producing splendid spikes of handsome flowers; succeeds best in light sandy loam mixed with vegetable mould. Greenhouse bulbs.

1123	Pancratium Illyricum. White; from south of Europe. 1 foot	.25
1124	— Maritimum. White; deliciously fragrant. From south of Europe. 2 feet	.25

PAULOWNIA. Nat. Ord., *Scrophulariaceæ.*

A noble, hardy tree, bearing panicles of dark-lilac flowers, resembling those of the Gloxinia. Thrives in any good soil.

| 1125 | Paulownia Imperialis. Blue; from Japan. 20 feet | .10 |

PEAS. Nat. Ord., *Leguminosæ.*

The Sweet-Peas are among the most popular annuals which enrich the flower-garden. They may be planted and trained on sticks the same as common peas; or they may be sowed along the sides of fences, forming a highly ornamental covering: in any situation, they are always admired.

NO.				PRICE
1126	Sweet Peas, Black. From Ceylon. 6 feet			$0.05
1127	— — White. From Ceylon. 6 feet			.05
1128	— — Purple. From Ceylon. 6 feet			.05
1129	— — Painted Lady. From Ceylon. 6 feet			.05
1130	— — Scarlet. From Ceylon. 6 feet			.05
1131	— — Scarlet Striped. From Ceylon. 6 feet			.05
1132	— — Mixed. The above mixed			.05
1133	— Everlasting. (See Lathyrus)			.05
1134	— Lord Anson's. Light-blue. 1½ foot			.05
1135	— Tangier. Scarlet; from Barbary			.05

PELARGONIUM. Nat. Ord., *Geraniaceæ*.

A genus of indispensable and beautiful greenhouse plants: whether for the adornment of the conservatory or the drawing-room, they stand unrivalled. Greenhouse perennial.

1136	Pelargonium. Finest mixed. From named prize flowers	.25

(For other varieties, see Geranium.)

PENSTEMON. Nat. Ord., *Scrophulariaceæ*.

A genus of well-known and highly ornamental hardy herbaceous plants, with long, graceful spikes of fine-shaped and richly-colored flowers. One of the most effective and free-flowering of border and bedding plants; succeeds in any light soil.

1137	Penstemon Cordifolius. Fine; scarlet; from Mexico. 2 feet	.10
1138	— Gentiunoides. Purple and white; from Mexico. 2 feet	.10
1140	— — Coccineus. Scarlet and white; from Mexico	.10
1141	— Jeffreyanus. Sky-blue; fine	.25
1142	— Lobbianus. Beautiful yellow, of good habit; fragrant. 2 feet	.25
1143	— Murrayanum. Light-scarlet, in long spikes, fine foliage; from Texas	.10
1144	— Digitalis. White, striped with red. 2 feet	.10
1145	— Finest Mixed	.10

PERILLA. Nat. Ord., *Labiatæ*.

Among the recent introductions of ornamental-foliaged plants for flower-garden decoration, the Perilla deserves a more than ordinary share of attention. Its habit of growth is neat and shrubby, whilst its foliage is a deep mulberry or blackish purple, and forms a fine contrast to the silvery foliage of Cineraria Maritima, or the lively green of other plants. Half-hardy annual.

1146	Perilla Nankinensis. Leaves, a deep mulberry or purplish-black; from China. 2 feet	.05

PETUNIA. Nat. Ord., *Solanaceæ*.

A highly ornamental and profuse-flowering, easily cultivated garden favorite, equally effective and beautiful whether grown in pots for the decoration of the greenhouse and sitting-room window, or planted out in beds or mixed borders. The brilliancy and variety of its colors, combined with the duration of its blooming period, render it invaluable. Seeds sown in spring make fine bedding-plants for summer and autumn display; succeeds in any rich soil. Half-hardy perennials.

1147	Petunia Phœnicia (the original variety). Flowers small; deep purple	.05
1148	— — Grandiflora Hybrida. Mixed; saved from named flowers	.25
1149	— — Marginata. Green-bordered; a fine variety	.10
1150	— — Buchanan's Hybrids. Beautifully blotched and marbled; a fine variety	.25
1151	— — Inimitable. Red-margined and blotched, with pure white; fine	.25
1152	— — Countess of Ellesmere. Deep rose, with white throat	.10
1153	— — Striatifolia. A beautiful striped variety	.25
1154	— — Flore Pleno. These are fecundated with great care, and are sure to produce a large percentage of double flowers	.25
1155	— Large-flowered Alba. White; fine	.10
1156	— — Purpurea. Purple	.10
1157	— — — Roses. Rose-colored	.10
1158	— — — Violet. Violet	.10
1159	— — — Good Mixed	.05
1160	— — — Finest Mixed	.10

| NO. | | PRICE |

PHASEOLUS (Scarlet-Runner Beans). Nat. Ord., *Leguminosæ*.

This is a popular climbing annual, with spikes of showy scarlet flowers, and a variety with white flowers. They are extensively grown to cover arbors, walls, or to form screens, for which purpose they are admirably adapted on account of their vigorous and rapid growth. Hardy annuals.

1161	Phaseolus Coccinea. Brilliant scarlet	$0.10
1162	— Painted Lady. A beautiful variety	.10
1163	— Alba. White	.10

PHLOX DRUMMONDII. Nat. Ord., *Polemoniaceæ*.

This magnificent genus of plants is unrivalled for richness and brilliancy of colors, profusion and duration of blooming. They are unsurpassed for bedding or pot culture, and produce a splendid effect in mixed borders. No garden should be without these beautiful plants. Succeeds best in light rich soil. Hardy annuals.

1164	Phlox Drummondii Alba. White	.10
1165	— — — Oculata. Pure white, with purple eye	.10
1166	— — Marmorata. Marbled	.10
1167	— — Louis Napoleon. Dark-crimson	.10
1168	— — Leopoldii. Purple; white eye	.10
1169	— — Queen Victoria. Violet; white eye	.10
1170	— — Purpurea. Deep purple	.10
1171	— — Chamois Rose. Delicate rose	.25
1172	— — Coccinea. Pure deep scarlet	.10
1173	— — Striata. Scarlet, striped with white	.10
1174	— — Radowitsky. Deep rose, striped with white	.10
1175	— — Variabilis. Light-blue marbled	.10
1176	— — Good Mixed	.05
1177	— — Finest Mixed. Including all the best varieties	.10
1178	— — Perennial Mixed. Saved from a collection of upwards of one hundred varieties, embracing all those splendid new varieties introduced during the last five years by the French and English florists, of which the produce may be expected to be fully equal or superior to the original	.25

PINK. Nat. Ord., *Caryophyllaceæ*.

A well-known and highly valued plant, remarkable as well for its great beauty and delightful fragrance as for its easy culture and accommodating habit, growing freely and flowering profusely either in pots, in the greenhouse, or in the open border; succeeding best in a rich loamy soil. Hardy perennial.

| 1180 | Pinks (Florist or Paisley). Finest mixed. From a named collection | .25 |
| 1181 | — Pheasant-eye. White or pink, with dark eye. The flowers are deeply fringed or feathered; very fragrant | .10 |

(For other varieties, see Dianthus.)

PICOTEE PINK. Nat. Ord., *Caryophyllaceæ*.

Favorite and well-known plants of great beauty, combining with the most perfect form the richest and the most beautiful colors. They have a delicate perfume, are easily cultivated, and bloom profusely, growing freely in any light rich soil. The seed we offer has been saved from flowers possessing all the requisite characteristics which constitute a first-class flower. Hardy perennial.

| 1182 | Picotee Pink. Good mixed | .10 |
| 1183 | — — Perpetual, or Tree. Saved from stage flowers. 1½ feet | .50 |

PITTOSPORUM. Nat. Ord., *Pittosporaceæ*.

A handsome genus of exceedingly ornamental shrubs; thrives in peat and loam. Greenhouse shrubs.

| 1184 | Pittosporum Undulatum. White and yellow; from New South Wales. 3 feet | .25 |
| 1185 | — Pendulum. From New South Wales. 3 feet | .25 |

PODOLEPIS. Nat. Ord., *Compositæ*.

A genus of pretty, graceful, free-flowering plants, succeeding best in a light, rich soil, and producing a fine effect in beds or mixed borders. Half-hardy annuals.

| 1186 | Podolepis Chrysantha. Yellow; from New South Wales. 1 foot | .05 |

TO THE FLOWER GARDEN.

NO.		PRICE
1187	Podolepis Gracilis. Pink; from New South Wales. 1 foot	$0.05
1188	—— —— Alba. White; from New South Wales. 1 foot	.05
1188½	—— Affinis. Yellow; new variety; the largest flowering kind	.10

CAMPANULA GRANDIS (see page 26).

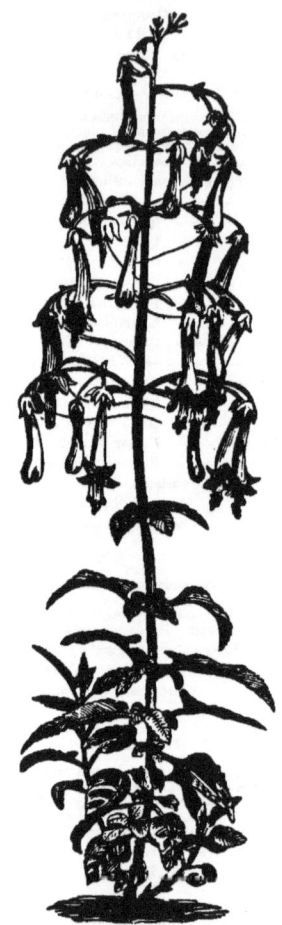

PHYGELIA CAPENSIS.

PHYGELIUS. NAT. ORD., *Scrophulariaceæ*.

A handsome free-flowering plant, with large, richly-marked, tubular blossoms; succeeds in light rich soil. Half-hardy perennial.

| 1189 | Phygelius Capensis. Large carmine, tubular flowers; inside golden-yellow; from Caffraria. 1½ feet | .25 |

NO.			PRICE

POINCIANA. NAT. ORD., *Leguminosæ.*

A very elegant and ornamental genus of greenhouse shrubs, requiring a good rich soil.

1190	Poinciana Gilliesii.	Yellow; from South America. 10 feet	$0.10
1191	—— Pulcherrima.	Orange; from East Indies. 10 feet	.25
1192	—— Regia.	Crimson; from Madagascar. 10 feet	.25

POLYGALA. NAT. ORD., *Polygalaceæ.*

A very handsome genus of greenhouse evergreen shrubs, which may be grown out of doors in summer; thrives best in peat and loam.

1193	Polygala Speciosa.	Purple; from Cape of Good Hope. 6 feet	.25
1194	—— Dalmatiana.	Purple; from Cape of Good Hope	.25
1195	—— Latifolia.	Rose; from Cape of Good Hope. 3 feet	.25
1196	—— Myrtifolia.	Purple; from Cape of Good Hope. 3 feet	.25

DOUBLE PORTULACA.

PORTULACA. NAT. ORD., *Portulaceæ.*

In praise of these charming flowers it is impossible to speak too highly: and it may be safely affirmed that a garden without them is devoid of its brightest ornaments; for the Portulacas are unsurpassed for brilliancy and richness of color. They are adapted for beds, clumps, edgings, pots, vases, or rock-work. The plants should stand at least eight inches distant from each other. Easily transplanted.

1197	Portulaca Splendens.	Rich crimson; showy. Half foot	.05
1198	—— Thellusonii.	Splendid scarlet. Half foot	.05
1199	—— Aurea.	Yellow. Half foot	.05
1200	—— Alba.	A pure white; fine. Half foot	.05
1201	—— Thorburnii.	Deep orange. Half foot	.05
1202	—— Rosea.	Fine rose. Half foot	.05
1203	—— Caryophylloides.	Carnation-striped; white and crimson; superb. Half foot	.10
1204	—— Striata.	Light yellow; gold-striped; fine	.10

TO THE FLOWER GARDEN. 73

NO.   PRICE

1205 Portulaca Grandiflora Flore Pleno. Saved from double-flowering plants, reproducing a large proportion of double, in white, blood-red, purple, &c., resembling roses; one of the finest new plants introduced for a long time; rare. (See illustration) $0.25
1206 —— Blensonii. Vermilion; fine 10

POLYANTHUS. Nat. Ord., *Primulaceæ.*

This gay and profuse-flowering hardy plant is too well known to need description. The seeds which we offer may be expected to produce the richest and most varied color. Hardy perennial.

1207 Polyanthus (*Primula elatior*). Good mixed 10
1208 —— Extra Mixed. Saved from named flowers 25

POTENTILLA. Nat. Ord., *Rosaceæ.*

These are very handsome herbaceous plants, and from their hardiness and showy character are exceedingly useful and ornamental. They may be employed to advantage in filling up vacant nooks and corners. Even in single plants, and in all situations, their neatness of foliage and long duration in bloom render them objects of much beauty. Hardy perennials.

1209 Potentilla Atrosanguinea. Dark red; from Nepaul. 1½ feet 05
1210 —— Hopwoodiana. Rose. 1½ feet 05
1211 —— Aurea. Orange-color; from the Alps. Half foot 10
1212 —— Fromosa. Orange and crimson; from Nepaul 10
1213 —— Pedata. Fine yellow. 1 foot 10
1214 —— Macrantha. White; from Switzerland. 1 foot 10
1215 —— Mixed. Finest mixed 10

POPPY. Nat. Ord., *Papaveraceæ.*

A tribe of remarkably showy, free-flowering plants, producing a rich and effective display in large mixed borders, in shrubberies, or select plantations; grows freely in any soil. Hardy annuals.

1216 Poppy, Carnation (*Papaver somniferum*). Finest mixed; double. 2 feet . . .05
1217 —— French. Finest dwarf-mixed; double. 1 foot 05
1218 —— German. Finest mixed; double 05
1219 —— Peony-flowered. Fine mixed; double 05
1220 —— Ranunculus. Double mixed 05

PRIONIUM. Nat. Ord., *Gramineæ.*

The rare Silver Grass-Tree, in appearance, and habit of growth, like a Pandanus.

1221 Prionium Palmita. Rare and beautiful 25

PRINCE'S FEATHER. Nat. Ord., *Amarantaceæ.*

Ornamental plants, with elegant plumes of rich-colored flowers; succeeds well in any good garden soil. Hardy annuals.

1222 Prince's Feather (Amaranthus). Large-flowered; crimson; from Nepaul. 2 feet . .05

PRIMULA. Nat. Ord., *Primulaceæ.*

A very beautiful greenhouse plant, of various colors. All these are particularly valuable as forming neat little plants, and flowering all winter. Greenhouse perennials.

(See Chinese Primrose.)

PUNICA. Nat. Ord., *Myrtaceæ.*

Certainly amongst the handsomest of shrubs. Under the shelter of a south wall, they flower profusely throughout the summer. Succeeds best in strong rich loam. Half-hardy shrubs.

1224 Punica Granatum (Pomegranate). Waxy scarlet; from south of Europe . . .25

PYRETHRUM. Nat. Ord., *Compositæ.*

Handsome, free-flowering, highly ornamental plants, producing a fine effect in the mixed flower and shrubbery borders. Hardy perennial.

1225 Pyrethrum Delehayi. New; crimson; fine. 1½ feet 10
1226 —— Duchess of Brabant. Rosy-purple. 1½ feet 10
1227 —— Gloire de Nimy. Bright crimson. 1½ feet 10

74 AMATEUR CULTIVATOR'S GUIDE

NO.		PRICE
1228	Pyrethrum Themistori. Reddish rose; orange centre. 1½ feet	$0.10
1229	—— Album. Double white. 1½ feet	.25
1230	—— Finest Mixed	.25

RHODANTHE MACULATA. (For full-sized flower, see engraving on page 75.)

RHODANTHE. Nat. Ord., *Compositæ*.

Charming everlasting flowers, of great beauty, equally valuable for the decoration of the conservatory and flower-garden. Its neat, compact growth makes it a suitable plant for bedding or ribboning, while its bright-colored flowers, elegant style of growth, and profuse blooming, render it an object of universal admiration. The flowers, if gathered when young, make valuable winter bouquets. Succeeds best in a light rich soil, and a warm, sheltered situation. Half-hardy annuals.

1231 **Rhodanthe Manglesii.** One of the prettiest of all the everlasting flowers; neat, unique, and beautiful; small, erect branching plant, with numerous semi-double, daisy-like flowers, of rich rose-color, suffused with white, retaining their transparency and beauty for a considerable period. 1 foot 10

TO THE FLOWER GARDEN. 75

NO.   PRICE

RHODANTHE MACULATA (full size of flower).

1232 **Rhodanthe Maculata.** This splendid novelty is larger in all its parts than Rhodanthe Manglesii; about two feet high, very robust, and more hardy; fine, glossy, heart-shaped foliage, of graceful bearing, with flowers from one and a half to two inches in diameter, of a bright, deep, rosy carmine, rendered more brilliant by a broad, velvety, blackish, purple-crimson belt, surrounding the bright-yellow disk; in brilliancy of color, and graceful habit, far surpassing Acroclinium Roseum. From Australia $0.10
1233 —— —— **Atrosanguinea.** New dwarf; densely-branching species, with longer and more pointed leaves than Rhodanthe Maculata, with flowers of a dark, purplish-crimson; very brilliant 20
1234 —— —— **Alba.** Pure, silvery-white variety, of same size of flower as Rhodanthe Maculata. This is one of the finest everlasting flowers introduced for a long time. When cut in the bud, and placed under a glass, it makes a beautiful ornament 20

RHODODENDRON. Nat. Ord., *Ericaceæ*.

A well-known and magnificent genus of free-flowering evergreen shrubs; should occupy a prominent place in every garden; thrives best in peaty soil. Hardy shrubs.
1235 **Rhododendron.** Finest mixed varieties, from choice named flowers 25

RIVINA. Nat. Ord., *Phytolaceæ*.

An exceedingly ornamental shrub when fruiting. The berries of this genus form the principal portion of the food of the American nightingale. Grows freely in any light soil. Greenhouse shrub.
1236 **Rivina Humilis.** White fruit, in bunches; from West Indies. 2 feet 25

RICINUS (Castor-Oil Bean). *Euphorbiaceæ*.

A magnificent and highly ornamental genus. The picturesque foliage and stately growth, combined with brilliant-colored fruit, of the new varieties, impart to select plantations, shrubberies, and mixed-flower borders, quite an Oriental aspect. In the gardens round Paris, they form one of the principal features of attraction; and if planted out and grown as single specimens on our lawns and pleasure-grounds, as an ornamental foliaged plant, they would form a new and striking feature. Half-hardy annuals.
1237 **Ricinus Africanus Hybridus.** Rose-colored hybrid; very handsome; new. 7 feet . .25
1238 —— **Giganteus.** Plant and leaves of enormous size; new. 12 feet 25
1239 —— **Insignis.** New; splendid. 7 feet 25
1240 —— **Major** (Castor-oil Bean). Very ornamental foliage. 6 to 8 feet 05
1241 —— **Sanguineus.** A very stately growing plant, seven feet high, with large and highly ornamental foliage of Oriental aspect, with clusters of red fruit. 6 feet . .10

NO.		PRICE

1242   Ricinus Sanguineus Tricolor. This effective species has its stems and leaves colored green, brown, and red. 7 feet $0.10
1243 —— Braziliensis. Rich green fruit; from Brazil 10
1244 —— Obermannii. Deep red; fine; from Africa. 8 feet 10

ROSE CAMPION. NAT. ORD., *Caryophyllaceæ.*

The Rose Campions are perfectly hardy, and very easily raised from seed, and will well repay the little care they require. The flowers are produced on long stems, blooming freely throughout the season. Hardy perennial.

1245   Rose Campion (*Lychnis coronaria*). Crimson; from Italy 05
1246 —— —— Alba. White; from Italy 05
1247 —— —— Mixed 05

ROSE, AFRICAN. NAT. ORD., *Papaveraceæ.*

1248   Rose African, Mixed (*Papaver rhæas*). A beautiful annual, of the easiest culture, producing double, semi-double, and single flowers, all handsome, sporting in a thousand different varieties of scarlet, crimson, purple, pink, white, variegated, and party-colored, and continuing a long time in bloom. 1½ feet 05

ROSE. NAT. ORD., *Rosaceæ.*

1249   Rose Seed. Saved from a large collection of hybrid Perpetual, Tea, Bourbons, &c. . .25

ROCKET (HESPERIS). NAT. ORD., *Cruciferæ.*

A well-known free-flowering spring plant, very fragrant; growing in any soil. Hardy perennial. From Europe.

1250   Rocket, Sweet. Purple. 1½ feet 05
1251 —— —— Alba. White. 1½ feet 05
1252 —— —— Mixed 05

RUDBECKIA. NAT. ORD., *Compositæ.*

Fine large flowers, with broad streaks of fine yellow, marked with a lively stripe of purple at the base; a prominent disk of deep brown. Very showy, and of the easiest culture.

1253   Rudbeckia Amplexicaulis. Hardy annual. 2½ feet 05
1254 —— Hirta. Light-yellow; hardy perennial. 2 feet 05
1255 —— Lasciniata. Golden-yellow, black disk; hardy perennial. 2 feet . . .05
1256 —— —— Fulgida. Yellow; hardy perennial. 2 feet 05
1257 —— —— Purpurea. Purple-red. Hardy perennial 05

SABBATIA. NAT. ORD., *Gentianeæ.*

1258   Sabbatia Campestris. A very pretty tender annual, with rose-colored flowers, yellow eye; from Texas. Half foot 25

SALPIGLOSSIS. NAT. ORD., *Scrophulariaceæ.*

The Salpiglossis are beautiful annuals, with very picturesque and richly colored, erect-lobed, funnel-shaped blossoms; colors beautifully marbled, purple, scarlet, crimson, clear yellow, and buff, with elegant shades of blue. The new dwarf varieties form a very desirable section of this pleasing flower. Half-hardy annual.

1259   Salpiglossis Atrococcinea. Rich scarlet, richly spotted. 1½ feet 10
1260 —— Atropurpurea. Deep purple. 1½ feet 10
1261 —— Azurea. Sky-blue. 1½ feet 10
1262 —— Coccinea. Scarlet. 1½ feet 10
1263 —— Sulphurea. Sulphur-yellow. 1½ feet 10
1264 —— Finest Mixed. The above mixed 10
1265 —— Nana Alba. Dwarf white. 1 foot 10
1266 —— —— Atropurpurea. Purple. 1 foot 10
1267 —— —— Coccinea. Scarlet. 1 foot 10
1268 —— —— Sulphurea. Light-yellow. 1 foot 10
1269 —— —— Finest Mixed. Above dwarf varieties 10
1270 —— —— Mixed 10

SAXIFRAGA. NAT. ORD., *Saxifrageæ.*

1271   Saxifrag, Mixed Species. Fine border perennials 25

TO THE FLOWER GARDEN. 77

NO.   **PRICE**

SALVIA. Nat. Ord., *Labiatæ*.

Strikingly ornamental plants for conservatory and out-door decoration, growing freely in any light rich soil, and producing a magnificent effect in beds, ribbons, or edgings, where their beautiful spikes of bloom are produced in the greatest profusion. They all bloom the first season from seed. Half-hardy annual.

1272 Salvia Coccinea. Small, bright scarlet flowers, very pretty for beds; from South America. 2 feet $0.10
1273 * —— —— Splendens. A fine scarlet variety; from South America. 2 feet . . .10
1274 —— Pumila. A dwarf dark-red variety; forming a dwarf, compact, handsome bush; fine for bedding. 1½ feet 10
1275 —— Romeriana. Deep crimson; fine. 2 feet 10

The following varieties are very fine for the conservatory or autumn flowering; remarkable for their spikes of rich-colored flowers. Half-hardy perennials.

1276 —— Amabilis. Lavender-blue; from South America. 2 feet 10
1277 —— Argentea. Fine large silvery foliage, of great substance; from Crete. 2 feet . .10
1278 —— Aurea. Yellow; from Cape of Good Hope 10
1279 —— Patens. Splendid deep blue; from Mexico. 3 feet 25
1280 —— Splendens. Beautiful scarlet. 3 feet 25
1281 —— Azurea. Fine azure-blue. 2 feet 25
1282 —— Lilleana. Blue and white; very fine. 3 feet 25
1283 —— Tenorii. Blue. Hardy perennial 05
1284 —— —— Rosea 05

SAPONARIA. Nat. Ord., *Caryophyllaceæ*.

One of the best and longest blooming of all dwarf annuals, producing masses of minute cross-shaped blossoms; admirable for bedding.

1285 Saponaria Calabrica. Bright rosy-pink; from Calabria. Half foot 10
1287 —— Rosea. Rose-colored. Half foot 10
1288 —— Alba. Pure white. Half foot 10

SCABIOUS (Mourning Bride). Nat. Ord., *Dipsaceæ*.

"The Scabious blooms in sad array,
A mourner in her spring."

A hardy ornamental plant, suitable for borders. It may be sown at any time in May, and will produce its flowers from July to October. There is a great variety in the flowers of different plants: some of them are almost black, others a dark puce-purple, and various shades, down to lilac; they are produced in heads. Hardy annuals.

1289 Scabiosa Atropurpurea. A mixture of the finest dark colors. 2 feet 05
1290 —— New Dwarf. Mixed; very fine. 1 foot 05
1291 —— Dwarf, Scarlet. Very fine. 1 foot 05
1292 —— —— Carmine. 1 foot 05
1293 —— Candidissima. Pure white; very desirable. 1 foot 05
1294 —— Starry. The blooms of this, if picked early, are well adapted for winter bouquets .25
1295 —— Ochroleuca. Light-yellow. Hardy perennial 10
1296 —— Tartarica. Blue. Hardy perennial 10

SCHINUS. Nat. Ord., *Teribinthaceæ*.

An elegant, ornamental, and highly fragrant greenhouse shrub, with beautiful bunches of waxy, currant-like fruit. The plant forms a desirable drawing-room ornament, and is easily cultivated; seeds sown in spring make handsome autumn plants. It succeeds out of doors in summer.

1297 Schinus Molle (Pepper Shrub). From Peru. 6 feet 25

SCOTANTHUS. Nat. Ord., *Leguminosæ*.

A beautiful fast-growing annual climber, with elegant foliage, covered with pure white flowers, imitating those of Mandevillea suaveolens, and splendid oblong scarlet fruits.

1298 Scotanthus Tubiflorus. A magnificent novelty 25

SCHIZANTHUS. Nat. Ord., *Scrophulariaceæ*.

Elegant slender-branched annuals, with very conspicuous lobed or cut-petaled flowers of white, lilac, purple, and rich red, orange, and violet-crimson spots and marks, very picturesquely blended; well adapted for either garden or pot-culture. For winter flowering, they should be sown in August, and grown in pots. Half-hardy annuals.

AMATEUR CULTIVATOR'S GUIDE

NO.			PRICE
1299	Schizanthus Grahamii. Lilac and orange; very fine. 1½ feet		$0.05
1300	—— Gracilis. Lilac and spotted; a very graceful variety		.05
1301	—— Grandiflorus Occulatus. Various shades, with blue centre; fine new variety. 1½ feet		.10
1302	—— Humilis. Lilac and crimson. Three-quarters		.05
1303	—— Pinnatus. Pinnate-leave, rosy-purple, and yellow spotted; very pretty. 1 ft.		.05
1304	—— —— Priestii. Pure white. 1 foot		.05
1305	—— Retusus. Deep rose, and orange-crimson tip; fine. 1½ feet		.05
1306	—— —— Alba. White, crimson tip; superb. 1½ feet		.05
1307	—— Good Mixed		.05
1308	—— Finest Mixed. Including all best varieties		.10

SEDUM (Stone-Crop). Nat. Ord., *Crassulaceæ*.

A useful and exceedingly interesting genus of pretty little plants, growing freely on rock or rustic work, also on ornamental mounds, old walls, &c., where, during summer, they expand their brilliant star-shaped flowers in the greatest profusion. Hardy perennial.

1309	Sedum Cœruleum. Blue; from Africa. One-quarter foot	.10
1310	—— Kamtschatkense. Orange; from Kamtschatka. Half foot	.10
1311	—— Mixed	.05

SIDA. Nat. Ord., *Malvaceæ*.

Handsome, free-flowering, easily cultivated greenhouse plants. Succeed well in any rich soil.

1312	Sida Angustifolia. Yellow; from Bourbon. 4 feet	.25
1313	—— Behriana. From India. 4 feet	.25
1314	—— Indica. Yellow, centre dark-red; from India. 4 feet	.25
1315	—— Mixed	.25

SCHIZOPETALON. Nat. Ord., *Cruciferæ*.

1316	Schizopetalon Walkerii. White, fragrant; pretty for pots or edging. Hardy annual. Half foot	.10

SILENE, or CATCHFLY. Nat. Ord., *Caryophyllaceæ*.

Among the tribe of Silenes will be found some of the brightest ornaments of the flower-garden, either in respect to brilliancy of color, or length of duration in bloom; fine for beds, borders, or ribbons. Hardy annuals.

1317	Silene Compacta. Beautiful pink, growing in clusters; from Caucasus. 1½ feet	.05
1318	—— Pendula. Rosy-purple; a favorite species; from Sicily. 1½ feet	.05
1319	—— Alba. White; fine; 1½ feet	.05
1320	—— Pseudo Atocion. Rosy-pink flower, with white centre; very free-blooming	.05
1321	—— Rubella. Red; from Portugal. 1 foot	.05
1322	—— —— Alba. White; fine. 1 foot	.05
1323	—— Schafta. Rosy-lilac; from Russia. Hardy perennial	.05
1324	—— Saxifraga. Pink. Hardy perennial. Half foot	.05

SNAPDRAGON (Antirrhinum). Nat. Ord., *Scrophulariaceæ*.

The Snapdragon, or Antirrhinum, is one of our most showy and useful border-plants. Amongst the more recently improved varieties of this valuable genus are large, finely shaped flowers, of the most brilliant colors, with beautifully marked throats; will bloom the first season from seed, and are very effective in beds or mixed borders. Half-hardy perennials.

(See Antirrhinum.)

SOLANUM. Nat. Ord., *Solanaceæ*.

A genus of most beautiful ornamental fruit-bearing plants, some of them among the most interesting of greenhouse shrubs. Others are the most valuable of ornamental climbers.

1326	Solanum Atropurpureum. Dark purple. 1½ feet	.10
1327	—— Capsicastrum. Miniature orange-tree, covered with a profusion of scarlet fruit all winter; fine for parlor or conservatory. Half-hardy perennial	.10
1328	—— Giganteum. Scarlet fruit	.25

TO THE FLOWER GARDEN. 79

NO.		PRICE
1329	Solanum Heteroganum. Large; black-fruited; from East Indies. 1½ feet .	$0.10
1330	—— Laciniatum Elegans. A beautiful shrub, producing a large quantity of blue flowers, with bunches of orange-colored fruit; fine. Half-hardy . . .	.25
1331	—— Jasiminoides. Flower white, in clusters; fine. Greenhouse climber. 30 feet .	.25
1332	—— Cabiliense Argenteum. Yellow fruit, with silvery three-lobed fruit. Shrub .	.25
1333	—— Texanum. Waxy scarlet fruit, of great beauty; from Texas. 2 feet . . .	.25

SPERGULA. Nat. Ord., *Caryophyllaceæ.*

Extremely neat, moss-like plants, of a beautiful, lively green, largely used as a substitute for grass on lawns, which they quickly cover, and require no further attention than rolling and keeping free from weeds: are found to thrive best on a stiff soil.

| 1334 | Spergula Pilifera. From Corsica. One-eighth foot . . . . | .10 |

SPHENOGYNE. Nat. Ord., *Compositæ.*

A very showy, free-flowering plant; very effective for beds, mixed borders, edging, or ribbons. Hardy annual.

| 1335 | Sphenogyne Speciosa. Bright yellow; black centre; from South America. 1 foot . | .05 |

SPRAGUEA. Nat. Ord., *Portulaceæ.*

A charming plant, resembling the Calandrina, with Amaranthus-like flowers; extremely graceful and beautiful; very effective as an edging, and valuable for rock-work; delighting in a rich loamy soil. Half-hardy annual.

| 1336 | Spraguea Umbellata. New; white, shaded and spotted with purple; from California. Three-quarters foot . . . . | .25 |

STATICE. Nat. Ord., *Plumbaginaceæ.*

A magnificent genus of beautiful greenhouse and out-door plants, remarkable alike for variety of their foliage and the brilliancy and beauty of their flowers. The hardy kinds are splendid for rock-work and the flower-borders, while the half-hardy make fine conservatory plants. Half-hardy perennial.

1337	Statici Armeria. Suitable for edging. Half foot	.10
1338	—— Bonduellii. Deep golden-yellow; from Levant. 1½ feet	.10
1339	—— Formosa. Rose-color; fine. 1 foot	.10
1340	—— Fortunii. White and yellow; from China. 1 foot	.25
1341	—— Pseudo Armeria. Very ornamental and effective; rose-color. 2 feet .	.10
1342	—— —— Alba. White; from China	.10
1343	—— Rosea Superba. Bright rose; fine	.25
1344	—— Halfordii. A beautiful greenhouse variety. 2 feet	.25
1345	—— Texana. Red. Hardy annual	.10
1346	—— Latifolia. Blue	.10

STOCKS (German, French, and English). Nat. Ord., *Cruciferæ.*

The Stock Gillyflower is one of the most popular, beautiful, and important of our garden favorites; and whether for bedding, massing, edging, or ribboning, it is unsurpassed, either for brilliancy and diversity of color, or profusion and duration of bloom.

The Ten-week Stock is the most universally cultivated, and usually blooms ten to twelve weeks after being sown. They grow from six to fifteen inches high, and when cultivated in rich soil, and occasionally watered with weak guano water, throw out an immense quantity of lateral spikes of bloom, so that each plant forms a perfect bouquet; and it would, indeed, be difficult to surpass the grand effect produced in beds or ribbons by these exquisite gems.

1347	Stocks, Ten-week. Large-flowered, comprising only the finest and most distinct colors, yielding fifty per cent of double flowers; mixed	.25
1348	—— —— Dwarf. One of the most popular varieties; several splendid colors mixed	.10
1349	—— —— New Large-flowered Pyramidal. The most popular stock in cultivation; very choice; received from one of the most celebrated florists in Germany. Twenty brightest and most distinct colors mixed	.25
1350	—— —— Good Mixed. A great variety of colors	.05
1351	—— —— Pure White	.10
1352	—— —— Scarlet	.10
1353	—— —— Purple	.10
1354	—— —— Carmine	.10
1355	—— —— Wallflower-leaved. Mixed	.10

AMATEUR CULTIVATOR'S GUIDE

NO.		PRICE
1356	**Stocks, Ten-week, New Hybrid.** Mixed between the rough and smooth-leaved varieties; very fine	$0.10
1357	—— —— Dwarf German (saved from pot-plants). This is one of the finest. Fifteen colors mixed	.10
1358	—— —— Miniature. A dwarf variety, growing four inches high; fine for edgings; finest mixed	.10
1359	—— Semperflorens, or Perpetual. A fine variety, remaining in flower a long time; finest mixed	.25
1360	—— —— Giant, or Tree. A very valuable acquisition, by its large flowers being from one and a half to two inches in diameter; height of plants two to two and a half feet; unsurpassed for bedding purposes; finest mixed	.25

The Intermediate or autumn-flowering varieties, if sown early in spring, will bloom the same autumn. For winter-flowering, they should be sown in June. They are also valuable for early spring-blooming, for which purpose they should be sown the last of July or in August, and kept from hard frost during winter. Plants treated in this way, and planted out in beds in May, make a rich display during the early summer months.

The Emperor, or perpetual-flowering. This magnificent class of Stocks may be treated in the same manner as the Intermediate, and used for the same purposes. They frequently last several years, if protected from frost; hence its name, — Perpetual.

1367	**Intermediate, or Autumn-flowering Stock.** Finest (twelve distinct colors) mixed	.10
1368	**Perpetual, or Emperor Stocks.** Finest mixed	.10
1369	—— —— New Large-flowering. Finest mixed; superb	.25
1370	**Hybrid Giant Cape, or Cocardean Stocks.** Finest (five distinct colors) mixed	.25

The Brompton and Giant Cape are generally called Winter Stocks on account of their not flowering the first year. The former is robust and branching. The latter possesses the characteristics so much esteemed by some; viz., immense pyramidal spikes of bloom.

1371	**Brompton, or Winter Stocks.** Finest mixed	.10
1372	—— —— Crimson. Dwarf; beautiful	.10
1373	—— —— Rose-color. Dwarf; beautiful	.10
1374	—— —— Dark Blue. Dwarf; beautiful	.10
1375	—— —— New Large and Early-flowering. A splendid acquisition, the habit of which is extremely robust; foliage is exceedingly strong-growing, and of a most striking green, by which the lively colors produce the greatest effect; finest mixed	.25

(For splendid assortments of Stock, see Collections.)

STIPA. NAT. ORD., *Graminaceæ*.

1377	**Stipa Gigantea.** Fine ornamental grass	.10
1378	—— Pennata (Feather Grass). Beautiful	.05
1379	—— Capitata. Ornamental grass	.10

STEVIA. NAT. ORD., *Compositæ*.

Mexican perennials, with tufts of very pretty white or pinkish flowers, which should be grown in sandy peat; fine for pots or borders. Tender perennials.

1380	**Stevia Purpurea.** Purple. 2 feet	.05
1381	—— Serrata. White; the variety usually grown for cutting. 2 feet	.05

SUTHERLANDIA. NAT. ORD., *Leguminosæ*.

An exceedingly beautiful little greenhouse shrub, with handsome Clianthus-like flowers; succeeds best in peat and loam.

1382	**Sutherlandia Frutescens.** Scarlet; from Cape of Good Hope. 3 feet	.25
1383	—— Speciosa Coccinea. A splendid new flowering shrub, with racemes of dark-red flowers, much like Clianthus	.25

SULTAN. NAT. ORD., *Compositæ*.

Handsome border annual, of easy culture; native of Persia, with fragrant flowers from July to September.

1384	**Sultan Sweet.** White. 2 feet	.05
1385	—— —— Purpurea. 2 feet	.05
1386	—— —— Yellow. Fine. 2 feet	.05

TO THE FLOWER GARDEN.

SUNFLOWER. NAT. ORD., *Compositæ.*
(See Helianthus.)

SWEET WILLIAMS. NAT. ORD., *Caryophyllaceæ.*

A useful and well-known tribe of plants, perfectly hardy, and easily raised from seed; a bed of fine varieties presenting a rich sight: it sports into endless varieties; viz., pink, purple, crimson, scarlet, white, variously edged, eyed, and spotted. Our seeds were saved from the finest-named varieties, together with Hunt's (a celebrated English amateur), which we can confidently recommend as superior to any thing ever before offered in this country. Hardy perennials.

No.		Price
1388	Sweet Williams. Fine mixed	$0 05
1389	—— —— Double-flowering. Finest mixed, from a splendid collection of double flowers	.10
1390	—— —— Auricula-flowered. New. This is one of the most desirable, differing from other varieties only in the markings of the flowers, which closely resemble the Auricula. The flowers have a large white disc, with a broad middle zone of rich crimson, purple, and violet; trusses large and perfect	.25
1391	—— —— Hunt's Perfection. Saved from Bragg's finest strain in cultivation; has taken the first prize at all the London exhibitions the past season; truly gorgeous in size, color, and variety	.25

SWEET ALYSSUM. NAT. ORD., *Cruciferæ.*
(See Alyssum.)

TAGETES SIGNATA PUMILA (full size of the flower).

TAGETES. NAT. ORD., *Compositæ.*

Elegant free-flowering plants, with pretty foliage; very effective in mixed borders; succeeds best in a light rich soil. Half-hardy annuals.

1392 Tagetes Signata Pumila. (See cut.) An elegant new dwarf variety, about one foot high; and, when full grown, the plant will measure two feet in diameter, forming a beautiful compact bush, completely covered with flowers, and continuing in bloom until hard frost sets in. Recommended as one of the most showy plants for borders and dwarf beds yet introduced; of the easiest culture. Plants should stand at least two and a half feet apart 10

82 AMATEUR CULTIVATOR'S GUIDE

NO. PRICE

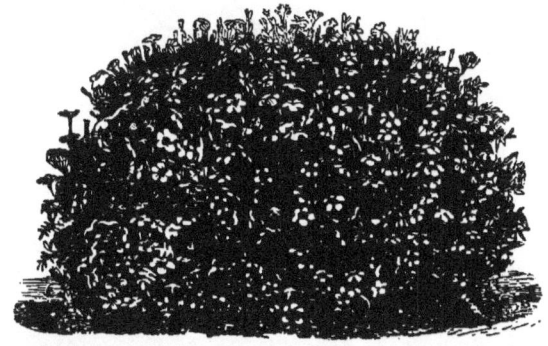

TAGETES SIGNATA PUMILA (full-grown plant, reduced to one-tenth of its natural size).

1394	Tagetes Lucida. Deep yellow; from South America. 1 foot	$0.10
1395	——— Signata. Orange, streaked with brown; from Peru. 2 feet	.10

TACSONIA. Nat. Ord., *Passifloreæ.*

1396 Tacsonia Ignea. This is a splendid orange-scarlet-colored "Passion-flower," like conservatory climbing shrub; showing the unequalled vermilion tint of the Genesera Cinnabarinna, each blossom being relieved by contrast with a circle or band of purple filaments in the centre 50

THALICTRUM. Nat. Ord., *Ranunculaceæ.*

1397	Thalictrum Aquilegiafolium. Light purple. Hardy perennial	.25
1398	——— Flavum. Orange. Hardy perennial	.10
1399	——— Floribundum. Yellow. Hardy perennial	.25

THALIA. Nat. Ord., *Marantaceæ.*

A curious and interesting aquatic plant, which should be planted in light rich soil, about two feet beneath the surface of the water.
1400 Thalia Dealbata. Black and white; from South Carolina 25

TOURNEFORTIA. Nat. Ord., *Boragineæ.*

A very pretty plant, flowers of which resemble the Heliotrope, but without its fragrance; fine either for pot or garden culture. Half-hardy annual.
1401 Tournefortia Heliotropoides. Lilac; trailer; from Buenos Ayres. Half foot . . .10

TRIFOLIUM. Nat. Ord., *Leguminosa.*

Remarkably showy plant, with large handsome flowers; grows freely in any soil. Hardy annual.

1402	Trifolium Atropurpureum. Dark purple. 1 foot	.05
1403	——— Odoratum (sweet-scented Clover). White; very fragrant. 4 feet	.05

TRACHELIUM (Throatwort). Nat. Ord., *Campanulaceæ.*

1404 Trachelium Cœruleum. Blue; pretty Campanula-like plants; from Italy. Hardy biennials. 2 feet 10

TRITOMA. Nat. Ord., *Hemerocallidaceæ.*

Splendid half-hardy, evergreen, herbaceous plants, forming large, robust, stemless leaf crowns, from the centre of which their tall flower-stems, three to five feet in height, are produced in summer and autumn, with large dense-flowered terminal racemes of rich pendant orange-red and scarlet tubulous flowers, each raceme a foot or more in length.

They are admirably adapted for bedding out; and the numerous terminal flame-colored blossoms form a stately distant or mediate effect. They thrive in any rich light garden soil. On approach of winter, they should be taken up and placed in the greenhouse or cellar, for replanting out again in spring.

1405 Tritoma Uvaria. Finest mixed 25

TO THE FLOWER GARDEN. 83

NO.   PRICE

THUNBERGIA ALATA.

THUNBERGIA. Nat. Ord., *Acanthaceæ.*

Extremely ornamental climbers; much admired; very free bloomers; good for trellis, stems of trees, and in the greenhouse, or out of doors in summer in a warm situation. Tender annuals.

1406	Thunbergia Alata. Winged, buff, with dark eye. 4 to 6 feet	$0.05
1407	—— Alba. White, with dark eye. 4 to 6 feet	.05
1408	—— Aurantiaca. Bright orange; dark eye. 4 to 6 feet	.05
1409	—— Bakerii. Fine; white. 4 to 6 feet	.10
1410	—— Sulphurea. Pale yellow. 4 to 6 feet	.05
1411	—— Americana. Clear buff. 4 to 6 feet	.10
1412	—— Mixed. All the above mixed.	.10

TIGRIDIA. Nat. Ord., *Tridaceæ.*

1413	Tigridia Pavonia (Tiger Flower). Red and yellow, spotted with dark crimson-purple. Tender bulbs.	.25
1414	—— Conchiflora. Bright yellow, spotted with crimson	.25

TROPÆOLUM. Nat. Ord., *Tropæoleæ.*

The following varieties, as hybrids from Tropæolum Lobbianum, are unsurpassed by any collection ever offered. They are all of the easiest culture, and flower profusely the first year. Though not in all cases perpetuating their respective kinds true from seed, they nevertheless often produce still more beautiful ones, and among them varieties of the perpetual-flowering, which are invaluable for decoration in the greenhouse or conservatory, and for bouquets in winter.

In the greenhouse or conservatory they may be had in bloom the greater part of the year; and in favored situations in the open air, for edgings, covering trellis-work, or handles of rustic baskets, or trailing from vases, their elegance of form and brilliancy of color render them peculiarly valuable.

1415	Tropæolum Lobbianum. Orange. 4 feet	.20
1416	—— —— Caroline Schmidt. Deep scarlet. 6 feet	.25
1417	—— —— Duc de Malakoff. Straw color; edged rose, spotted with red. 6 feet	.25
1418	—— —— Brilliant. Dark scarlet. 6 feet	.25
1419	—— —— Schultzi. Deep carmine; foliage dark green; fine. 4 feet	.10
1420	—— —— Flamula Grandiflora. Yellow; beautifully streaked with carmine; very choice. 6 feet	.20
1421	—— —— Geant des Batailles. Brilliant crimson. 6 feet	.25
1422	—— —— Garibaldii. Fine orange, shaded with scarlet. 6 feet	.25
1423	—— —— Duc de Vicence. Sulphur, with vermilion spots. 6 feet	.25

TROPÆOLUM LOBBIANUM.

NO.				PRICE
1424	Tropæolum Lobbianum Duc de Luynes. Dark crimson			$0.25
1425	— — Masiliense. Deep carmine			.25
1426	— — Monsieur Turuell. Orange-yellow, striped with vermilion; flower very fine form. 6 feet			.25
1427	— — Monsieur Calmet. Lemon, spotted with crimson; very beautiful			.25
1428	— — Napoleon III. Orange yellow, striped with vermilion. 6 feet			.25
1429	— — Peraguanum. Scarlet, with black spots; very fine. 6 feet			.25
1430	— — Roi des Noirs. Nearly black. 4 feet			.25
1431	— — Tricolor Grandiflora. Carmine; spotted. 4 feet			.25
1432	— — Triomphe de Gand. Fine orange-scarlet. 4 feet			.25
1433	— — — Du Prado. Yellow-scarlet flamed. 4 feet			.25
1434	— — Versicolor. Orange-striped. 4 feet			.25
1435	— — Victor Emmanuel. Brilliant carmine and gold. 4 feet			.25
1436	— — Zanderii. Vivid scarlet; one of the strongest growing varieties. 4 feet			.25
1437	— — Lillie Schmidt. Scarlet. 6 feet			.25
1438	— — Von Humboldt. Fine orange-shaded. 6 feet			.25
1439	— — Mixed. Finest varieties			.25

The following are beautiful tuberous varieties for the greenhouse:—

1440	Tropæolum Brachyceras. Yellow and red; fine foliage; splendid trailer			.25
1441	— Pentaphyllum. Scarlet and green; delicate foliage; fine for open borders			.25
1442	— Jarattii. Scarlet and yellow			.25
1443	— Tricolorum. Scarlet, yellow, and black			.25

TO THE FLOWER GARDEN. 85

NO.   PRICE

TYDÆA. NAT. ORD., *Gesneraceæ.*

A stove plant of great beauty. Greenhouse perennial.

1444   Tydæa Hybrida. Very fine $0.25

VALERIAN. NAT. ORD., *Valerianceæ.*

Perennial plants; mostly natives of Europe; will grow in almost any soil. The dwarf species are very suitable for rock-work.

1445   Valeriana Rubra. Red. 1¼ feet 05
1446   —— Alba. White. 1½ feet 05

VENIDIUM. NAT. ORD., *Compositæ.*

An exceedingly showy plant, with large handsome flower, having a very gay appearance in beds or mixed borders; thrives best in turfy loam. Half-hardy annual.

1447   Venidium Calendulaceum. Deep orange; rich brown centre; from Cape of Good Hope. 1 foot 05

VENUS'S LOOKING-GLASS. NAT. ORD., *Campanulaceæ.*

A free-flowering, pretty little plant, of nice habit of growth, especially adapted for beds, ribbons, or edgings; grows well in any garden soil. Hardy annual.

1448   Venus's Looking-Glass (*Campanula*). Finest mixed; from south of Europe. Half foot, .05

VALLOTA. NAT. ORD., *Amaryllidaceæ.*

A splendid bulbous-rooted plant, allied to the Amaryllis and Lily. It blooms in August, throwing up its strong stems about one foot high, with from five to eight brilliant scarlet lily-like flowers; very ornamental for bedding out in summer or for culture in pots.

1449   Vallota Purpurea Superba. Fine 25

VENUS'S NAVELWORT. NAT. ORD., *Boraginaceæ.*

A very pretty little plant, useful for ribbons, and forms a neat edging to shrubbery borders, &c.; grows freely in every soil. Hardy annual.

1450   Venus's Navelwort (*Cynoglossum Linifolius*). White; from Portugal. 1½ feet. . .05

VERONICA. NAT. ORD., *Scrophulariaceæ.*

A genus of the most beautiful and showy evergreen shrubs, producing their handsome spikes of flowers in the greatest profusion.

1451   Veronica Glauca (New). Blue; very fine; from England. Hardy perennial. 2 feet . .10
1452   —— Devoniana. Red and white. Half-hardy shrub. 2½ feet 10
1453   —— Syriaca. Bright blue and white; fine for pot-culture, edgings, vases, or rock-work. Half-hardy annual. Half foot 10
1454   —— —— Alba. White variety of preceding 10
1455   —— Andersonii. Lilac and white; greenhouse shrub. 2 feet 10
1456   —— Austriaca. Blue. Hardy perennial 05
1457   —— Imperialis. Blue. Greenhouse shrub 25
1458   —— Lindleyana. Lilac. Greenhouse shrub 25
1459   —— Virginica. Rose-color. Hardy perennial 05

VERBENA. NAT. ORD., *Verbenaceæ.*

A charming genus of universally admired and easily cultivated plants, simply requiring the treatment of half-hardy annuals to have them bloom during the summer; for winter decoration they are invaluable. Half-hardy perennial.

1460   Verbena Aubletia. Reddish-purple; from North America. Half foot 05
1461   —— Drummondii. Lilac; from Texas 10
1462   —— Pulcherrima. Violet; fine. Half foot 10
1463   —— Teucroides Odorata. Fine white; from Germany 10
1464   —— Venosa. Rich purple; free-bloomer; trailer. From Buenos Ayres 05
1465   —— Fine Mixed 10
1466   —— Hybrida. From finest named sorts; extra mixed 25
1467   ——— Snow's. From Dexter Snow's celebrated collection of several hundred varieties; fine mixed 25
1468   —— —— New Italian Striped. One of last season's novelties; brilliant colors of carnation-like, striped with rose, lilac, purple, on various colored ground . . .25

| NO. | | PRICE |

BASKET OF VERBENAS.

1469 **Verbena Hybrida Auriculæflora.** A splendid novelty, large and well formed; blooms in various shades, with a distinct eye of white or rose, and properly called Auriculæflora, as the disk comes near the Polyanthus and Auricula. Extra fine mixed, $0.50
1470 — — Coccinea. From most brilliant scarlet flowers 25
1471 — — Cœrulea. Deep-blue; fine 25

VIOLA TRICOLOR. Nat. Ord., *Violaceæ*.
(See Pansy or Heartsease.)

VINCA. Nat. Ord., *Apocynaceæ*.

A genus of the most beautiful greenhouse plants; succeeding out of doors in warm, sheltered situations. Seed sown early in spring will bloom the same season.
1473 Vinca Rosea. Rose-color; from East Indies 10
1474 — Alba. White, with crimson eye 10
1475 — Alba Nova. A new variety; pure white 25

VICTORIA REGIA. Nat. Ord., *Nymphaceæ*.

One of the most beautiful of all the aquatic plants, which requires a house for its special use. To succeed in growing them from seed, keep the pot immersed in water until the seed vegetates, when it should be repotted in a large pot, and sunk in a pond or fountain about one foot below the surface of the water. From the River Amazon.
1476 Victoria Regia. The most magnificent of all lilies. Per seed 1.00

VISCARIA. Nat. Ord., *Caryophyllaceæ*.

A genus of remarkably pretty profuse-flowering plants, producing a striking effect in beds, ribbons, or mixed borders; growing freely in any good garden-soil. Hardy annual.
1477 Viscaria Burridgii. White. 1½ feet 05
1478 — Cœli Rosea (Rose of Heaven). Bright rose, with white centre; from Levant. 1½ feet 05
1479 — — Alba. Pure white; fine . . . . . . , ...05
1480 — — Nana. Dwarf; bright rose, white centre 10
1481 — Oculata. Pink, with rich crimson eye. From Algiers 05
1482 — — Dunnetti. White, with dark eye 10
1483 — — Coccinea Nana. Bright scarlet, with rosy-purple centre. 1 foot . . .10
1484 — — Hybrida Splendens. A handsome perennial variety 25
1485 — Finest Mixed 10
1486 — Good Mixed 05

VIMINARIA. Nat. Ord., *Leguminosæ*.

Exceedingly curious plants, with leafless stems, which very much resemble a bundle of twigs; these are covered with handsome flowers, giving the plant a very striking and remarkable appearance. Greenhouse shrubs.
1487 Viminaria Pressii. Yellow; from New South Wales. 3 feet 25

TO THE FLOWER GARDEN.

WALLFLOWER. Nat. Ord., *Cruciferæ.*

A useful and ornamental class of plants; very fragrant. Half-hardy perennial.

No.		Price
1488	Wallflower. Good mixed	$0.05
1489	—— Dwarf. Large-flowering; mixed	.10
1490	—— Double. Finest German; mixed	.10

(For separate colors, see Collections.)

WIGANDIA CARACASANA.

WIGANDIA. Nat. Ord., *Hydroleaceæ.*

1491 Wigandia Caracasana. Greenhouse perennial 25

WHITLAVIA. Nat. Ord., *Hydrophyllaceæ.*

A very handsome free-flowering plant, suitable for beds and borders; from California. Hardy annual.

1492 Whitlavia Grandiflora. Violet-blue. 1 foot 05

XERANTHEMUM. Nat. Ord., *Compositæ.*

A fine everlasting flower, good for winter bouquets. Hardy annual.

1493 Xeranthemum Double. Purple. 2 feet 10

88 AMATEUR CULTIVATOR'S GUIDE

NO.		PRICE
1494	Xeranthemum Double, White. 2 feet	$0.10
1495	—— —— Campacta. New dwarf; purple. 2 feet	.10
1496	—— —— —— Alba. White. 2 feet	.10
1497	—— —— Lutea. Yellow. 2 feet.	.10

ZAUSCHNERIA. Nat. Ord., *Onagrariæ*.

1498 Zauschneria Californica. A very interesting and valuable hardy autumn-flowering plant, with a profusion of scarlet flower-tubes in September, October, and November; well adapted for dry, gravelly soils in sunny situations. Exceedingly handsome for beds and borders. Hardy perennials. 1 foot 25

DOUBLE ZINNIA.

ZINNIA. Nat. Ord., *Compositæ*.

A grand genus of autumn-flowering plants, combining the greatest richness and diversity of color with unequalled profusion and duration of bloom.

Among the novelties of recent introduction, the New Double Zinnia has proved a most important acquisition. Its splendid double flowers rival, in beauty, size, and form, moderate size dahlias.

1499 Zinnia Elegans. Mixed. 2 feet 05
1500 —— Double. Mixed (see engraving). No new annual has excited so much attention as this. First introduced by Messrs. Vilmorin, Andriex, & Co., Paris, 1860; and since that time has been much improved in size, form, and color. The seed we offer was saved only from the finest double flowers, and will produce a large percentage of double-flowering plants. Finest mixed 10

TO THE FLOWER GARDEN.

NO.   PRICE

MEXICAN ZINNIA.

A	Zinnia Double Aurea.	Splendid double; golden-yellow; rich	$0.10
B	—— —— Coccinea.	Double; scarlet	.10
C	—— —— Carmine.	Beautiful light rose or carmine; full double	.10
D	—— —— Violacea.	Very dark crimson-purple; full double	.10
1501	—— Mexicana.	This proves to be a new and desirable species. It is a neat dwarf plant of compact habit, scarcely one foot high, much branched, with numerous flower-heads, about two inches across, the ray florets being of a full orange color in the centre, and paler at the margins. It is offered in some lists under the name of Zinnia Haageana, and also Aurea and Sanvitalia Mexicana . . .	.10

(For separate colors, see Collections.)

Splendid Assortments

OF

FRENCH AND GERMAN FLOWER-SEEDS.

We invite the attention of our numerous customers to the following list of assortments of flower-seeds. They have all been selected expressly for us, by our special correspondents in France and Germany, from the various noted flower-seed growers, whose well-known reputation is a sure guaranty of their superior excellence, both as regards distinctness of color, and freshness of seed. We have no hesitation in recommending them as equal, if not superior, to any to be obtained in Europe. Our Asters are, many of them, of our own growth; and the best guaranty we can give of their extra quality is the award of the highest premium of the Massachusetts Horticultural Society for the best thirty flowers exhibited in 1865, and EVERY YEAR but FOUR for the previous twenty years; and this, too, in competition with the choicest French seeds.

ASTERS.

NO.		PRICE
1501½	Truffaut's Peony Flowered Aster. Sixteen splendid varieties; distinct colors	$1.50
1502	Truffaut's Peony Pyramid Flowered. Twelve splendid varieties, of the most beautiful colors	1.25
1502½	—— —— —— —— Eight splendid varieties; distinct colors	1.00
1503	—— —— —— Six splendid varieties, of the most beautiful colors	.75
1504	—— —— Perfection. Twelve splendid varieties, of the most beautiful colors	1.50
1505	—— —— —— Six splendid varieties, of the most beautiful colors	.75
1506	Dwarf Large-flowering Peony. Six superb varieties, of the most beautiful colors	1.00
1506½	Imbricated Pompone. Twelve splendid varieties	1.50
1507	Truffaut's Imbrigue Pompone. Ten splendid varieties, of the most beautiful colors	1.00
1508	New Dwarf Chrysanthemum-flowered. Ten splendid varieties, of the most beautiful colors	1.25
1509	New Giant Emperor. Ten splendid varieties, of the most beautiful colors	1.50
1510	New Cocardeau, or Crown-flowered. Six beautiful varieties, of the most splendid colors	1.00
1511	Globe-flowered Pyramidal. Twelve superb varieties, of the most beautiful colors	1.00
1512	Double Globe Quilled. Twelve splendid varieties, of the most beautiful colors	1.00
1513	Ranunculus-flowered. Eight superb varieties, of the most beautiful colors	.75
1514	Reid's Improved Quilled. Eight splendid varieties, of the most beautiful colors	1.00
1515	Double Dwarf Aster. Twelve splendid varieties, of the most beautiful colors	.75
1516	Double Dwarf Bouquet Pyramid. Twelve splendid varieties, of the most beautiful colors	1.00
1517	Boltze's New Miniature Bouquet Pyramid. Five superb varieties, of the most beautiful colors	.75
1518	New Peony Globe. Seven superb varieties, of the most beautiful colors	.75
1519	New Rose-flowered. Twelve superb varieties, of the most beautiful colors	1.50
1520	Porcupine, or Hedgehog. Nine superb varieties, of the most beautiful colors	.75

BALSAMS.

1521	Double Camellia-flowered Balsams. Ten splendid varieties, of the most beautiful colors	1.00
1522	Double Dwarf Balsams. Ten splendid varieties, of the most beautiful colors	.75
1523	Double Spotted Rose-flowered Balsams. Twelve splendid varieties, of the most beautiful colors	1.00
1524	Improved Double Rose-flowered Balsams. Ten splendid varieties, unsurpassable in quality. Twenty-five seeds of each	1.25
1524½	New Rose-flowered. Eight splendid varieties	1.00

GERMAN STOCKS.

1525	Dwarf Early Flowering. Sixteen varieties	1.25
1525½	Dwarf Early-flowered Ten-weeks Stocks. Twelve splendid varieties, of the most beautiful colors	1.00
1526	Large-flowered Improved Dwarf Ten-weeks Stocks. Six splendid varieties, of the most beautiful colors	.75
1527	New Large-flowered Pyramidal Ten-weeks Stocks. Twelve splendid varieties, of the most beautiful colors	1.00
1527½	New Large-flowered Pyramidal. Eight varieties	.75

TO THE FLOWER GARDEN. 91

NO.		PRICE
1528	Dwarf Pyramidal Ten-weeks Stocks. Twelve splendid varieties, of the most beautiful colors	$1.00
1529	Miniature, or Lilliputian Ten-weeks Stocks. Six splendid varieties, of the most beautiful colors	.75
1530	Dwarf Bouquet Ten-weeks Stocks. Six splendid varieties, of the most beautiful colors	.75
1531	Giant, or Tree Ten-weeks Stocks. Ten splendid varieties, of the most beautiful colors	1.00
1532	New Early Autumn-flowering Stocks. Eight splendid varieties, of the most beautiful colors	1.00
1533	Giant Cape Stocks. Five splendid varieties, of the most beautiful colors	.50
1534	Brompton Stocks. Twelve splendid varieties, of the most beautiful colors	1.00
1535	New Early Large-flowered Brompton Stocks. Eight splendid varieties, of the most beautiful colors	1.00
1536	Emperor, or Perpetual Stocks. Eight splendid varieties, of the most beautiful colors	1.00
1537	Semperflorens, or Perpetual. Eight splendid varieties, of the most beautiful colors,	1.00
1538	New Hybrid. Hybrid between the Wall-flower and the rough leaves. Six splendid varieties, of the most beautiful colors	.75
1539	New Robust. A beautiful acquisition. Six splendid varieties, of the most beautiful colors	1.50

LARKSPURS.

1540	Double Dwarf Rocket Larkspur. Ten splendid varieties, of the most beautiful colors	.75
1541	Double Tall Rocket Larkspur. Eight splendid varieties, of the most beautiful colors,	.50
1542	Double Branching Larkspur. Eight splendid varieties, of the most beautiful colors	.50
1543	Double Hyacinth-flowered Larkspur. Ten splendid varieties, of the most beautiful colors	.75

VARIOUS COLLECTIONS.

1545	Antirrhinum Majus (Snapdragon). Twelve splendid varieties, of the most beautiful colors	1.00
1546	Antirrhinum Majus Nanum. Five splendid varieties ; dwarf; the most beautiful colors,	.75
1547	Acacia. Twenty-five splendid varieties, of the most beautiful colors	3.00
1548	—— Twelve splendid varieties, of the most beautiful colors	1.50
1549	Canna. Twenty-five splendid varieties, of the most beautiful colors	3.00
1550	—— Twelve splendid varieties, of the most beautiful colors	1.50
1551	Capsicum. Six splendid varieties, of the most beautiful colors	1.00
1552	Convolvulus Major. Ten splendid varieties, of the most beautiful colors	.50
1553	Coxcomb Twelve splendid varieties, of the most beautiful colors	1.00
1553½	Everlasting Flower. Twenty-four varieties	1.50
1554	Everlasting Flowers. Twelve splendid varieties, of the most beautiful colors	1.00
1555	Gladiolus. Six splendid varieties, of the most beautiful colors	1.00
1556	Gourds. Twenty-five splendid varieties, of the most beautiful colors	1.50
1557	—— Twelve splendid varieties, of the most beautiful colors	.75
1558	Helichrysum. Eight splendid varieties, of the most beautiful colors	.75
1559	Hollyhock. Twelve splendid varieties, of the most beautiful colors	1.50
1559½	Hollyhock. Eight varieties	.75
1560	Heartsease. or Pansies. Eight splendid varieties, of the most beautiful colors	1.50
1561	Petunia. Eight splendid varieties, of the most beautiful colors	.75
1562	Phlox, Drummondii. Twelve splendid varieties, of the most beautiful colors	1.00
1563	Poppies. Twelve splendid varieties, of the most beautiful colors	.75
1564	Portulaca. Eight splendid varieties, of the most beautiful colors	.50
1565	—— Double. Four splendid varieties, of the most beautiful colors	1.00
1566	Salpiglossis. Eight splendid varieties, of the most beautiful colors	1.00
1567	Sweet Peas. Eight splendid varieties, of the most beautiful colors	.50
1568	Scabiosa. Eight splendid varieties, of the most beautiful colors	.50
1569	Solanum. Twelve splendid varieties, of the most beautiful colors	1.50
1570	Ipomea. Half-hardy and tender. Twelve splendid varieties, of the most beautiful colors	1.00
1571	Jacobea. Eight splendid varieties, of the most beautiful colors	.50
1572	—— Dwarf. Eight splendid varieties, of the most beautiful colors	1.00
1573	Kennedya. Twelve splendid varieties, of the most beautiful colors	2.00
1574	—— Six splendid varieties, of the most beautiful colors	1.00
1575	Marvel of Peru. Eight splendid varieties, of the most beautiful colors	.50
1576	Marygold, African and French. Eight splendid varieties, of the most beautiful colors	.50
1577	Ornamental Grasses. Twenty-five splendid varieties, of the most beautiful colors	1.25
1578	—— Twelve splendid varieties, of the most beautiful colors	.75
1579	Penstemon. Six splendid varieties, of the most beautiful colors	.75
1580	Ornamental Fruits. Twelve splendid varieties, of the most beautiful sorts	1.25
1581	Tropæolum Lobbianum. Twelve splendid varieties, of the most beautiful sorts	1.50
1582	Wallflower (from pot-plants). Ten splendid varieties, of the most beautiful colors	1.50
1583	—— Six splendid varieties, of the most beautiful colors	1.00
1584	Zinnia Elegans. Eight splendid varieties, of the most beautiful colors	.75
1585	—— Finest Double. Six splendid varieties, of the most beautiful colors	1.00

NOVELTIES OF 1866-7,

AND OTHER

CHOICE AND RARE FLOWERS.

NO.   PRICE

1586 **Arbronia Fragrans.** This beautiful plant is a native of the Rocky-Mountain country, and can hardly be surpassed for beauty and elegance. It is a hardy perennial, of trailing habit, sending up immense numbers of flowers of a pure white color, in clusters resembling the Snowball. It opens its flowers towards evening, which possess a delightful fragrance. In bloom from June to September. Seeds per packet $0.25
1587 **Abutilon Venosum Striatum.** Greenhouse plant; striped 25
1588 **Acacia Balsamea.** Yellow; fine 25
1589 —— **Dolibriformis.** Yellow 25
1590 —— **Drummondii.** New and beautiful 25
1591 —— **Excelsa.** White 25
1592 —— **Floribundus.** Very free flowering 25
1593 —— **Glandulosa.** Yellow 25
1594 —— **Longiflora Magnifica.** Superb 25
1595 —— **Miesnerii.** Yellow; new; very fine 25
1596 —— **Spectabilis.** Deep golden yellow; very showy and beautiful 25
1597 —— **Adonis Vernalis Grandiflora Superba.** A beautiful variety, with larger flowers than Adonis Vernalis; bright yellow, with large dark-brown centre. Perennial . .25

AGROSTEMMA CŒLI ROSA, DWARF-FRINGED.

1598 **Agrostemma Cœli Rosa, Dwarf-fringed.** A fine variety of Agrostemma Cœli Rosa, of dwarf, compact growth (eight to ten inches high), thickly branched, vigorous, and free-blooming; flowers a fresh and lively rose-color, with a very white centre. The borders of the petals are finely fringed, giving to the whole plant a delicate and graceful aspect. Hardy annual 10
1599 —— **Cœli Rosa Hybrida Flore Pleno.** A new double variety of this very pretty plant, producing a profusion of densely-double flowers. A great acquisition . . .25
1600 **Ageratum Cœruleum Multiflorum.** Very free, flowering, blue, half-hardy annual. 3 feet 10
1601 **Anthemis Purpurea.** Dwarf bushy species, with very numerous flower-heads; ray flowers, yellow above and brown underneath 25

BOCCONIA JAPONICA. See page 94.

TO THE FLOWER GARDEN.

NO.		PRICE
1602	**Andropogon Argenteum.** A beautiful perennial grass, growing several feet high, with silver green foliage	.25
1603	—— **Formosum.** A new perennial grass from India, said to exceed in dimensions any ornamental grass at present in cultivation, and producing a majestic effect	.25
1604	**Antirrhinum Majus Pumilum Quadricolor.** A most beautiful Liliput variety, brilliant crimson, scarlet, white, and yellow	.25
1605	—— **Majus Tom Thumb.** A very handsome dwarf Antirrhinum or Snapdragon, of compact globular growth, with bright vermilion-colored flowers	.10
1606	**Anemome Species Nova Pontica.** Described as a very beautiful alpine plant; native of the subalpine regions of the Pontic Mountains	.50
1607	—— **Japonica, Honorine Jobert.** A vigorous, beautiful, and effective hardy perennial, with splendid large pure white flowers	.25
1608	**Aplopappus Rubiginosus.** A showy autumn-flowering annual, about three feet high, with lanceolate incised foliage, producing, in September, large terminal corymbs of yellow flowers, each nearly two inches in diameter	.25
1609	**Aquilegia Siberica Reddish Violet.** A fine variety, with upright double flower, of a pretty reddish-purple tinge; plant compact, and a profuse bloomer	.25
1610	—— **Glandulosa.** A splendid and newly-introduced species from Siberia. The plant is more dwarfish in its habits than the common Columbine. The flowers are large and rich sky blue, the inside and margin of the corolla pure white; about one foot high. (See cut.)	.10
1611	—— **Hybrida Lucida.** A beautiful hybrid; remarkably free flowering, with handsome foliage; flowers large, brilliant bronze scarlet, yellow margined. Perennial	.25
1612	—— **Spectabilis.** A new species, with large flowers of a bright blue, shaded red, with green-bordered sepals and golden-yellow margined corolla. Perennial	.25
1613	—— **Siberica Violacea.** Fine new variety, with upright double flowers of a pretty reddish-violet tinge; plant compact, and a profuse bloomer. Hardy perennial	.25
1614	—— **Siberica Rubro Violaceo Pleno.** A fine, compact, full-blooming variety, with erect, double, rich, reddish-violet flowers. Perennial	.25
	—— **Vulgaris Fl. Albo Pleno.** Pure white double Columbine	.25
1615	**Arundo Donax Fol. Variegatis.** A very ornamental reed-like plant, growing six feet high, with broad lance-shaped foliage of the deepest green, beautifully striped with white	.25
1616	**Asters.** The continued effort and rivalry among the French and German growers of Asters has resulted in great improvements in this beautiful and popular tribe of annual flowers; more than forty different classes or styles of this flower are now described in their catalogues, an indication of its great and increasing popularity. In habit of plant, form of flower, variety and brilliancy of colors, they now far excel those in cultivation a few years since. The following includes the newest and most desirable, among which, it will be noticed, are many entirely novel in style and color: —	
1617	—— **New Victoria Carmine Rose.** Flower as large as the Emperor Asters, with ten to twenty flowers; brilliant carmine, fine form	.25
1618	—— **New Victoria Snow White,** one foot in height; flowers three to four inches in diameter, very double and of the purest white	.25
1619	—— **New Large-flowered Dwarf Bouquet.** A beautiful class, growing in bouquet form, with full and perfect double flowers, of a great variety of exceedingly brilliant colors, and lasting unusually long in bloom; handsome branching habit, and finely adapted for edgings or dwarf-groups, beds, &c. Twelve varieties mixed	.25
1620	—— **New White-centred Pæony-flowered Dwarf Pyramidal Bouquet** of pyramidal nosegay form; very striking and beautiful colors, carmine, crimson, violet, rose, &c., all having white centres. Eight varieties mixed	.25
1621	—— **Brilliant Deep Blood-red, with pure white centre**	.25
1622	—— **New Pæony Perfection,** of vigorous upright growth, with very large full double flowers four inches or more in diameter, of the most perfect form, not showing an open centre to the last stage of blooming. Twelve varieties mixed	.25
1623	—— **New Dwarf Globe-flowered Imbricated Pompon.** A real gem among Asters; dwarf, bushy habit, not over fifteen inches high, closely set with beautiful globular flowers of most brilliant colors; the earliest flowering class, and extremely showy. Six varieties mixed	.25
1624	—— **New White-centred Pyramidal.** Very distinct and splendid, with pure white petals in the centre, surrounded by lavender, rose, violet, or carmine, producing a novel and very picturesque effect. Collection of six varieties	1.75
1625	—— **Mixed**	.25
1626	—— **New White Centre, Globe-flowered.** Very showy, of spreading habit, with fine double flowers, the following varieties separate: —	
1627	—— **Crimson.** With white centre	.25
1628	—— **Dark Violet.** With white centre	.25
1629	—— **Light Blue.** With white centre	.25
1630	—— **Rose.** With white centre	.25
1631	—— **Boltze's New Bouquet.** These novel and pretty varieties grow about eight inches high, are very double, rich, and free flowering, very fine for pots, beds, or groups. The two following separate: —	
1632	—— **Carmine.** With white, new and very fine	.25
1633	—— **Dark Rose.** With white	.25
1634	—— **New Hedge-hog or Crown.—**	
1635	—— **Carmine Rose.** With white centre, extra double	.25

94 AMATEUR CULTIVATOR'S GUIDE

NO. PRICE

Asters. New Hedge-hog or Crown,—
1836 —— Light Violet. With white centre, extra double 25
1637 —— Truffaut's Pæony-flowered French Asters. These are unsurpassed for size, beauty, and general effect, and too well known to need a description. Collection of ten splendid varieties 1.50
1638 —— New Large-flowered Dwarf German. A new and highly improved variety, growing only eight inches high, and very branching, with large double flowers, finely imbricated 10
1639 —— New Pæony-flowered la Superbe. This is the largest Pæony-flowered Aster; height two feet, with magnificent flowers, five inches in diameter; brilliant rose color .10
1640 —— Boltze's New Miniature Bouquet. Of pyramidal growth, eight inches in height, constant in habit, extremely pretty, and very free blooming; mixed colors . . .10
1641 —— Pæony-flowered Globe. Snow white; new and fine 10
1642 **Aubrietia Græca.** An admirable little spring-bloomer; can be strongly recommended as a most desirable plant, either for borders or beds, in early spring, blooming for several weeks in succession 50
1643 **Bartonia Nuda.** This is a perfect gem : it grows two to three feet high, and is literally covered with its large white flowers of the most delicate texture, surpassing even the finest lace-work. The flowers are two and a half inches in diameter, and produced in great abundance all the season. A perfectly hardy perennial. Per packet . . .25
1644 **Begonia Pearcei (Veitch).** A beautiful species introduced from South America, with large bright yellow flowers borne on slender stems, well above the leaves, the upper sides of which are of a dark velvety green, traversed by pale, straw-colored veins, while the under side is of a dull red. Greenhouse plant 50
1645 **Bryonopsis. Erythrocarpa.** Splendid climber, with beautiful scarlet fruits marbled with white. Annual 25
1646 **Blitum Capitatum.** Scarlet-fruited strawberry blite 05
1647 **Bisnaja Major.** A very handsome hardy annual, growing about two and a half feet high, with deep-green, finely cut foliage, and dense umbels of white flowers, elegantly disposed, producing a grand effect in groups or masses 25
1648 **Bocconia Japonica** (*B. Yokuhoma*). This noble plant, recently introduced from Japan, and not yet in the trade, has been an object of unusual admiration in the German gardens. Allied to the fine Bocconia Cordata, it surpasses this in point of beauty, of robust, free growth, habit of plant, size, shape, coloring of leaves, and showiness of flower-spikes. It is perfectly hardy, requiring no protection in winter; of luxuriant growth, forming a bush five to six feet in height, which is decorated, from the month of August, by beautiful pyramidal spikes of flowers, two to three feet or more in length. The beautiful, deeply serrated leaves, in the way of oak-leaves, are large, of an obtuse, cordate form, of a sombre green above, glaucous below. As a single object on the lawn, or grouped together, its effect is exquisite. It is a grand acquisition. (See our engraving of the plant.) 50
1649 **Calliopsis Diversifolia.** A very pretty dwarf, hardy plant about a foot high, covered with golden-yellow flowers, which have a reddish-brown centre, and slightly marbled margin. Perennial 25
1650 **Callirhoe Involucrata.** A trailing hardy perennial of great beauty ; from the Rocky Mountains. In bloom from May to September. The flowers rise singly, on stems six to ten inches high, and vary in color from bright rose to the deepest crimson. In size and color resembles the Portulacas. Per packet 25
1651 **Calceolaria New-spotted.** Saved from a superb collection of new-spotted sorts . .50
1652 —— Pinnata. Yellow; half-hardy annual. 1½ feet 10
1653 **Campanula Attica.** A charming Grecian annual, forming compact plants about one foot in diameter, covered with deep-blue bell-shaped flowers; well suited to sunny exposures 10
1654 —— Rhomboidea Soldanelliflora Plena. A beautiful novelty. The petals of the handsome, pale azure-blue double flowers, are finely cut or fringed, and the blossoms are borne on graceful, drooping, slender branches. Perennial 25
1655 —— Medium, Flore Roseo. Pink flowering Canterbury Bell. A new and very fine variety, with bright pink flowers ; a real novelty in color of this favorite and popular flower, and considered a most valuable introduction 25
1656 —— Leutweini. Beautiful azure-blue flowers, size of the Canterbury Bell. Hardy perennial. Flowers the first year from seed 26
1657 **Canna Bihorelli.** A new dwarf variety with large dark-red leaves and large dark-red flowers 50
1658 —— Nigricans. One of the most showy and attractive of the Cannas, excelling in the rich tints of its stem and leaves either of the others, and more nearly approaching the rich deep coloring of the Dracæna, having that dark bronzy metallic lustre peculiar to many of the tropical ornamental-leaved plants. Its growth is rapid, its aspect stately, and attaining the height of eight feet, terminated with spikes of scarlet flowers, is a superb object. (See engraving) 25
1659 **Celosia Pyramidalis Nana Aurantica.** Annual ; from Cochin-China ; erect, from fifteen to eighteen inches ; leaves oval, acuminated, bright green : trusses of flower-spikes pyramidal of a brilliant buff yellow. Fine novelty for forming masses which will contrast beautifully with the following 25
1660 —— Pyramidalis versicolor. Annual; from Cochin-China ; two to three feet high, bushy from the bottom, with oval acuminated leaves of red brown; all the spikes terminated by bright carmine trusses before opening, passing gradually to violet carmine 25

NO.		PRICE
1661	Celosia Pyramidalis Versicolor Var Hybrida Foliis Atrobruneis. A variety believed to be a hybrid of C. Versicolor and C. Nana Aurantica. It is distinct from the former by its darker colored leaves, and its flower-trusses, which have a tinge of orange. A pretty foliaged plant, which will produce a great effect in beds	.25
1662	Cedronella Cana. A fragrant foliaged plant, with long spikes of deep purple flowers, retaining the purple hue of the calyxes for a long time after the flowers have fallen; allied to Gardoquia Betonicoides; flowering abundantly the first season if sown early. Hardy perennial	.25
1663	Cerastium Biebersteini. Handsomer than Cerastium Tomentosum, more compact in habit, with larger leaves, of a dazzling, snowy whiteness. Six inches high. Perennial	.25
1664	Chamæpeuce diacantha. A beautiful, silvery, spiny, herbaceous plant, of magnificent effect as single specimens on the lawn. Was much admired during the past summer at the Sub-tropical Gardens, at Battersea Park. Half-hardy perennial	.50
1665	Chrysanthemum, Dunnetti, New Double Golden. A seedling from the annual Chrysanthemum tricolor, with flowers as double as Truffaut's Pæony Aster; color bright golden yellow, similar in habit and bloom to the C. Dunnetti; double white; introduced in 1865. Annual. Per packet	.50
1666	— Carinatum annulatum. A remarkably fine new variety of this popular annual; flowers orange, bordered with a broad scarlet ring; a beautiful design	.25
1667	— Louise Honor-ty. Charming miniature, raised from the Pompon tribe; but so widely different that we consider it a forerunner to an entirely different class of summer-flowering Chrysanthemums. This plant forms perfectly round tufts, from ten to twelve inches high, by fifteen to eighteen through. The small flowers, of purplish rose, shading off to white towards the centre, are produced in such quantity that the whole plant forms a single bouquet	.50
1668	— Japonicum, flore pleno. New double Japanese fancy varieties. This new tribe of Chrysanthemum is particularly recommended, as, from its sportive character, we feel convinced that the plants raised from seeds will always vary in the shape and color of their flowers, constantly producing new varieties	.50
1669	— Carinatum Atrococcineum. Blooming in the most various shades, from light scarlet to dark blood-red. Very beautiful. Hardy annual	.10
1670	— Carinatum Purpureum. Beautiful crimson and purple-violet flowers; very fine. Hardy annual	.25
1671	— Tricolor Dunnetti Flore Pleno. The flowers are of snowy whiteness, and its great charm consists in being as perfectly double as the Truffaut's Pæony Aster. Hardy annual	.10
1672	Cineraria Argentea Vera. A handsome, silvery, shrubby species	.50
1673	— Burgæi. 'With very handsome leaves and flowers	.50
1764	— Papyracea. A new and beautiful large-leaved species, with flower-stems four feet high	.50
1675	Clianthus Dampieri Alba. A new and remarkable variety, with large white flowers, delicately marked with a scarlet line around each petal	.50
1676	Clarkia Pulchella Alba Tom Thumb. A very compact and beautiful variety	.25
1676½	— Integripetala Alba Tom Thumb. A new and exceedingly dwarf and compact-growing variety of the entire-petalled Clarkia, producing a profusion of snow-white flowers, which are exceedingly showy, and of the highest decorative effect, either for bedding, edging, and ribboning. This variety has been selected with great care, and will be found very constant in its character. Height, eight inches	.25
1676¾	— Integripetala Fl. Albo Pleno. A new double variety, highly recommended by the raisers of this new acquisition	.25
1677	— Integripetala Flore Pleno. A magnificent double variety. The blossoms are very large, of a rich magenta color, and are produced in the greatest profusion. Hardy annual	.10
1677½	Clematis Erecta. White; one of the best hardy perennials. Three feet	.05
1678	— Florida. White; hardy climber; fragrant; hardy. Ten feet	.10
1679	Cosmidium Engelmani. A very handsome annual from Mexico, forming compact plants a foot high, with neat linear foliage, and intense-yellow flowers	.10
1680	Coreopsis Philadelphica. Hardy perennial, which flowers the first year. Its large flowers are of a fine yellow, and very ornamental	.25
1681	— Auriculata. Bright orange; fine; hardy perennial. Three feet	.10
1682	— Tenuifulla. Beautiful cut foliage and yellow flowers; hardy perennial. One foot	.10
1683	Coccinea Indica. Highly ornamental, with scarlet fruit. One foot	.25
1684	Cucurbita Melanocarpa. Hardy and handsomest gourd for covering verandas, &c. Very rapid grower, with fine foliage, and beautiful, marbled, glossy green, and silvery-white striped fruit	.15
1685	— Melo-pepo-capensis. A variety of gourd, producing extraordinary large fruit	.25
1686	— Argyrosperma. A new Mexican gourd, with fruit of a depressed spherical form, having large, handsome, white seeds; eatable, with the flavor of a hazel-nut; an addition to the dessert. Ten seeds	1.00
1687	Cucumeropsis Mackenni. A handsome cucurbitaceous plant, with green fruit of the size of a cedar-cone, with light-green and white stripes	1.00
1688	Cytisus Glabratus. Very beautiful, with large golden-yellow flowers; very fragrant	1.00
1689	Dahlia Imperialis. A splendid foliaged species, with white bell-shaped flowers, borne gracefully on large terminal pyramids	1.00

AMATEUR CULTIVATOR'S GUIDE

NO.		PRICE
1690	**Datura Huberiana fl. pl. New varieties, mixed.** A beautiful species; of robust habit, with very large, double flowers, in many new colors; white, violet, carmine, lilac, rose, &c.; also one of the finest foliaged plants.	.25
1691	—— **Ceratocauli.** Very large blush flowers. 3 feet	.05
1692	—— **Humilis Alba Plena.** A new double white variety of D. humilis fl. pl. with very large trumpet-shaped flowers	.25
1693	**Delphinium Chinensis Pumilum, Dark Blue.** A new color of this valuable acquisition sent out last season. Early from seed the first year; about one foot high, with large, rich, blue flowers, abundantly produced. Hardy perennial	.25
1694	—— **Chinense Pumilum Cæruleum.** Beautiful dwarf variety; dark blue; hardy perennial. ½ foot	.10
1695	—— —— —— **Cœlestis.** Beautiful; light blue; hardy perennial. ½ foot	.10
1696	—— **Formosa Cœlestinum.** New; light blue; hardy perennial. 2 feet	.10
1697	—— **Hendersonii.** Fine; blue; very large flowers and spikes; hardy perennial. 2 ft.	.10
1698	—— **Azureus.** A hardy perennial variety, growing two to three feet high, with spikes of delicate white flowers, tinged with pale blue. Native of Western Iowa and Nebraska. Seeds per packet	.25
1699	—— **Menziesii.** A very fine variety, growing one to two feet high, with dense spikes of flowers of the deepest blue. Perfectly hardy. Native of Nebraska. Seeds per packet	.25
1700	**Desmanthus Brachylobus.** A hardy perennial, with beautiful fern-like foliage, and white globular clusters of flowers of considerable beauty. New and rare. Seeds per packet	.25
1701	**Dianthus Chinensis Coronatus fl. pl.** A most beautiful new double Chinese annual Pink, with white flowers striped with lilac and crimson	.25
1702	—— **Heddewigii Striatus Grandiflorus fl. pl.** Pure-white double flowers, with broad crimson stripes, very striking and beautiful.	.50
1703	—— **Imperialis Plenissimus Pictus.** A new and splendid variety. White ground, and each petal marked with a dark spot, like a Paisley Pink.	.50
1705	—— **Caryophyllus Double Dwarf Mixed.** This new, and too little known, species is commendable on account of its compact and bushy habit, and the abundance of its double flowers, variously colored. The flower-stems are pretty nearly equal in height (about twelve to fifteen inches), and stand close to each other, making the whole plant look like a bunch of flowers.	.50
1706	—— **Dentosus Hybrid.** Very pretty, but exceedingly sportive; new species; new varieties are found every year in the seedlings; flowers single, semi-double, or double; plants blooming very freely and perpetually through the whole summer and autumn; the finest are easily preserved by propagating from cutting	.50
1707	—— **Heddewigii Nanus Flore Albo Pleno** (Benary). This is a new, double, white variety of the beautiful Heddewigii Pink. It is of quite compact, dwarfish habit, resembling Dianthus Heddewigii fl. pl.; and nearly, without exception, constant from seed, which it produces very sparingly	.50
1708	—— **Cincinnatus.** A new species from Japan, of the size of Dianthus Heddewigii, and with deeply-fringed petals. Superb	.50
1709	**Digitalis Tomentosa.** Herbaceous plant, very distinct from *D. purpurea*; its flowers are more erect, of dark purple color, spotted with bright carmine	.25
1710	—— **Winterii.** Rich amber color; dense tall spikes; hardy biennial. 4 feet	.10
1711	**Egg Plant. Giant White.** A new variety. Fruit, three times larger than those of the old white variety. Half-hardy annual, and very ornamental.	.25
1712	—— **Giant Striped.** The fruits of this are equally of extraordinary size, and their variegation very constant. Like the foregoing, it will be more effective when planted as a single specimen than in masses, as it is desirable that the curious fruits of these two varieties are well exposed to view. A highly-ornamental, half-hardy annual.	.25
1713	**Embothrium Coccineum.** A magnificent greenhouse climber, with brilliant scarlet flowers; clusters like Bignonia Venusta	1.00
1714	**Erianthus Ravennæ Violescens.** A new and beautiful variety of this perfectly hardy grass, rivalling the Pampas, growing twelve feet high. The violescens is a new and superb variety	.25
1715	**Erythræa Ramosissima.** Fine rose-flowered Gentianeæ, forming dwarf, compact, bushy plants, suitable for edgings and dwarf beds.	.25
1716	**Geranium Scarlet Tom Thumb.** A very fine dwarf; habited, compact-growing variety, attaining only to the height of six or eight inches, and very desirable and admirable for belts, edgings, and bedding purposes.	.25
1717	**Gilia Achillæfolia fl. rosea.** A new rose-colored variety of this well-known annual	.25
1718	—— **Agregata.** A hardy biennial of great beauty, growing two to three feet h'gh; flowers, scarlet, dotted with maroon. Very desirable; from Utah Territory. Seeds per packet	.25
1719	**Gloriosa Plantii.** Greenhouse plant, with red flowers. 3 feet	.25
1720	**Gourd Bonnet.** 10 feet	.10
1721	—— **Miniatum.** Small fruit. 10 feet	.10
1722	—— **Ostrich Egg.** 10 feet.	.10
1723	—— **Siphon.** 10 feet.	.10
1724	—— **Turban.** 10 feet	.10
1725	**Godetia Reptans.** New dwarf carmine rose, with purple spots, very profuse, blooming and pretty	.15
1726	—— **Reptans Alba.** A charming variety, of dwarf habit, blooming in profusion; flowers pure white, with crimson blotch at the base of each petal	.15

IPOMEA VOLUBILIS. Madame Anne.
See page 97.

SANVITALIA PROCUMBENS.
See page 100.

BALSAM SOLFERINO.
See page 146.

TO THE FLOWER GARDEN. 97

NO.		PRICE
1727	—— **Lindleyana Flore Pleno.** A startling novelty in this much-admired tribe of annual plants, the first double variety which has been produced. Rich rosy purple.	.10
1728	—— **Amœna Alba.** White; very fine; hardy annual. 1 foot	.10
1729	—— **Rosea Alba Tom Thumb.** New dwarf rose; hardy annual. ¼ foot	.10
1730	**Grevillea Thelemanni Splendens.** A splendid species, with flowers fine blood-red.	.50
1731	**Gunneri Scabra.** Large, ornamental foliage: greenish-white; half-hardy perennial. 2 feet	.10
1732	**Gynerium Argentium Kermesinum.** A new and superb variety of the magnificent Pampas Grass, the tall, silvery flower-spikes tinted with *rosy crimson*	.50
1733	**Gypsophilla Saxifraga.** A lovely miniature species, with delicate branches, covered with white flowers; very pretty for edgings and dwarf beds	.10
1734	**Helipterum Corymbiflorum.** A handsome, everlasting flower; from Australia; with silvery leaves, and white, star-like blossoms in corymbs. Hardy annual	.50
1735	**Hibiscus Cannabinus.** A biennial species, growing five feet high, with finely-cut foliage, and an elegant addition to the flower-border; flowering the first year from seed; white, with purple throat	.50
1736	—— **Macrophyllus.** A gigantic, shrubby species, with large, cordate, glossy leaves, and light-yellow, fragrant flowers; elegant for planting out in summer. Five seeds.	1.00
1737	**Iberis Linifolia.** A fine autumn-flowered annual species, with delicate rose-colored umbels of flowers	.25
1738	**Imperiata Sacchariflora.** A magnificent, hardy grass, quite recently introduced from Amoor, with graceful curved foliage, forming a fine bush about three feet high, throwing out numerous flower-spikes about five feet in height, bearing glittering, silvery plumes of flowers; extremely pretty. The leaves are lively green, with a broad, silvery line down the middle; and the habit and bearing of the plant are quite as handsome as Gynerium Argenteum, while it has the superiority of flowering very freely, and standing any degree of frost without the slightest protection	.25
1739	**Ipomœa Volubilis Madame Anne.** A very fine new variety, with variegated flowers, striped red on a white ground	.25
1740	—— **Minima Spectabile.** A pretty, hardy, annual species; with small, heart-shaped leaves and rosy-carmine flowers, remaining the whole day expanded. A lovely, extremely-full-blooming climber	.50
1741	—— **Coptica.** A beautiful climber; deep-lanceolated leaves; flowers, handsome rose with white, standing well in bouquets	.50
1742	**Iris Kæmpferi.** A magnificent new species; from Japan; received the Certificate of Merit from the Massachusetts Horticultural Society, 1865; hardy perennial. 2 ft.	.25
1743	—— **Gracilis.** Light blue; hardy perennial. 2 feet	.10
1744	—— **Pumila.** Very beautiful; saved from forty new varieties	.50
1745	**Lagenaria Sphœrica.** New Ornamental Gourd. Flowers large, snowy white, with bright yellow stamens; fruit, the size of an orange, smooth, of a dark-green color, marbled all over with white. Per packet	.25
1746	**Lathyrus Mauritanicus.** A new and pretty perennial and climbing species, with crimson flowers	.25
1747	—— **Cœruleus Coccineus.** A sweet pea, with a dark-red blotch on each petal	.25
1748	**Linum Macrayi.** A plant newly introduced from Chili; dwarf habit; with large, orange-colored flowers. P	
1749	**Lilium Colchicum.** A very beautiful and attractive Lily; flowers, fine primrose-yellow; in form, resembling those of the favorite Lilium Longiflorum. 10 seeds.	.50
1750	—— **Aurantiacum.** Fine yellow. 3 feet	.10
1751	—— **Eximium.** Beautiful white; large trumpet-shaped flowers. 2 feet	.25
1752	—— **Auratum, Golden Striped Lily.** This new and magnificent species of Lily, lately introduced from Japan; spoken of by Dr. Lindley as follows: "If ever a flower merited the name of glorious, it is this, which stands far above all other Lilies, whether we regard its size, sweetness, or its exquisite arrangement of color. Imagine upon the end of a purple stem, not thicker than a ramrod, and not above two feet high, a saucer-shaped flower, at least ten inches in diameter, composed of six spreading, somewhat crisp parts, rolled back at their points, and having an ivory-white skin, thinly strewn with purple points or studs, and oval or roundish, prominent purple stains. To this add, in the middle of each of the six parts, a broad stripe of light satin-yellow, losing itself gradually in the ivory skin. Place the flower in a situation where side-light is cut off, and no direct light can reach it, except from above, when the stripes acquire the appearance of gentle streamlets of Australian gold, and the reader who has not seen it may form some feeble notion of what it is. It should be sown in pots, and placed under a shaded glass in gentle heat, using very light loam, covering one-fourth inch deep; requires a number of months to vegetate. (See cut.)	.50
1753	**Lobelia "Snow-flake."** This variety is a pure white-flowered form of the well-known Lobelia Ramosa, being similar in its style of growth, and large-sized bloom, forming a very elegant and effective plant for pot-culture, and also for groups in the flower-borders	.50
1754	—— **Erinus Compacta Alba.** Pretty variety; of compact, low habit of growth; a profuse and continuous bloomer; flowers, pure white; finely adapted for pot-culture, small groups, or edgings	.25
1755	—— **Erinus Grandiflora Stellatus.** New; brilliant blue, with white eye; hardy annual. ¼ foot	.25
1756	—— **Siphilitica.** Blue; hardy annual. 2 feet	.10

13

98 AMATEUR CULTIVATOR'S GUIDE

NO.		PRICE
1757	**Lupinus Mutabilis Roseus.** A most beautiful variety, of a bright, rosy-carmine color, both buds and flowers; whereas the old kind is white in bud, changing into lilac red going out of flower. A most beautiful showy variety	.25
1758	——— **Hybridus Atrococcineus.** The most showy Lupin ever introduced. Large, handsome spikes of bloom; color, bright crimson scarlet, with white tip	.25
1759	——— **Cruickshankii Hybrid.** One of the finest annual Lupins. Flowers very fragrant, presenting various shades of color on the same spike; at first of a lovely blue, tinged with white, and yellow in the centre, afterwards changing to purple; very ornamental for groups or for cut flowers	.25
1760	——— **Cruikshankii Variegated.** Hardy annual. 2 feet	.05
1761	——— **Pubescens Elegans.** Violet rose; hardy annual. 2 feet	.05
1762	**Lychnis Haageana, Hybrida Mixed.** A beautiful perennial, with large flowers of sparkling color; the color ranging from the brightest scarlet to blood red, purple, orange, white, or flesh-color	.25
1763	——— **Grandiflora Gigantea.** New; with flowers of double the size of the beautiful Lychnis Haageana, in all the colors of white, chamois, rose, scarlet, &c.	.50
1764	**Machæranthera Glabra.** A neat, hardy perennial, diffusely branched, and covered with Aster-like, violet flowers, with a yellow centre more than an inch in diameter, and standing out in corymbs. Sown early, it flowers the first year. One and a half to two feet high	.25
1765	**Mairia Crenata.** A herbaceous composite, with large, rose-colored flowers, yellow in the centre; a native of the Cape of Good Hope. Per packet	.50
1766	**Malva Californica.** A beautiful shrubby species, with handsome foliage, and flowers like Malope Grandiflora. Flowers abundantly the first season, in the open ground, and blooms in the greenhouse all winter. A valuable acquisition	.25
1767	——— **Lateritia.** A trailing perennial, with dark-green leaves, the whole plant covered with rosy Nankin flowers. Half-hardy, blooming abundantly the second year. Elegant for rock-work	.25
1768	**Marigold Dwarf.** Dark velvet; double; fine; rich colored	.10
1769	**Maurandya Emeryana.** Bright pink; half-hardy annual. 10 feet	.10
1770	**Melothria Pendula.** Pretty, hardy climber, with handsome foliage and small fruits; black, on coming to maturity; fine for trellises; the fruit makes fine pickles.	.25
1771	——— **Cucumerina.** A species of Cucurbitacea, from China, with smooth foliage and yellow flowers; fruit very smooth, of the thickness of the finger, and about one and a half inches long; can be pickled like Gherkins	.25
1772	**Mimulus, New Double Spotted.** This beautiful variety is a fine acquisition for culture in pots, and remarkable for its double flowers, which are brilliant yellow, spotted, striped, and mottled with crimson; and remain in bloom much longer than the single sorts	.50
1773	——— **Pardinus (Tigrinus) Flore Pleno, Superb Double.** A new strain, obtained by the florists of Prussia, having all the variety of colors of the single, and come so true from seed that there is but a small percentage of single flowers. These are quite equal to any of the English varieties, and are now for the *first time* offered as the most beautiful yet produced.	.50
1774	——— **Quinquevulnerus Robustus.** A beautiful novelty of very vigorous growth, about a foot high, with large leaves of a brilliant green, blotched with black. The large, handsome flowers are curiously mottled, and marked in all the rich coloring peculiar to this tribe of plants	.25
1775	——— **Cupreus Hybridus.** Of the great variety of Mimulus, none can surpass this for richness and diversity of color, and free blooming. The plants are dwarf, bushy, and vigorous; with large, fine-shaped flowers, spotted, stained, marbled, speckled, and blotched in the most striking manner	.25
1776	**Mirabilis Jalapa Foliis Variegatis Tricolor.** Dwarf; tricolored variety; very beautiful	.25
1777	**Mukia Scabrella.** Another pretty climber, with lobed, heart-shaped, small leaves, and small scarlet berries	.25
1778	**Myosotidium Nobile.** The rare New-Zealand Forget-me-not, with broad, ovate-cordate, thick, fleshy leaves; subglobose racemes of deep azure; purple-eyed flowers, measuring five inches across. A magnificent acquisition	1.00
1779	**Nasturtium, Tom Thumb Rose.** An entirely new color in Nasturtiums; habits similar to scarlet Tom Thumb Nasturtium; color, the exact counterpart of Trentham Rose Geranium.	.25
1780	**Nemophila Oculata Grandiflora.** A seedling from the popular Maculata. The flowers are of the circumference of a crown-piece. Very showy	.25
1781	——— **Discoidalis Elegans.** Maroon, bordered with white; half-hardy annual	.05
1782	——— ——— **Vittata.** Chocolate; broad, white margin; hardy annual	.05
1783	**Nierembergia Frutescens.** An entirely new species, from the Andes; introduced by the Botanical Garden of Bordeaux. A hardy, small, shrub-like perennial; it forms a very graceful, rounded bush, its straight and upright stems branching at the top in every direction, and throwing out a profusion of thread-like, drooping branchlets, covered from May to October with an immense quantity of very pretty white and purple flowers, larger than those of N. Gracilis. It is nearly hardy, and deserves to become a general favorite, both for the open garden in summer, and greenhouse in winter.	.50
1784	**Nicotiana Macrophylla Var. Gigantea. Purple-Flowered.** The most remarkable of all the Nicotianas now cultivated. Its leaves are much larger than those of any other variety; it grows six to eight feet high; and the plants are crowned with immense bunches or corymbs of large purple flowers. The general habit of the plant, its huge foliage, and stately aspect, give it the advantage over most other ornamental-leaved plants, for lawns or groups in the flower-garden. (See engraving.)	.25

TO THE FLOWER GARDEN. 99

NO.		PRICE
1785	**Nymphia Cœrulea.** Elegant blue lily; greenhouse plant	.25
1786	**Nolana Lasciniatus.** New; large blue flowers; from Chili; hardy annual. 1 foot	.05
1787	**Onothera Drummondi Nana Alba.** Similar in habit and flower to the Œ. Drummondii Nana, but with beautiful pearly-white blossoms. Exceedingly fine	.25
1788	— **Macrantha.** Large yellow flowers; hardy annual. 2 feet	.10
1789	— **Odorata.** Sweet-scented, yellow flowers; hardy annual. 1 foot	.05
1790	— **Rosea.** Small rose-colored flowers; hardy annual. 1 foot	.05
1791	**Onopordum Arabicum.** An immense ornamental-foliaged biennial, attaining ten feet in height, and thirty feet in circumference at the base. The glaucous cottony leaves are large and spiny, rendering the plant striking and attractive. Of magnificent aspect on the lawn	1 00
1792	**Orobus Niger.** Dark purple; hardy perennial. 1 foot	.10
1793	— **Verna.** A fine early-flowering variety, with rare flowers; hardy perennial. 1 ft.	.10
1794	— — **Alba.** The same, with white flowers; hardy perennial. 1 foot	.10
1795	— **Flaccida.** With grass-like foliage and rose flowers; hardy perennial. ½ foot	.10
1796	**Papaver Croceum.** Beautiful orange; hardy perennial. 1 foot	.10
1797	**Pardanthus Sinensis.** With beautiful, spotted, lily-like flowers; hardy perennial. 2 ft.	.10
1798	**Passiflora Acerifolia.** A new perennial Passion-flower, with beautiful maple leaves, and small bluish-white flowers	.25
1799	**Palafoxia Hookeriana.** This new Texas plant is one of the finest of recent acquisitions. It is much dwarfer and more branching than Palafoxia Texana, and the flowers — which have very much broader florets — are larger, and of a bright rosy-crimson color, with a dark centre. It is an annual, and will flourish finely in light and dry soils, and blooms throughout the summer. Messrs. Hovey & Co. were awarded the CERTIFICATE OF MERIT of the Massachusetts Horticultural Society, for the exhibition of superb specimens in 1865	.25
1800	**Pea, Scarlet Invincible.** A beautiful new variety; flowers intense scarlet, very free	.10
1801	**Pennisetum Longistylum.** An ornamental grass; half-hardy annual. 2 feet	.10
1802	**Penststemon Hartwegii Coccinea.** Scarlet; half-hardy perennial. 3 feet	.10
1803	— **Pubescens.** Light purple; hardy perennial. 1½ feet	.10
1804	— **Torreyi.** Superb, with long spikes of scarlet flowers; hardy perennial. 1½ feet	.10
1805	— **Wrightii.** With spikes of flame-colored flowers. 2 feet	.10
1806	— **Grandiflorus.** This is the finest of the genus, and is perfectly hardy. It grows two to three feet high, blooms in June and July, and is a decided acquisition to our hardy perennials. It is a native of the Platte Valley, Nebraska. Seeds per packet	.25
1807	— **Cobæi.** A new and hardy variety from the Rocky Mountains. Grows two feet high, with flowers of a delicate purple; throat dotted with maroon. One of the finest of the genus. Seeds per packet	.25
1808	— **Barbatus.** A fine variety, with scarlet flowers, blooming in succession all the season. Grows two to three feet high, and is perfectly hardy. Seeds per packet.	.25
1809	**Petalostemon Violacum.** Grows two to three feet high; flowers in dense spikes of a rich violet-purple color. In bloom most of the season. Native of Iowa and Nebraska. Seeds per packet	.25
1810	— **Candidum.** This is precisely like the above, except in color of its flowers, which are pure white. Seeds per packet	.25
1811	**Penicellaria Spicata.** Ornamental grass, from Africa; annual; stems four feet high, with large broad leaves; spikes, or panicles, long, almost cylindrical, large and compact, containing thousands of flowers, which are succeeded by white flowery grains, useful as food for poultry. Beautiful plant for growing in isolated tufts	.25
1812	**Pectis Angustifolia.** A new dwarf annual, of a dense-leafed habit, forming bushes a foot across, with opposite linear foliage; remarkable for its strong, citron-like fragrance. The flowers are nearly half an inch in diameter, of a bright yellow, so abundant as to completely cover the surface of the plant. This fine acquisition received a certificate from the Floral Committee of the Royal Horticultural Society of London	.25
1813	**Petunia Multiflora.** A small-flowered variety; red, with dark centre; flowering most abundantly. Constant from seed, and fine for bedding	.25
1815	— **Picturata.** Dwarf; large-flowered, velvety-scarlet crimson, marbled with white; a beautiful variety	.25
1816	— **Hybrida Coronata.** A most magnificent dwarf, compact variety; with beautiful, regularly-formed flowers of great substance, of a brilliant, velvety purplish crimson, with five broad, pure white stripes	.10
1817	— **Inimitable Marmorata.** A beautiful variety; flowers marbled and blotched.	.50
1818	**Phycella Coruscus.** A magnificent, free-flowering amaryllidaceous plant, with lily-like crimson-scarlet flowers, standing in many-flowered umbels. It may be grown in pots, or planted in the spring in the open ground, like Amaryllis Formosissima. Per packet	1.00
1819	**Phlox Drummondii Isabellina.** A very fine new variety, producing constant, pale-yellow flowers, entirely new and distinct in color	.25
1820	**Phlomis Abasicus.** A new and fine hardy herbaceous species, with golden-yellow flowers in spikes, much resembling the Salvia in form	.25
1821	**Pink, Sarah Howard.** A new white monthly Pink, with slender foliage and stems; two feet high; loaded with flowers the whole autumn. The flowers are medium size, double, pure white, and very beautiful	.50
1822	**Potentilla Hybrida, Double.** These are improved and beautiful varieties of this well-known hardy perennial; flowers, Ranunculus-formed, and of brilliant and various colors	.25

NO.		PRICE
1823	**Polemonium Cæruleum.** Blue; handsome; hardy perennial. 1 foot	.05
1824	—— **Album.** White-flowered; hardy perennial. 1 foot	.05
1825	**Portulaca Grandiflora.** A magnificent collection, saved by one of the best German growers; all from the most beautiful double flowers; in six distinct colors, — alba, alba striata, aurantiaca, splendens, Thellusoni, Thorburni. Each separate	.25
1826	—— **Mixed.** The six varieties mixed	.50
1827	**Primula Sinensis Flore Pleno. Double Prize Varieties.** We have the pleasure of offering to amateurs the choicest varieties of Chinese Primrose, unequalled by any yet produced, comprising a proportion of double flowers. These seeds were received directly from the celebrated London growers, who received one special and three first-class certificates in 1866, from the Royal Horticultural Society. The following is a description of these flowers, taken from the *Gardener's Chronicle*: — "This strain of Primula is a remarkable one. The flowers are large, full, and frilled; and in color, vary from white, through shades of pale flesh-color, to blush of deepest hue; and from that again to the carmine-rose of Mr. Benary's Carminata; and on, through the ordinary rose-tint, to a very dark purple rose; the pale ones especially are also remarkable for having a large, yellow, star-like eye, sometimes measuring fully five-eighths of an inch across, the flowers themselves being about two inches. Some others are splashed and flaked with rose, on a white ground; and both pure white, and flesh-tinted white, as well as rose, and rosy purple, full, double flowers were amongst those sent for inspection." Our collection comprises five distinct colors, viz., white, deep blush, purple, lilac, striped, and deep carmine rose, and their intermediate shades, beautifully fringed; large, and producing immense trusses of flowers, thrown well up above the foliage. Another valuable property of them is, that, from each bloom being specially hybridized, a proportion of beautiful double flowers may be expected. Sealed packets	1.00
1828	—— **Chinensis Fimbriata Punctata.** Splendid variety; with large bouquets of flowers, finely fringed; brilliant crimson, spotted with white	.50
1829	—— **Polyantha.** The tall English Oxlip, in various colors; very pretty and interesting; spring-flowering; hardy perennial	.10
1830	**Ranunculus Asiaticus Superbissimus.** It is with great pleasure that we bring before our amateurs and lovers of beautiful plants this rare class of garden Ranunculus as one of the greatest acquisitions; supplying the place of the Persian tuberous sorts, — so elegant, but so difficult to grow. This is grown as a biennial, flowering freely the second year; producing unusually large double varieties, of an unsurpassed brilliancy of colors, of all shades, of white, yellow, rose, crimson, blood-red, scarlet, purple, &c. The plants are very vigorous in growth, and very profuse bloomers, and have claimed universal admiration. Good seeds are now offered, which will produce but a small percentage of single flowers.	.25
1832	**Reseda Crystallina.** A very interesting species; similar in habit to Reseda Odorata (Mignonette), but with larger capsules, or seed-pods, which are covered with transparent granulations or crystals, in the manner of the Ice-plant	.10
1833	**Rumex Vesicarius Roseus.** An ornamental, annual species; with triangular leaves and curious fruits, borne on long panicles; also pretty, grown in pots	.25
1834	**Rhyncocarpa Dissecta.** A fine, hardy climber; with handsomely divided foliage, and bearing small, conical, brilliant, orange-colored fruits	.25
1835	—— **Welwitschi.** One of the Gourd family; very ornamental, with thick, five-lobed foliage, and acorn-like scarlet fruit. Ten seeds	1.00
1836	**Sanvitalia Procumbens Fl. Pl. New Double Sanvitalia.** A novelty of last year, which has proved to be one of the most beautiful acquisitions. We cultivated it extensively last year, and the dense masses of perfectly double flowers, like Pompon Chrysanthemums attracted unusual attention. It is without doubt the only dwarf, compact plant of a yellow color, suited to beds and masses of low growth. The seeds are saved from the finest flowers, and will give from 80 to 90 per cent of double blossoms. (See engraving.)	.25
1837	**Salvia Splendens Compacta.** Dwarf flowered Splendid Salvia. A new French variety, distinguished from the old Splendens by its more tufted and compact habit, its dwarfer growth, and by the spikes of flowers, which are more numerous, bloom earlier, and more dense on the stems. Its brilliant color and abundance of flowers render it one of the most attractive and effective plants for the summer garden	.25
1838	—— **Graciliflora.** Annual, one foot in height, habit of S. Roemeriana; flowers fine violet red, and very abundant and showy	.25
1839	—— **Sibthorpi.** Hardy perennial, with fine large leaves, and long spikes of lilac-blue flowers. Very ornamental	.50
1840	—— **Splendens Compacta.** A new, dwarf, compact-growing variety, of the old beautiful species	.50
1841	—— **Graciliflora.** A new species, with long flowers of a rosy-lilac color. Very delicate.	.25
1842	—— **Chionantha.** A hardy perennial, with large white flowers on pyramidal spikes, about two feet in height	.25
1843	**Salpiglossis Hybrida Grandiflora.** (*Vilmorin.*) These fine annuals have been greatly improved by careful selection and cultivation, and their flowers are unparalleled for size, shape, and color	.25
1844	**Saxifraga Cymbalaria.** A miniature perennial species, with handsomely crenated, roundish, glossy leaves, above which rise the pretty light-yellow flowers in great profusion; extremely pretty	.50
1845	—— **Hypnoides.** Grows in moss-like tufts; hardy perennial. ½ foot	.10

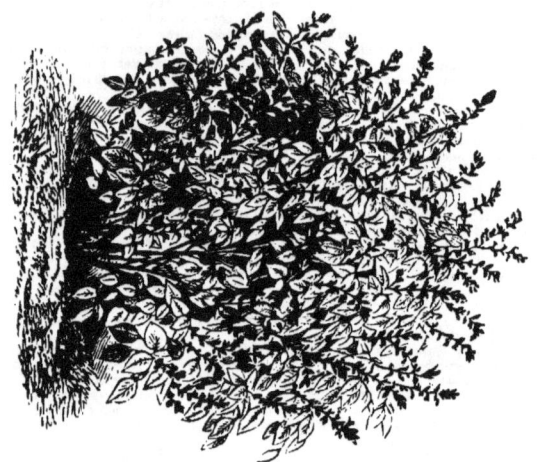

NICOTIANA MACROPHYLLA GIGANTEA. See p. 98.

SALVIA SPLENDENS COMPACTA. See page 100.

TO THE FLOWER GARDEN. 101

NO.		PRICE
1846	**Saxifraga Umbrosa** (London Pride). Pink; beautiful; hardy perennial. 1 foot	.10
1847	—— **Rotundifolia.** White; hardy perennial. 1 foot	.10
1848	**Scabiosa Nana Fl. Pl. Varieties** (*Benary*). New, double, dwarf Scabious. This beautiful novelty will be found a valuable improvement of the well-known Dwarf Scabious. The flowers, which have all the beautiful varieties of colors of this tribe, are perfectly double, and form round, globular heads; the petals are shorter, so that the stamens become almost invisible, making the flower resemble a double Pompon Chrysanthemum. It is of a dwarfer and more compact habit than the old varieties, and will prove a most valuable acquisition	.25
1849	**Schizanthus Oculatus Atropurpureus.** A seedling of the S. Grandiflorus Oculatus, with large handsome blooms of a rich crimson purple, with black eye	.25
1850	—— **Grandiflorus Albus.** A very showy and beautiful variety, with large, pure-white flowers, with sulphur eye	.25
1851	—— **Retusus Nana.** A most desirable variety of this ornamental greenhouse or half-hardy annual, forming a compact well-branched plant, with a profusion of rich red blossoms. A very effective plant for pot-culture and conservatory decoration	.25
1852	**Schizostylis Coccinea.** A new African plant, which appears to be a rival to the Gladiolus, resembling it, not only in general habit, but in the brilliancy of its long spikes of broad open flowers, varying from deep rosy crimson to vivid scarlet, and measuring two inches across. It appears quite hardy, and blooms in the autumn, remaining long in flower. It is easily cultivated, and will be very valuable for the open garden or for greenhouse decoration. The flowers are striking and brilliant	.50
1853	**Sedum Denticulata.** Rose; fine; hardy perennial. ¼ foot	.10
1854	**Silene Alpestris.** White; hardy perennial. ½ foot	.05
1855	—— **Pendula Ruberrima.** A very remarkable variety, worthy of general cultivation, as vigorous and free-flowering as Silene Pendula; but its flowers are of a deeper crimson tinge, and its stems, leaves, and petals of a brownish-purple color, which extends also to the calix, and imparts to the whole plant a very peculiar and striking aspect	.25
1856	—— **Saxifraga.** Charming little miniature species, very fine for borders or rock-works. Its foliage, of a shining green, resembles a fine, short grass, and is dotted with numerous pretty, white flowers; grows two to four inches in height	.25
1857	**Solanum Fontanesianum.** An annual species, with large canary-yellow flowers, deeply-cut foliage, and spinous fruits of the size of a walnut	.25
1858	—— **Reclinatum.** Similar to Lasciniatum, with large azure-blue flowers	.25
1859	**Sonchus Macranthus.** A splendid foliaged plant, with leaves above eighteen inches in length, throwing out its flower-spikes more than six feet in height, set with double flowers two inches in diameter. Highly valuable and ornamental	.50
1860	—— **Pinntus.** A beautiful foliaged plant, with thin glossy leaves very finely cut	.05
1860½	**Silybum Eburneum.** A fine variety of the Thistle; native of Algeria; leaves broad, dark, green, and glossy, beautifully spotted with white; very showy for groups or scattered on grass-plats; biennial, flowering second year, from seeds	.25
1861	**Stock Large-flowered Canary.** Yellow; splendid new variety; hardy annual 1 ft.	.25
1862	—— —— **Aurora-Colored.** Yellow, tinted with rose; hardy annual. 1 ft.	.10
1863	—— **New Rose-flowered Autumnal.** Rose-shaped, double flowers; fine for pot-culture. 1 foot	.25
1864	—— **Ten Week, New, Tall, Large-Flowering, Giant German Bomb.** This, is without doubt, the most perfect stock ever produced, and, well-grown, forms a compact and giant plant. Its immense truss, and long duration of flowering, make it a most useful variety, either for the garden or bouquet	.50
1865	**Statice Thouinii.** A splendid novelty of 1867; of dwarf, bushy habit, with spreading heads of flowers, the corollas of which are white, with porcelain-blue calyces: very fine for bedding. Per packet	.25
1866	**Stipa Elegantissima.** An extremely elegant grass from Australia, one and a half feet high; with silvery, feathered flower-stalks; beautiful for bouquets. Perennial; flowering the first year from seed	.50
1867	**Trachelium Cæruleum Carmine.** A beautiful pink variety of this old but greatly admired plant; of a dwarfer and more compact growth	.25
1868	**Tropæoleum, King Theodore.** A new variety, selected from King of Tom Thumb, having the same bluish-green foliage, and novel blossoms of an intense black; forms a fine contrast with the scarlet	.25
1869	—— **Lobbi Crown Prince of Prussia.** A splendid acquisition of strong habit; flowers, brilliant scarlet; said to surpass all others	.50
1870	—— **Lilli Schmidt Crimson.** A bright crimson variety of the Lilli Schmidt	.25
1871	—— **King of Tom Thumbs.** Magnificent. The lustrous, blue-green foliage, contrasting vividly with the intense scarlet of the blossoms, produces an unequalled blaze of brilliance, and the plant must become a universal favorite	.25
1872	**Tritoma Uvaria Grandiflora.** One of the finest summer and late-autumn flowering herbaceous plants known, forming magnificent groups in flower-gardens, borders, &c., and admirably adapted for single specimens. The very brilliant orange-red and flame-colored, sceptre-like flower-heads, three to four feet high, elevated above the foliage, are unequalled for effect in masses or for border decorations. The plants should be lifted, and placed in a frame or cellar during winter. Per packet	.50
1873	**Tricyrtis Hirtus Nigra.** A new and distinct Japan plant; growing about three feet high; foliage, resembling Lilium Lancifolium; flowers, nearly black, and lily-shaped; new, curious, and beautiful	.50

NO.		PRICE

1874 **Verbena Montana.** This is another gem, truly: it has the habit of the common Verbena, but is perfectly hardy, and blooms more profusely. The plant literally covers itself with its bright, rose-colored flowers, from early in May until winter sets in. A native of the gold regions of Colorado Territory. Seeds per packet 25
1875 **Veronica Perfoliata.** A fine greenhouse plant, two feet high, with glaucous-green leaves and purple blossoms; free blooming 50
1876 **Viscaria Cardinalis.** A seedling Viscaria, of an exceedingly brilliant and showy character; color brilliant magenta (a new color in Viscarias); the foliage, a bright lively green, contrasts effectively with the very brilliant bloom, of which there is a profusion. In its way, this Viscaria is quite as important an introduction as was the Linum, to which it is a suitable companion 25
1877 —— **Purpurea.** Purple; new; fine; hardy annual. 1 foot 12
1878 —— **Splendens.** Rosy red; beautiful; hardy annual. 1 foot 10
1879 **Violet. The Czar.** A new, very large, and beautiful variety of the Violet. The leaves are large; and the flowers, which are of the deepest blue violet, are borne on very long foot-stalks (five to six inches in length), and are nearly twice as large and much sweeter than the old Russian Violet. It is so hardy that it commences blooming in September, and continues flowering until May, even during the frost and under the snow. "The Gardener's Chronicle" says that, "in point of size and vigor, it eclipses all that have preceded it." Mr. Graham, the originator of the variety, writes us that "it is in great demand among the flower-dealers in Covent-Garden Market, and that he has made heaps of money with it." It has been awarded numerous first-class certificates. Our plants have been in flower since last September, and the few seeds we now offer were raised from the original plants obtained of Mr. Graham. .50
1880 **Viola Cornuta.** One of the finest of all known Violets for summer and autumn decoration. A neat, compact, perennial, herbaceous plant. Six to nine inches high, with small heart-shaped leaves; and yielding a succession of conspicuous, delicate, light-mauve-blue flowers as large as the leaves, in succession, from April to October. A beautiful plant for clumps or edgings, forming a rich, compact mass of green foliage, set off by the profusion of deep purple, mauve-color, and violet blossoms. The seed vegetates best if sown early in a cold frame, and the young plants removed to the border where they are to bloom 50
1881 **Wallflower, Brown's Early.** This variety is commendable, and deserves to be preferred to the old variety, its spikes of flowers being longer and thicker, the flowers larger, more numerous, and blooming more regularly; at the same time, very good either for cut flowers or for bedding out 25
1882 **Waitzia Corymbosa.** Another very fine annual species of Everlasting; of bushy, compact habit, growing about one foot high, and as much in diameter, each branch terminating in clusters of elegant flowers of a deep amaranth color, with small yellow disk; succeeds well in light soil in the open ground, blooming from August to October. Also fine for pot-culture 25
1883 —— **Acuminata Citrina.** A fine Australian Everlasting, of bushy, compact growth, twelve inches high, with narrow foliage, bearing numerous terminal corymbs of flowers, each flower an inch across, and in all the various shades of yellow . . .25
1884 —— **Albo Purpurea.** A variety of the former, with amaranth-colored flowers, in the various shades from crimson to purplish-red, with a yellow disk. Both are suited to pot-culture, and, if planted in the open ground, require a light sandy soil . .50
1885 —— **Corymbosa Sulphurea.** A beautiful yellow variety of the amaranth-colored species sent out last year, but much more showy 25
1886 —— **Grandiflora.** Resembling the W. Aurea, but more robust in habit, and with larger flowers. A very fine Everlasting, which received a first-class certificate from the Royal Horticultural Society of London 50
1887 **Whitlavia Gloxinoides** An elegant novelty of the same habit as W. Grandiflora, and produces a multitude of Gloxinia-like flowers; the tube of the corolla being pure white, and the limb of upper portion a delicate light blue 25
1888 **Wigandia Vigieri.** A splendid acquisition, obtained from seed, by far surpassing W. Caracasana in beauty. Leaves much larger, of a lovely green, glaucous underneath. Seeds of easy growth 50
1889 **Xeranthemum Annuum, Caryophylloides. Double Striped.** (*Benary.*) A really striking variety of this well-known Everlasting; the densely double flowers are white and pink-like, striped and sprinkled rose, red, crimson, and purple. This new variety will prove an invaluable acquisition for dried bouquets, as the colors remain unaltered. It is strongly recommended for bedding and grouping, as it is very double, and just as profuse blooming as the other varieties of this Everlasting; of a regular, compact habit, and quite constant in character 50
1890 **Zea.** The new striped Japanese Maize. One of the most valuable acquisitions. Among ornamental-foliaged plants of rapid growth and immediate effect, the new Striped Japanese Maize holds the most conspicuous place. It is a native of Japan. It appears to be a variety of Maize, but differs in many respects from our common Indian Corn. It grows from five to six feet high, and has alternate foliage: the foliage is about four feet long, and two to three inches wide. The variegation does not show itself until the fourth or fifth leaf: it then begins to show its true character of great white stripes, and in a short time the long wavy and gracefully recurved leaves become evenly and perfectly striped or ribboned with alternate colors of clear white and the brightest green, occasionally showing faint tinges of rose-color at the edges. In general appearance, it approaches the beautiful Arundo Donax Variegata. For groups on the lawn, or for a back row in the flower-border, nothing can be more imposing, effective, and grand 25

THE
AMATEUR CULTIVATOR'S GUIDE
TO THE VEGETABLE GARDEN.

IN again presenting our Catalogue of VEGETABLE SEEDS, we embrace the opportunity to add that our stock, as heretofore, has been selected with a view to secure only the freshest and most reliable seeds. Most of the staple seeds are raised expressly for us by experienced growers; and such as are imported are purchased from the most reliable seedsmen in Europe, with whom we have long dealt, and from whom we have received only such as we could with perfect confidence recommend. It is our invariable rule to test all our seeds ourselves, and never to send out any thing but what we are certain will vegetate freely, and prove true to name. Nothing causes greater disappointment than poor seeds; for not only is the season lost if they fail to grow, but an inferior crop will not pay for the trouble of planting. American-grown seeds always have our preference; but some kinds it is impossible to obtain in sufficient quantity to fill our orders, and those are obtained only from reliable dealers abroad.

Our prices are affixed by the ounce, quart, and packet; but no quantity is sold less than the ounce or quart at these prices: when less is ordered, they will be supplied in packets at that rate. All the kinds can be supplied by the pound or bushel at the lowest market rate for prime seeds.

Prices of seeds vary, to some extent, from the time of harvesting to the time of planting, and we do not feel bound by these prices unless orders are sent in early. We can only advise our customers to give their orders in good season to secure the most favorable terms.

VEGETABLE SEEDS.

Artichoke (CYNARA SCOLYMUS).

German, *Artischoke.* — French, *Artichaut.* — Spanish, *Alcachofa.*

The Artichoke is a native of the south of Europe, and is principally cultivated in the gardens of the French, by whom it is considered more as a luxury than as a profitable esculent. There are two varieties, the Globe and the Green. The former is so called from its globular head, of a dull purplish tint. The scales are turned in at the top more than the other varieties, and it is preferred; as the scales or edible parts are thicker, and possess more flavor. The Green is more hardy and prolific, the scales are more open, and the plant better adapted for culture in cold climates, than the former. The heads, in their immature state, and before their blue thistle-like flowers open, are cut, and boiled in salt and water. The edible part is merely the fleshy substance on the bottom of the scales, which, to make palatable, has to be dipped in a nicely prepared sauce of butter and spices. They are frequently eaten as salad in a raw state.

CULTURE. — The Artichoke may be grown from seed or offset suckers, separated early in spring. The best way to obtain a supply from seed is to sow the seeds in April in a bed of good rich earth, or it may be planted in drills one inch deep and about twelve inches apart. It should be transplanted the following spring to a permanent place. Either in beds or drills, plants should stand two feet apart each way, requiring a deep, rich, moist loam; also should be protected with leaves or straw during winter.

per oz.
Large Globe. A very large sort, much esteemed, and most generally cultivated. Heads or buds very large, nearly round, and with a dusky-purplish tint. Per pkt., 10 . . 50
Green, or Common. Heads large, of a conical or oval form; scales deep green, thick, and fleshy; pointed at the tips, and turned outwards. Per pkt, 10 . . . 50
per lb.
Jerusalem. Produces tubers resembling potato. Cultivated by planting tubers as early as the ground will admit 12

Asparagus (ASPARAGUS OFFICINALIS).

German, *Spargel.* — French, *Asperge.* — Spanish, *Esparrago.*

This universal vegetable is supposed to be a native of Great Britain, where it is found on the banks of sandy soil contiguous to the sea, growing luxuriantly under the salt breezes. There are, it is said, several varieties of Asparagus; but the difference mainly arises from the nature of the soil.

CULTURE. — Sow the seed early in spring one inch deep, and three or four inches apart, in rows one foot apart. When two years old, they may be transplanted into permanent beds, the plants placed a foot apart in each direction, and at least four inches beneath the surface.

To make it "Giant," be particular to select for the bed warm rich soil. Trench it at least eighteen inches deep, working in six inches or more depth of well-rotted manure. Every fall cover the bed with manure, and in spring dig it in lightly, care being taken not to disturb the roots.

Fine Asparagus beds may be formed by sowing the seed where it is to remain. With this end in view, sow the seed in beds prepared as directed above. Sow the seed in rows lengthwise, twelve inches apart. When a year old, thin out the plants to one foot apart.

per oz.
Giant Purple Top. Sprout white; top, as it breaks ground, purple; grows to a good size; excellent. Per pkt., 5 10
Green Top. When grown under same treatment as Giant Purple Top, it is generally smaller or more slender. Per pkt., 5 10

English Bean (FABA VULGARIS).

German, *Gartenbohne.* — French, *Feve de Marais.* — Spanish, *Haba.*

The following varieties are much grown in England, but find little favor in this country.

CULTURE. — Sow as early as the ground will admit, in rows two feet apart, and three inches apart in the rows. They will come sooner into bearing if the tops of the plants are pinched off as soon as they are in full bloom. Succeed best in a deep, strong, loamy soil.

By Mail, 8 cents a pint extra. per qt.
Early Mazagan. This variety, though originally from Mazagan, on the coast of Africa, is one of the hardiest sort now in cultivation. Stems from two to three feet high; rather slender 35
Long Podded. This variety grows from three to four feet high; remarkably productive, and a few days later than the Mazagan 35
Broad Windsor. This familiar sort is much esteemed and extensively cultivated, remaining fit for use longer than any other variety. A sure bearer 40

Beans, Dwarf or Bush (PHASEOLUS VULGARIS).

German, *Bohne.* — French, *Haricot.* — Spanish, *Frijolenano.*

The plants of this class vary from a foot to two feet in height. They require no stake or pole for their support.

CULTURE. — Drop the beans two or three inches apart, in rows two and a half feet apart; plant in light rich soil; hoe often, never when the vines are wet, or they will rust. All varieties of beans are very sensitive to frost and cold, and should not be planted before the middle of spring. As they require but about six weeks to make green pods, they can all be sown as late as July.

By Mail, 8 cents a pint extra. per qt.
Early Yellow Six Weeks. Excellent for string or shell; one of the earliest . . 40
Early Turtle Soup. Much esteemed, when dry, for cooking 30
Early Valentine. Long tender pod; an excellent string-bean 40
Early Mohawk. Early, productive, and very hardy 40
Early China. Red eye; one of the most productive 40
Early Half-moon. Large and productive 40
Early Marrowfat. White; an excellent shell-bean; valuable, when dry, for baking . . 30
Red Bush Cranberry. One of the best string-beans 50
Refugee, or Thousand to One. A favorite string with many; very productive . . 40
White Kidney, or Royal Dwarf. Late and productive 30
Dwarf Horticultural, or Zebra. Excellent, green or dry 40

Beans, Pole, or Running (PHASEOLUS VULGARIS).

German, *Stanger Bohne.* — French, *Haricots a rames.* — Spanish, *Judias.*

As a class, these are less hardy than the dwarfs, and are not usually planted so early in the season. The common practice is to plant in hills three feet or three and a half apart, with a stake or pole to run upon. By Mail, 8 cents a pint extra.

per qt.
London Horticultural, or Speckled Cranberry. Sometimes called Wren's Egg; an excellent variety; may be used as a snap, or, when more advanced, shelled, as the Lima; very productive 50
Red Cranberry. This is one of the oldest and most familiar of garden beans; excellent as a string or snap bean 50
White Cranberry. Similar to the preceding, but not as prolific 50
White Case Knife is the most prolific of the running varieties. As a shelled bean, it is of excellent quality in its green state, and, when ripe, farinaceous and well-flavored in whatever form prepared 50
Indian Chief, or Wax. One of the best varieties for general cultivation, either for snaps or shelled; remarkable for its fine, tender, succulent, and richly colored pods, which are produced in great abundance, continuing a long time fit for use . . . 75

Beans, Flowering-Runners (PHASEOLUS MULTIFLORUS).

German, *Grosse Bunte Bohne.* — French, *Haricot d'Espagne.* — Spanish, *Judia Vastago d'Espana.*

per qt.
Scarlet-Runner. A very prolific variety; fine for covering arbors, trained over pales, up the walls of cottages, which they enliven by the brightness of their blossoms, at the same time yielding a supply of wholesome and nutritious food . . . 50

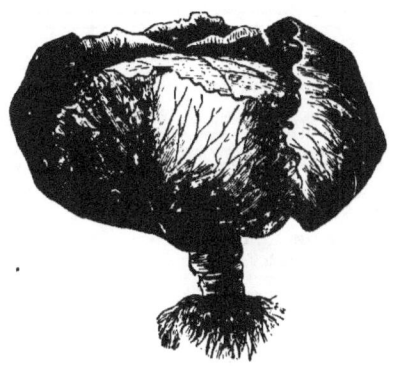

MARBLEHEAD MAMMOTH DRUMHEAD CABBAGE. See page 131.

CABBAGE. EARLY SCHWEINFURTH. See page 130.

TO THE VEGETABLE GARDEN.

per qt.
White-Runners. A variety of the Scarlet-Runner. The plants are less vigorous, and the flower and seeds pure white. As a shell-bean, either green or ripe, they are considered superior to the scarlet, and often seen in our markets under the name of Lima, from which they may be distinguished by their greater thickness, and more rounded form 50
Painted Lady. A sub-variety of the Scarlet-Runner, with variegated flowers; the upper petals being scarlet, the lower white 60

Beans, Lima (PHASEOLUS LUNATUS).
German, *Bohne von Lima.* — French, *Haricot de Lima.* — Spanish, *Haba Vastago de Lima.*

per qt.
Large Lima. This is one of the latest, as well as the most tender, of all garden beans. Little will be gained by very early planting, as the seeds are not only liable to decay before vegetating, but the plants suffer greatly from cold, damp weather; the best time being from the first to the middle of May. In planting, be sure to place the eye downwards, or otherwise it might not come up 75
Small Lima, Carolina, Sewee, Sieva, or Saba. This is one of the most productive of all varieties. The beans, in their green or ripe state, are similar to the Lima, and are nearly as delicate and rich flavored. It is from two to three weeks earlier than the large Limas 75

Beet (BETA VULGARIS).
German, *Runkle Rube.* — French, *Betterave.* — Spanish, *Bettaraga.*

CULTURE. — Beets are always raised from seeds. For early use, sowings are sometimes made in November; but the general practice is to sow the seed in April, as soon as the frost is out of the ground, or as soon as the soil can be worked. For use in autumn, the seed should be sown about the middle or twentieth of May; and for the winter-supply, from the first to the middle of June. Lay out the ground in beds five or six feet in width, and of a length proportionate to the supply required; spade or fork the soil deeply and thoroughly over; rake the surface smooth and even; and draw the drills across the beds fourteen inches apart, and about an inch and a half in depth. Sow the seeds thickly enough to secure a plant for every two or three inches, and cover to the depth of the drills. Should the weather be warm and wet, the young plants will appear in eight or ten days. When they are two inches in height, they should be thinned to five or six inches apart. The surplus plants will be found an excellent substitute for Spinach, if cooked and served in a like manner. The after-culture consists simply in keeping the plants free from weeds, and the earth in the spaces between the rows loose and open by frequent hoeing.

per oz.
Early Flat Bassano. An Italian variety; generally considered the earliest of garden beets, being from seven to ten days earlier than the Early Turnip Blood. Flesh white, circled or zoned with bright pink; very tender and juicy; not suited for winter use unless sown quite late. Per pkt., 5 20
Early Turnip Blood. One of the best varieties for general use. Flesh deep blood-red, sometimes circled and rayed with paler red; remarkably sweet and tender. Per pkt., 5 15
Early Yellow Turnip, or Orange. A sub-variety of the Blood Turnip, differing principally in color, and to some extent in form, which is less compress. Flesh yellow, comparatively close grained, sweet and tender. Per pkt., 5 15
Long Blood Red. One of the most popular of winter beets. The seed should not be sown before the middle of June, as the roots, when large, are frequently tough and fibrous. Per pkt., 5 15
Long Smooth Dark Blood. This is an improved variety of the common Long Blood. Flesh dark blood-red, sweet, tender, and fine grained, with but few side roots; fine winter beet if sown late. Per pkt., 5 15
Henderson's Pineapple. Short top, medium size. Flesh very deep blood-red, fine grained, sweet, tender, and of excellent quality. Per pkt., 10 30
Carter's St. Osyth. Medium sized, good shape, short top, rich deep blood-red color; fine flavor. Per pkt., 10 30
White Sugar. A large variety, grown extensively for feeding stock, although the young roots are tender, sweet, and well flavored. Per pkt., 5 10
Nutting's New Dwarf Red. A new English variety, said to be one of the best. Per pkt., 10.
Long Red Mangel Wurzel. A large variety, grown principally for feeding stock. When young, is sometimes used for the table. Flesh white, zoned and clouded with different shades of red; is hardy, and keeps well. Per pkt., 5 10
Yellow Globe. A large, round, orange-colored variety; excellent quality, which keeps better than the Long Red, and produces better crops on shallow ground. Per pkt., 5 10
Swiss Chard, or Silver. This variety of beet, sometimes called Sea-Kale Beet, is cultivated for its leaf-stalks, which are served up much like Asparagus, and for its leaves cooked as Spinach. If cut often, new and more tender stalks will be reproduced. Per pkt., 5 15
New Perpetual Spinach. Leaves large, of good color; flavor superior to Spinach, for which it is used as a substitute. In use the whole season. Per pkt., 10. . . 25

Borecole, or Kale (BRASSICA OLERACEA ACEPHALA).
German, *Blatter Kohl.* — French, *Chou vert.* — Spanish, *Breton.*

Borecole, German Greens, or Scotch Kale, is a very delicate vegetable. It is essential to its perfection that it be acted upon by the frost before it is cut for the kitchen. The part used are the tops or crown of the plant, with any of the side sprouts. It boils well, and is tender and sweet.

CULTURE. — The seeds are sown at the time of sowing the seeds of the Cabbage or Cauliflower, and in the same manner: early plants may be started in a hotbed, or the seed may be sown in the open ground in May. In transplanting, treat the plants same as young cabbages, setting them more or less remote, according to the size or habit of the variety; requires a light rich soil.

per oz.

Green Curled Scotch. This is one of the most popular varieties. It is very hardy, and is much improved by frost. Per pkt., 10 15
Dwarf Curled Kale, or German Greens. This is a very hardy and comparatively low-growing variety; the leaves are finely curled. A fine variety for winter and spring use when planted in a light cellar, or other protection from the severity of the weather. In the Southern and Middle States, it stands well in the open beds. Per pkt., 10 15
Tall Green Curled. A fine hardy and productive variety; height two and a half feet. Per pkt., 10 20
Cottager's Kale. A new English variety. It is exceedingly hardy, of excellent flavor, and very productive. It should be planted in March, in a frame, and transplanted early about three feet apart; requires a light rich soil. Per pkt., 10 . . . 35
Carter's Improved Garnishing. This will produce more than twenty varieties, some of which are worthy of a place in a greenhouse, being quite equal in color to the new Coleus. The colors vary from rich crimson to white laced and fringed Per pkt., 10 75
Ragged Jack. A very fine English variety. Per pkt., 10 20

Brussels Sprouts (BRASSICA OLERACEA VAR).

German, *Kopf, Kohl, Gruner.* — French, *Chou de Bruxelles.*

Cultivated for the small heads, which are produced in great numbers on the main stem of the plant, and are in perfection in the autumn. They are very tender, and of fine flavor after early frosts. Sow in seed-beds in May; transplant and cultivate as directed for Cabbage.

per oz.

Roseberry. A new and superior English variety; one of the best. Per pkt. 10 . . . 35
Own Saving. A new English variety; very fine. Per pkt., 10 35
The Albert Sprout. This is a hybrid between the Drumhead Savoy Cabbage and the Brussels Sprouts. It comes in after the other varieties of the Sprout. The flavor, after cooking, is all that could be desired, — mild, mellow, and very fine. Per pkt., 20 50
New Feather-Stem Savoy. A true hybrid, possessing the growth and habit of Brussels Sprouts. A delicate and delicious vegetable, requiring same treatment as Brussels Sprouts. Per pkt., 10 35

Broccoli (BRASSICA OLERACEA BOTRYTIS)

German, *Brocoli, Spargel-kohl.* — French, *Chou Brocoli.* — Spanish, *Broculi.*

In its structure and general habit, the Broccoli resembles the Cauliflower. It is very hardy, and surer to head, but inferior in flavor.

CULTURE. — The seeds should be sown in hotbeds in April, or in open ground in May, in a very deep rich soil, on an open exposure, where the plants grow much stronger than near trees or fences. Sow the seeds tolerably thick on the surface. If dry, tramp them down, and rake in lightly. If drought continues, give the beds a few waterings till the plants appear, which will be in two or three weeks. Transplant in June or July, when the weather is moist, in rows two feet apart, and twenty inches in the row. Their further culture is to keep them clear of weeds by hoeing and stirring the ground. When they have advanced in growth, draw some earth to their stems, which greatly promotes their luxuriance.

per oz.

Early Purple Cape. This has a close compact head of a purple color, and, in favorable seasons, comes as large as a Cauliflower. Hardy, and of excellent flavor. Per pkt., 10 60
White Cape. Later than the preceding, and should be planted here, at the North, early in April. The heads, when perfected, are large and white and compact, resembling the Cauliflower. Per pkt., 10 75
Chappell's Large Cream-Colored. A very large and fine sort; flower cream-yellow; very early. Per pkt., 10 60
Snow's Superb White Winter. This is a dwarf variety. The leaves are broad, with short stems; the heads are large, white, very compact; considered by many equal to the Cauliflower. Per pkt., 25 . . . . 3.00
Walcheren. Comparatively new, and so closely resembling a Cauliflower as to be scarcely distinguishable from it. The leaves, however, are more curbed, and it is hardier. Per pkt., 10 75
Grange's Autumn. A fine fall variety; close compact head; one of the best. Per pkt., 10 75
Adam's Early White. A fine variety; strong and robust grower, with a compressed head, so as to render it invisible when ready for cutting; and this protects it from rain, and effect of frost; heads large and pure white. Per pkt., 10 . . . 60
Carter's Champion. Dwarf, compact-growing, large-headed; the best late variety in cultivation. Per pkt., 25.
Elletson Emperor. A new and fine English variety. Per pkt., 10 60

TO THE VEGETABLE GARDEN. 107

Cabbage (BRASSICA OLERACEA CAPITATA).
German, *Kopfkohl.* — French, *Chou Pomme.* — Spanish, *Repollo.*

One of the most popular vegetables grown.

CULTURE. — The Cabbage can be cultivated by the most simple and easy means. It grows in most soils, and produces its beneficial heads nine months in the year. The ground must be rich, or made so by a good coat of manure, as they have strong tapering roots. Digging or ploughing deep is very essential. To produce a constant succession of the Cabbage, it is necessary to plant at a number of times; also different varieties. For early use, sow in hotbeds in February or March; and for winter, the seeds may be sown in the open ground in May or June. When five or six inches high, transplant to from twelve to thirty inches apart. The plants should not be allowed to stand too thickly together, as this causes them to grow weak and feeble.

WINTERING CABBAGES. — If you have not a dry, airy, vegetable cellar nor open shed to spare for burying them, take a sheltered part of the garden, and bury the roots, stalks, and part of the head, in the earth; over which, in severe weather, place a good sprinkling of straw and a few boards. In southern latitudes, this is unnecessary: there they can withstand the climate.

The plants, before heading, are used extensively at the South for greens, under the name of Collards. We recommend the Sugar-loaf for this purpose; but any early cabbage will answer.

per oz.

Early York. One of the oldest, most familiar, and, as an early market sort, one of the most popular, of all the kinds now cultivated. The head is of rather less than medium size, roundish-ovoid, close, and well-formed, of a deep or ash green color; tender and well-flavored. Per pkt., 5 25
Early Sugar-loaf. Conical heads, with leaves erect; of a peculiar ashy or bluish-green hue; spoon-shaped; a fine variety for the Northern States, but in the South it loses its flavor and tenderness; said to be more affected by the heat than most early varieties. Per pkt., 10 30
Early Wakefield. An English variety, similar in form to the Early York, and nearly as early; grows to a good size; a favorite with market-gardeners. Per pkt., 10 . 40
Early Champion. Very early; dwarf and compact heads. Per pkt., 10 . . . 30
Early Drumhead, or Battersea. This is a round, flat-headed variety, of excellent quality; one of the latest among the early sorts. Per pkt., 5 25
Early Queen. Very fine; medium size; quite early. Per pkt., 5 35
Green Glazed. Heads large, rather loose and open. Its texture is coarse and hard; extensively grown in warm latitudes, where it appears to be less liable to the attacks of the cabbage-worm than any other sort. Per pkt., 5 40
Large York. This is a larger variety than the Early York, which it somewhat resembles. The head is broader, and more firm and solid; a favorite at the South, as it bears the heat well; two weeks later than Early York. Per pkt., 5 25
Large Late Drumhead. Heads very large; round, sometimes flattened a little at the top; close and firm; very hardy, and keeps well for a winter cabbage. Per pkt., 5 . 40
Large French Oxheart. A French variety, which is taking the place of many others, as it comes in after the Early York. It is tender, forms its heads readily, and well-flavored; a fine intermediate sort. Per pkt., 10 40
Little Pixie. A comparatively new variety; makes a small delicate-flavored head; one of the very earliest and best. Per pkt., 10 40
Large Bergen, or Great American. Head remarkably large, round, flattened at the top; compact; one of the largest and latest of all the Cabbages, and, when not fully perfected before being harvested, has the reputation, if reset in earth in the cellar, of heading, and increasing in size, during the winter. It is a popular market sort. Plants should stand three feet apart. Per pkt., 10 40
Stone Mason. This variety was originated by Mr. John Mason, of Marblehead, Mass. It is characterized for its sweetness and for its reliability for forming a solid head. It is also an excellent variety for extreme northern latitudes. Under good cultivation, nearly every plant will set a good head. Per pkt., 10 40
Mason's Drumhead. Large, round, solid heads; a very popular market Cabbage. Per pkt., 10 40
Marblehead Mammoth Drumhead. One of the largest of the Cabbage family; produced from the Mason or Stone Mason; in good soil, and with proper culture, will average thirty pounds per head. Per pkt., 25 . . . . 1.00
Pomeranian. An intermediate variety; heads are of medium size; has the form of an elongated cone, and is very regular and symmetrical; quite solid. Per pkt., 10 . 40
Premium Flat Dutch. A low-growing variety; heads large, bluish-green, round, solid, broad and flat on the top, and often tinted with red and brown. As a winter variety, it has no superior. Per pkt., 10 50
Red Dutch, or Pickling. This sort is used mostly for pickling, and often cut in shreds and served as a salad; medium size, oblong shape, and very solid; of a deep-red or purple color. Per pkt., 10 35
Winnigstadt. This is a German variety, somewhat similar to the Oxheart, but more regular; conical; heads very full and solid. It is an intermediate variety, which comes in after the Early York. All things considered, this is one of the best for general cultivation. Per pkt., 10 40

SAVOY.

None of the Cabbages are hardier or more easily cultivated. They should be sown early, and, when the seedlings are five or six inches high, transplanted or thinned out to three feet apart. The Savoys have more of the delicious richness of the Cauliflower than any of the Cabbages.

	per oz
Drumhead Savoy. Head large, round, compact, yellowish at the centre, and a little flattened; in the form of the common Drumhead, which it nearly approaches in size; excellent for winter. Per pkt., 10	50
Green Globe, or Curled Savoy. One of the best and most familiar of the Savoys; medium size; does not make as firm a head as some, but, being very tender, the inner leaves will be found very good for the table. Per pkt., 10 . . .	25
Russian Savoy. A new and hardy variety of the Savoy, with fine solid heads. Per pkt., 25.	
Victoria Savoy. A new variety, highly recommended. Per pkt., 10	40
Early Dwarf Ulm. Heads small, round, solid; leaves small, thick, fleshy, of a fine deep-green color, of first-rate quality; valuable for small gardens; should be planted early; Per pkt., 10	40

Cauliflower (BRASSICA OLERACEA BOTRYTIS).

German, *Blumen Kohl.* — French, *Choufleur.* — Spanish, *Coliflor.*

This very delicate vegetable was first introduced into England from the Island of Cypress, and is classed among the most delicious of vegetables.

CULTURE. — The proper seasons for sowing seeds are, for the early spring or summer crop, between the 8th and 20th of September; and for the late autumn crop, about the 1st of April. The plants, as soon as they are two or three inches high, should be planted out in a bed of rich light earth, three inches apart each way, so as to grow firm and stocky, to remove to their final place of growth. For the purpose of growing them to perfection, use a bed of the richest light earth, two feet deep, made very rich, with well-decomposed manure, surrounded by a frame covered with glass or shutters. Lift the plants carefully with a trowel from where they were transplanted, and plant them eighteen inches apart each way into the pit or frame prepared for it; give a gentle watering, and press the soil down firmly. The frame should be surrounded with straw or litter of some kind; also the glass or shutters should be covered with mats or dry straw in severe weather, observing to give plenty of air on mild and pleasant days to prevent the plants from drawing or damping off at the neck; should be kept well watered; soap-suds is beneficial. For a late autumn crop they require no particular care or skill, and not much labor, simply keeping them free from weeds, and the ground stirred frequently.

	per oz.
Early Paris. Heads rather large, white, and compact; leaves large, stalk short; a very early sort; should be planted in spring; one of the best. Per pkt., 15 . . .	3.00
Early London. A well-known variety; good for general use. Per pkt., 10 . . .	75
Early Dutch. An intermediate variety, coming in after the above; heads large, white, and compact; fine. Per pkt., 10	1.25
Carter's Dwarf Mammoth. A very early hardy variety, of dwarf and compact habit, with a firm white head; larger than the Walcheren; stand dry weather; said to be one of the finest. Per pkt., 25.	
Erfurt Earliest Dwarf. One of the best, if not the best, in general cultivation for early forcing and open ground; very dwarf, leaves small, heads large and very firm; pure white. Per pkt., 25.	
Stadtholder. A large strong-growing variety, with compact heads, considered by many superior to the Walcheren; fine for market. Per pkt., 15	1.00
Large Asiatic. A large and well-known variety; one of the best. Per pkt., 10 . . .	60
Walcheren. A very early variety, with close compact head; a general favorite. Per pkt., 10	75
Le Normand. A French variety; heads large, compact, and fine flavor; a superior variety in all respects. Per pkt., 25	3.00
Hovey's Early American. One of the earliest and best varieties. Per pkt., 15 . .	1.50
Large White French. An excellent variety, coming in after the earliest sorts. Per pkt., 10.	75
Waite's Alma. A new variety, represented as being of large size and firm. Per pkt., 15 .	1.25

Carrot (DAUCUS CAROTA).

German, *Mohre.* — French, *Carotte.* — Spanish, *Zanahoria.*

The Carrot in its cultivated state is a half-hardy biennial. It is generally served at table boiled with meats; it also makes an excellent ingredient for soups. As an agricultural root, it is not surpassed for feeding cattle.

CULTURE. — The Carrot flourishes best in a good, light, well-enriched loam. If possible, the ground should be stirred to the depth of twelve to fifteen inches, incorporated with a liberal application of well-rotted compost, and well pulverizing the soil in the operation. The surface should next be levelled, cleared as much as possible of stones and hard lumps of earth, and made mellow and friable; in which state, if the ground contains a sufficient moisture to color the surface when stirred, it will be ready for the seed. This may be sown from the 1st of April to the 20th of May: early sowing succeeds best. The drills should be one inch in depth, and from twelve to fifteen inches apart. The plants should stand from four to five inches apart.

HARVESTING. — The roots attain their full size in the autumn of the first year. When large quantities are raised for stock, they are generally placed in the cellar in bulk, without packing; but the finer sorts, when intended for the table, are usually packed in earth or sand, in order to retain their freshness and flavor: with ordinary precaution, they will remain sound and fresh until May or June.

	per oz.
Earliest French Short Horn. A very early variety; small size, and of excellent flavor. Fine for forcing; one of the best. Per pkt., 10	25

per oz.
Early Horn. A very early variety, and as a table Carrot is much esteemed, both on account of the smallness of its heart, and the tenderness of its fibres. As the roots are very short, it will grow well on shallow soils. Per pkt., 5 20
Orange Intermediate. Size medium; skin bright orange-red; flesh orange-yellow. Sweet, well flavored, and, while young, excellent for the table. Per pkt., 5 . . . 15
Long Orange. A well-known standard sort. Roots long, thickest at or near the crown, and tapering regularly to a point; one of the best for table or field-culture, and requires a very deep soil. Per pkt., 5 15
Improved Long Orange. Similar to the above in form, but is larger, and of a deeper color; one of the best for general cultivation. Per pkt., 5 20
Altringham. Flesh bright and lively, crisp and breaking in its texture; the heart, in proportion to the size of root, smaller than that of the Long Orange. A fine variety Per pkt., 5 15
Large White Belgian. Very large, and valuable for field-culture. Per pkt., 5 . . 15
Large Orange Belgian. Similar to above, except in color. Per pkt., 5 . . . 15

Celery (APIUM GRAVEOLENS).

German, *Seleri*. — French, *Celeri*. — Spanish, *Apio*.

Celery is one of the most popular salads used in this country. Succeeds well throughout the Northern and Middle States, and, in the vicinity of some of our large cities, is produced of remarkable size and excellence.

CULTURE. — The seed should be sown in hotbeds in March, or in the open ground the last of April or first of May; but, when sown in the open ground, it vegetates very slowly, often remaining in the ground several weeks before it comes up. A bushel or two of stable manure put in a hole in the ground, against a wall or any fence facing south, and covered with a rich fine mould three or four inches deep, will bring the seed up much sooner. Sufficient plants for any family may be started in a large flower-pot or two, placed in a sitting-room, giving them plenty of air and moisture. As soon as the young plants are about three inches high, prepare a small bed in the open ground, and make it rich, and the earth fine. Here set out the plants for a temporary growth, placing them four inches apart. This should be done carefully; and they should be gently watered once, and protected for a day or two against the sun. A bed ten feet long and four feet wide will contain three hundred plants, and, if well cultivated, will more than supply the table of a common-sized family from October to May. In this bed the plants should remain till the beginning or middle of July, when they should be removed into trenches. Make the trenches a foot or fifteen inches deep, and a foot wide, and not less than five feet apart. Lay the earth taken out of the trenches into the space in the middle, between the trenches, so that it may not be washed into them by heavy rains; for it will, in those cases, injure the crop by covering the heart of the plants. At the bottom of the trench put some good, rich, but well-digested, compost manure; for if too fresh the Celery will be rank and pipy, or hollow, and will not keep nearly as long or well. Dig this manure in well, making the earth fine and light; then take up the plants from the temporary bed, and set them out carefully in the bottom of the trenches, six or eight inches apart.

BLANCHING. — When the plants begin to grow, hoe on each side and between them with a small hoe. As they grow up, earth their stems; that is, put the earth up against the stems, but not too much at a time, and always when the plants are dry. Be particular and not allow the soil to get between the stems of the outside leaves and the inner one, as it is injurious to the plants. In frosty weather, they should be protected by covering the tops of the trenches well with dry litter; this should not be allowed to remain longer than is absolute'y necessary: it is well to cover the whole with boards to shed the rain.

per oz.
White Solid. Large, strong-growing variety; clear white, solid, and crisp. One of the best for market or general use. Per pkt., 10 30
Seymour's Superb White. A large-sized, vigorous-growing variety. Stalks white, round, very crisp, and perfectly solid; considered one of the best. Per pkt., 10 . 30
Boston Market. A medium-sized, white variety; hardy, crisp, succulent, and mild-flavored. A variety much grown by market-gardeners about Boston. Per pkt., 25. . 50
Cole's Crystal White. A fine variety for general use; dwarf, solid, crisp, and fine flavored. Per pkt., 10 30
Cole's Defiance Red. This is a comparatively new sort; medium-sized, solid, dark-red color. Per pkt., 10 35
Cole's Superb Dwarf Red. One of the best; dwarf, crisp, and fine flavored. Per pkt., 10, 35
Hood's Dwarf Imperial. A stout-growing, very compact, solid, and hardy variety, of superior flavor, and distinct habit. Per pkt., 25.
Sealey's Leviathan Celery. A very large, solid, white variety; highly recommended. Per pkt., 10 35
Laing's Improved Mammoth Red. This is considered the largest variety yet produced; specimens under good cultivation having attained the extraordinary weight of eight to ten pounds, and, at the same time, perfectly solid. It is nearly perennial in its habit, as it will not run to seed the first season. Color bright red; flavor unsurpassed, if equalled. Per pkt., 10 40
Nonesuch Red (Ivery's). A very late variety; remaining fit for use late in the spring. Very fine flavor; solid and crisp; one of the best. Per pkt., 10 . . . 40
Manchester Red. A large, strong-growing variety; not so compact at heart as some, yet grown largely for flavor; excellent for soups or stewing. Per pkt., 10 . . . 40
Turner's Incomparable. Dwarf white variety, of stiff, close habit; solid, crisp, and juicy. Said to keep in good order later in the season than any other variety; highly recommended. Per pkt., 10 40

per oz.
Carter's Incomparable Dwarf Dark Crimson. This is a new variety, highly recommended; of very dwarf habit; exceedingly solid; of a deep crimson color. Per pkt., 25.
Turkish Giant Solid. One of the largest white sorts, and considered by many superior to the common White Solid. Per pkt. 10 30
Celery Seed. For flavoring soups, &c. Per oz., 15. Per lb., $1.00.

Chervil (Scandix Cerifolium).

German, *Gartenkerbel.* — French, *Cerfeuil.*

Is a warm, mild, and aromatic plant. A native of Europe, and, in olden times, of great repute. After being boiled, it was eaten with oil and vinegar, and considered a panacea for courage, comfort to the heart, and strength to the body. It is much cultivated by the French and Dutch, who use the tender leaves in soups and salads as we use Parsley, and is considered by many to be a milder and more agreeable ingredient.

CULTURE. — Chervil is an annual plant, and should be sown in March, April, and May, in drills about a quarter of an inch deep, and nine inches apart. Cover lightly, and press the soil firm with the foot; rake evenly, and give a gentle watering in dry weather. The leaves are fit for use when two to four inches high. Cut them off close; they will come up again, and may be gathered in succession throughout the season.

per oz.
Chervil. Per pkt., 10 25

Chicory (Cichorium Intybus).

A hardy perennial, introduced from Europe, often abounding as a troublesome weed in our pastures and mowing-lands; is much used in Europe as a substitute for coffee, and large quantities of the prepared root are annually exported to this country for the same purpose. It may be raised to good advantage, and will pay a large profit, as its culture is simple. In the fall, the roots require to be taken up and cut in small pieces, and put where they will dry, requiring the same treatment used for drying apples. When required for use, it should be roasted and ground like coffee. Persons who suffer from the deleterious effects of coffee, will find, by adding a portion of this, the difficulty removed, and the flavor of the coffee greatly improved; requires similar treatment to Carrots.

per oz.
Large-rooted, or Coffee. Per pkt., 10 20

Corn, Indian (Zea Mais).

German, *Welschcorn.* — French, *Mais.* — Spanish, *Mais.*

per qt.
Adams's Early. Much grown for early use and the market; very early. Per pkt., 10 . 25
Early White. One of the earliest of the table varieties; of low growth. Per pkt., 10 . 25
Early Burlington. A very early variety, much grown for the market; the ear good size · an excellent table variety. Per pkt., 10 25
Darling's Extra Early Sugar is early, very tender, and sugary; yields well, produces little fodder, ears near the ground, and is one of the best sorts for early use, as it seldom, if ever, fails to perfect its crops. This we consider the best for early use. Per pkt., 10 30
Red Cob Sweet. Medium; early; usually twelve, but sometimes fourteen rowed; quality good; cob red; kernels large. Per pkt., 10 30
Burr's Improved Sweet. An improved variety of the twelve-rowed Sweet. The ears are from twelve to sixteen rowed, and, in good soils and seasons, often measure eight or ten inches in length, and nearly three inches in diameter; cob white; hardy, productive, tender, and sweet; the best for general use. Per pkt., 10 . . 30
Mammoth Sweet. A very large and late variety; cob white; fine flavored; one of the best. Per pkt., 10 30
Stowell's Evergreen Sweet. This variety is intermediate in its season, and, if planted at the same time with the earlier kinds, will keep the table supplied till October. It is hardy and productive, very tender and sugary, remaining a long time in a fresh condition, and suitable for boiling. Per pkt., 10 30
Tuscarora. A very large variety; eight-rowed; cob red; remaining a long time in a boiling state. Per pkt., 10 30
Golden Sweet. A hybrid between the common yellow and Darling's Early; quite tender, and sweet. Per pkt., 10 40
Old Colony Sweet. A remarkably sweet and delicious sort, with twelve to twenty rowed ears; one of the best. Per pkt., 10 50
Nonpareil, or Pop-corn. A fine parching variety. Per pkt., 10 30
Rice. Hardy and prolific; good for parching. Per pkt., 10 40
Early Canada Yellow. Productive and early 20
King Philip, or Brown. Very productive, and is recommended as one of the best field sorts now in cultivation. In good soil and favorable seasons, the yield per acre is from seventy-five to ninety bushels; sometimes reaches as high as a hundred and ten . 25
Early Dutton, or Golden Sioux. One of the handsomest of the field varieties; productive, and of good quality 30

Cress, or Peppergrass (LEPIDIUM SATIVUM)

German, *Kresse.* — French, *Cresson.* — Spanish, *Mastruco.*

The leaves, while young, have a warm, pungent taste, and are eaten as a salad, either separately, or mixed with Lettuce or other salad-plants.

CULTURE. — Sow rather thick in shallow drills, and at short intervals during the season. The Water-cress requires to be grown on the edge of a running stream or brook where it does not freeze too hard during the winter.

	per oz.
Curled. A well-known sort. Per pkt., 5	10
Broad-leaved. A coarse variety, with broad spatulate leaves; sometimes grown for feeding poultry; also used for soups. Per pkt., 5	10
Henderson's Australian. Fine piquant flavor; for salads. Per pkt., 10	25
Water. This is an aquatic plant, with small oval leaves and prostrate habit. The leaves are universally used and eaten as an early spring salad. Per pkt., 10	50

Corn Salad, or Fettleus (VALERIANA LOCUSTA).

German, *Lammersalat.* — French, *Mache.* — Spanish, *Canonigos.*

per oz.

An annual plant, cultivated for its tender leaves, which are esteemed as a winter and early spring salad. The seed is usually sown in shallow drills, early in September. On approach of winter, cover the plants lightly with straw 15

Cucumber (CUCUMIS SATIVUS).

German, *Gurke.* — French, *Concombre.* — Spanish, *Cohombro.*

CULTURE, in the open air, is of the simplest character. Merely dig out a hole about a foot wide and deep; fill it with rich sandy soil; raise it above the surface about six inches. The hills should be six feet feet apart each way. Any time in May sow a few seeds therein, and the result is certain. It the weather be warm, they will grow in a few days. If the nights are cold, protect them. There is frequently a little bug which preys upon the tender leaves; if so, soot and wood-ashes, sprinkled over them while wet with the dew, will retard the progress of the depredator. As soon as the vines have made three rough leaves, nip the points off to make them branch out: they will fruit sooner by it. Three vines to one hill is quite enough. To have young fruit in February and March is rather a nice operation; but any one who can command a few loads of warm horse-manure can have them from April to October. That the amateur cultivator may have the article either for family use or for sale, a few hints may be in place on forcing cucumbers. Prepare a frame, following the instructions laid down in the first part of this work for hotbeds. After the beds are in order, put in a good quantity of good, light, rich loam, — none better than the surface of the woods. In two or three days, the earth will be sufficiently warm for sowing the seeds. If the plants are to be removed into other frames, sow them in pots; if not to be removed, sow them in a hill made in the centre of the bed by placing a barrowful of soil in it. Cover the sash at night with straw mats, or any similar protection, and surround the beds with litter or boards to protect it from the piercing winds. The seeds vegetate quickly, and soon grow into strong plants. During their growth, admit air every day at the back of the frame, giving as much light as possible to the young plants. If the soil or plants appear dry, give them water in the forenoon which has been kept in the bed during the night that it may be in a warm state, — the requisite temperature of the bed at night, from 65° to 75° day, 75° to 100°.

per oz.

Early Russian. This is a comparatively new variety, resembling in some respects the Early Cluster; fruit from three to four inches long, an inch and a half in diameter; generally produced in pairs; flesh tender, crisp, and well flavored; comes into use ten days in advance of the Early Cluster, and makes a fine small pickle. Per pkt. 10 25

Early Cluster. A very popular early Cucumber, producing its fruit in clusters near the root of the plant. Its usual length is about five inches; skin prickly; flesh white, seedy, tender, and well flavored; comes in about ten days later than the Early Russian. Per pkt., 5 15

Early Frame. One of the oldest of the garden sorts, justly styled a standard variety; fruit straight and well formed; flesh greenish-white, rather seedy, but tender, and of an agreeable flavor; a few days later than the Early Cluster. Per pkt., 5 . . . 15

Early White Spine. One of the best table sorts, and greatly prized by market-men on account of its color, which never changes to yellow. The fruit is of full medium size, straight, and well-formed; skin deep green; prickles white; flesh white, tender, crispy, and of remarkably fine flavor; very productive, and good for forcing; sometimes known under the name of New-York Market. Per pkt., 5 20

Long Green Prickly. This is a large-sized variety, and somewhat later than the White Spine; skin dark green, changing to yellow as the fruit approaches to maturity; flesh white, somewhat seedy, but crisp, tender, and well-flavored; hardy and productive; makes a good pickle if plucked while young; well deserving of cultivation. Per pkt., 5 20

Extra Long Green Turkey. A distinct and well-defined variety; when full grown, sometimes measuring nearly eighteen inches in length; form long and slender, with but few seeds; flesh remarkably firm and crispy; very productive and excellent. Per pkt., 10 25

AMATEUR CULTIVATOR'S GUIDE

per oz.
Haage's White Cylindric. A new long white variety; very prolific bearer, and recommended as a most valuable acquisition. Per pkt., 25.
Haage's Striped Giant. One of the largest and longest varieties; green, with yellow stripes; new and fine. Per pkt., 25.
Long Green Smooth. A very long-growing variety. Flesh greenish-white, firm, and crisp; flavor good. A German variety, twenty to twenty-four inches in length. Per pkt., 10 50
Charlwood's Ridge. An English variety, highly recommended; productive, and good flavored. Per pkt., 10.
Stockwood Ridge. A very productive black-spined variety, having three to four fruit, twelve to eighteen inches long, at each joint; one of the best. Per pkt., 10 . . 50
New-Jersey Hybrid. Very productive, and good average growth of fruit; about twenty inches. Per pkt., 15 50
Giant of Arnstadt. One of the very best, and of fine quality. Per pkt., 25.
White Giant of Arnstadt. A new and beautiful snow-white variety, growing twenty to twenty-four inches long. Per pkt., 25.
West-India Gherkins. Used only for pickles. Per pkt., 15 50
English Gherkins. Fine for the table, or pickles. Per pkt., 10 50

ENGLISH FRAME VARIETIES.

per pkt.
Berkshire Champion	25
Carter's Champion, selected	25
Cuthill's Black Spine	25
Cuthill's Highland Mary	25
Carter's White Spine	25
Manchester Prize	25
Minster Abbey	25
Lynch's Star of the West	25
Lynch's Conqueror of the West	25
Star of the West	25
Sion House Improved	25
Sir Colin Campbell	25
Surprise	25
Stilwell's Matchless	25
Weedon's Surprise	25
Kenyon's Favorite	25
Walker's Rambler	25
Napoleon III.	25
Roman Emperor	25

General Grant (for forcing). A new and superb variety, either for exhibition or the table; perfect in form, solid and crisp, and of a most agreeable flavor. Many specimens were grown the past season, averaging twenty-four to thirty inches in length; succeeds well in the open ground . . . . ¶. 25

Egg-Plant (SOLANUM MELONGENA).

German, *Cierpflanze.* — French, *Aubergine.* — Spanish, *Berengena.*

The Egg-Plant was introduced from Africa, and is called by some the Guinea Squash. It is generally cultivated, and is becoming more so every year. They are cut into thin slices, and fried, which have a taste very similar to oysters: others use them in stews and soups.

CULTURE. — Sow in hotbed very early in spring; transplant, when two inches high, into a second hotbed; if that is not done, thin to four inches apart. Do not plant out till the weather becomes settled and warm. Keep plants watered for a few days if hot when put out. Where hotbeds are not convenient, a few plants can be started in flower-pots or boxes, and, when planted out, must have a deep rich soil, and full exposure to the sun. Till and hoe same as for Cabbages.

per oz.
Early Long Purple. Earliest, hardy, and most productive; of superior quality. Per pkt., 10, 75
New-York Improved Purple. One of the largest and best varieties. Oval-shaped, of a dark-purple color; fine flavored. Grown extensively for the market. Per pkt., 10 1.00
White-fruited. Fruit milk-white, egg-shaped, varying from three to five inches in length, and from two and a half to three inches in diameter; grown principally for ornament. Per pkt., 5 . . . . 1.00
Scarlet-fruited. A highly ornamental variety. In general appearance, it resembles the common Egg-Plant; but the fruit, which is about the size of a hen's egg, is of a most beautiful scarlet: principally cultivated for its peculiar, richly colored, and ornamental fruit, which makes a fine garnish. Per pkt., 10.
Gaudaloupe Striped. Fruit nearly ovoid; smaller than the large purple; skin white streaked, and variegated with red. Per pkt., 10.
Pekin New Black. A new variety, from Pekin, China, producing very remarkable, large, round fruit, weighing six to eight pounds each. Per pkt., 25.

Endive (CHICORIUM ENDIVIA).

German, *Endivien.* — French, *Chicorée.* — Spanish, *Endvia.*

The garden Endive is a native of Northern China, and has been cultivated in Europe the past three centuries for a winter salad. The French are particularly fond of it, using it raw, pickled,

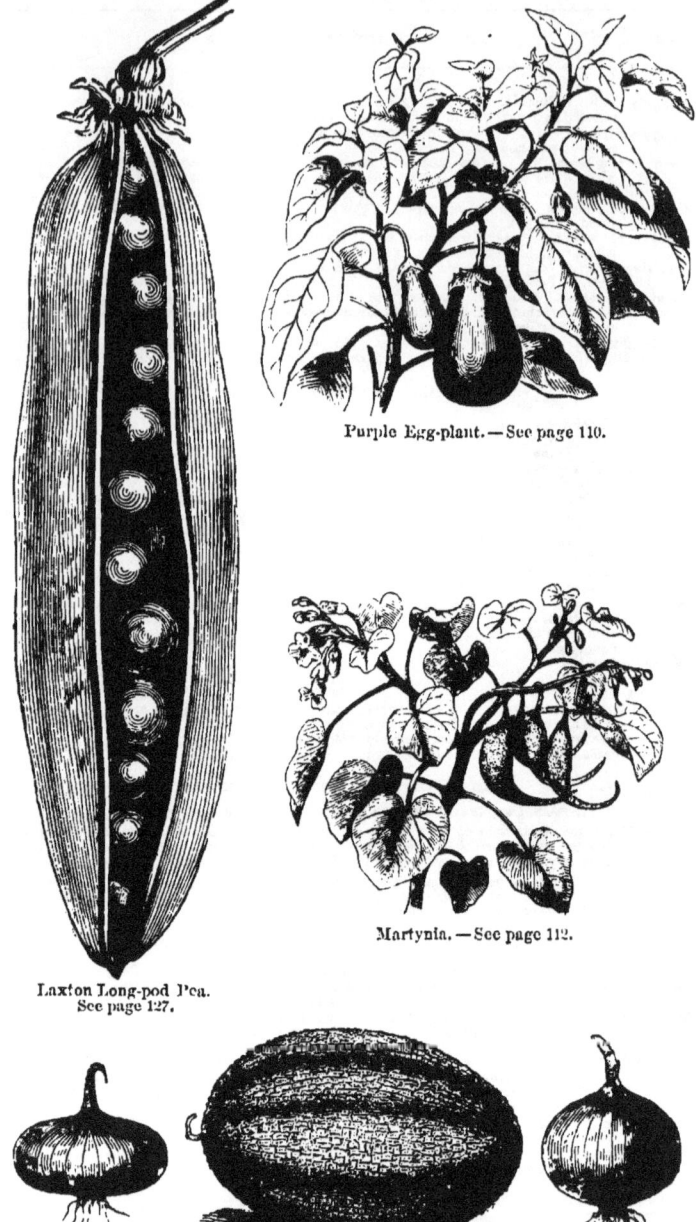

Purple Egg-plant.—See page 110.

Martynia.—See page 112.

Laxton Long-pod Pea.
See page 127.

Yellow Dutch Onion.
See page 115.

Large Musk Melon.—See page 113.

Yel'w Danvers Onion.
See page 115.

fried, and boiled, esteeming it exceedingly wholesome in every form. It agrees with every constitution.
CULTURE. — For the early crop, sow about the 1st of July. It will do on the ground where early Cabbages or Peas have come off, by giving it a coat of manure. Draw drills the depth of the hoe, one foot apart, and sow therein; sprinkle a little earth in the bottom of the drill, sufficient to cover the seed, which will be up in a few days. If dry weather ensue, water once or twice till the plants get hold. Thin them out, when about two inches high, to ten inches apart; hoe freely, and keep clear of weeds. Being grown in these shallow drills, they are more easily earthed up, and grow better in warm, dry weather. When the leaves have attained about eight inches long, they are fit for blanching: for this purpose a dry day must be chosen. Gather up the leaves in your hand, in a close and rounded form; see that there is no earth or litter in their centre. Tie them up with a piece of cotton-twist or matting, which is to go several times round the plant, causing it to close at the top to prevent the rain from penetrating to and injuring its centre; then draw a little earth round its base for support. If the leaves are not perfectly dry when tied up, they will rot, or become so stained as to be unfit for the table. They will take about ten days in warm, and twenty days in cool weather to blanch for use: a judgment may thus be formed of the quantity to be tied up at a time. For late crops, sow about the end of July.

per oz.
Green-curled. Easily blanched; very hardy, and well adapted for winter use. One of the best. Per pkt., 10 35
White-curled, or Ever-blanched. Leaves pale yellowish-green, nearly white when young; long, rather narrow; lobed, cut, and beautifully frilled or curled. Not so hardy as the Green. Per pkt., 10 35
Broad-leaved Batavian. Leaves yellow-green, large, long, and broad; thick and fleshy. Chiefly used in stews, soups, &c. Called, by the French, Chicorée Scarolle. Per pkt., 10 35
Fine Curled, or Moss. A new variety, with very fine curled leaves, much resembling moss. Per pkt., 10.

Kohl-Rabi, or Turnip-rooted Cabbage.

German, *Kohl-rabiuber*. — French, *Chow-rave*. — Spanish, *Col de nabo*.

The Kohl-Rabi is a vegetable intermediate between the Cabbage and the Turnip. The stem, just above the surface of the ground, swells into a round fleshy bulb, in form not unlike a turnip; on the top, and about the surface of this bulb, are put forth its leaves, which are similar to those of the Swedish Turnip. The part chiefly used is the turnip-looking bulb, formed by the swelling of the stem. This is dressed and eaten with sauce or with meat, as turnips usually are. While young, the flesh is tender and delicate, possessing the combined flavor of the Cabbage and Turnip.

CULTURE. — Cultivate same as Cabbage; only that, in earthing up the plant, be careful not to cover the globular part. They should not be used before they have attained their full growth.

per oz.
Early White Vienna. Above ground; early and fine. Per pkt., 10 40
Early Purple Vienna. Above ground; similar to the preceding. Per pkt., 10 . . . 40
Large Purple. Above ground; very large. Per pkt., 5 25
Large White. Below ground; similar to the White Ruta-baga. Per pkt., 5 . . . 25
Late Purple Giant. Very large and tender variety, often weighing from seven to eight lbs.; new. Per pkt., 10.

Leek (ALLIUM PORRUM).

German, *Lauch*. — French, *Poireau*. — Spanish, *Puerro*.

This is a branch of the Onion family, — a native of the north of Europe; is very hardy, and, from its mild qualities, is preferred by many families to the Onion. History records it as having been cultivated many hundred years. The Welsh indulge in Leeks on their patron St. David's Day, in commemoration of a victory which they obtained over the Saxons, which they attributed to the Leeks they wore, by order of St. David, to distinguish them in battle.

CULTURE. — There is no part of the garden too rich for Leeks. They require the best ground, well worked, and manured the full depth of the spade. Sow the seed thinly on a small bed of light rich ground, in drills six inches apart and half an inch deep; rake it evenly, and give it a beat with the back of the spade.

When they come up, they should stand an inch apart; if thicker, thin them out. When grown to about eight inches high, they will be of sufficient size to plant out. As we have remarked, choose the best ground, draw thereon drills a foot apart, and as deep as the hoe will go. When ready, the plants are to be taken up from the seed-bed. Shorten their roots to about an inch from the plant, and cut two inches or more from the extremity of the leaves. Both these operations are done for convenience and neatness in planting. Dibble them in the drills eight inches apart, and as deep as the plant will admit of, not to cover the young leaves pushing from its centre. Choose moist or cloudy weather for the operation; but, if dry, give the plants a copious watering. Hoe the ground frequently, to keep down weeds, and, as the plants are observed to grow, draw the soil around them. By good culture, they will be fit for use early in October. On the approach of severe frost, lift sufficient for winter use, and store them away in earth or sand.

per oz.
Large London is hardy, and of good quality. It is more generally cultivated in this country, than any other variety. Per pkt., 10 30
Broad Scotch, or Flag. This variety is remarkably hardy, and well suited for open culture; large and strong-growing, with broad leaves growing on two sides. Per pkt., 10 30

Lettuce (LACTUCA SATIVA).

German, *Lattich.* — French, *Laitue.* — Spanish, *Lechuga.*

The Lettuce is generally divided into two classes; viz., Cabbage Lettuces and Cos Lettuces. The Cabbage have round heads and broad-spreading leaves; the Cos varieties have long heads, and upright, oblong leaves.

CULTURE. — A very rich soil is necessary to produce fine head Lettuce. Its crisp and tender quality depends very much on a luxuriant and vigorous growth. The earliest sowing may be made in February or March, under glass with slight heat. Keep the plants thin, and admit plenty of air to the frame every fine day. For later supplies, sow in the open ground as soon as the season will permit: transplant or thin out the plants gradually to a foot apart, and keep well cultivated. The Cos Lettuces are excellent if grown very early in the spring, but run to seed quickly in hot weather. The large Cabbage kinds are best, and most suitable for summer crops.

per oz.

Early-curled Silesia. Standard sort; very early; the best for forcing and the first spring sowing; makes a loose head; tender, and of excellent flavor. Per pkt., 10 . . . 40

Early Tennisball. One of the oldest and most esteemed of the Cabbage Lettuce. The head is below medium size; dark-green; very solid if grown in cool weather; one of the earliest and best. Per pkt., 10 40

Early Royal Cape, or Summer Cape. Head roundish, usually well-formed, and moderately close and firm; good size; as a summer Lettuce, is one of the best. Per pkt., 10 40

Early Drumhead, or Malta. Head remarkably large, somewhat flattened, compact; pale green without, and white at the centre; crisp and tender; fine summer variety. Per pkt., 5 25

Boston Curled. A new variety; one of the best for general cultivation. The elegant frilling of the leaves, and fine form, make it very attractive; flavor very fine. Per pkt., 10 40

Royal Summer Cabbage. Head medium-sized, round, somewhat flattened, firm, and close. Per pkt., 5 30

Large India. Heads large and compact, similar to the Curled Silesia, but is less curled, and whiter; sometimes tinted with brown; heads round, crispy, and fine flavor; very popular as a market variety; one of the best for summer culture. Per pkt., 10 40

Wheeler's Tom Thumb. A new English variety; very dwarf and compact; excellent flavor; crisp and refreshing. Per pkt., 10 50

Ivery's Nonesuch. A new English variety, highly recommended as a summer variety. Per pkt., 10 40

Brown Dutch. A very hardy sort, enduring the winter with less protection than most other varieties; heads medium size, rather long, and loose; good flavor; generally sown in the autumn. Per pkt., 10 40

Hammersmith Hardy Green. A very popular old variety. It is considered the hardiest sort in cultivation, and is one of the best for growing in winter or forcing. Per pkt., 10 40

Victoria Cabbage. An excellent early and hardy variety; is larger than Tennisball; heads freely, and is crisp and well-flavored; should be planted early. Per pkt., 10 . 40

White Paris Cos. This variety is grown mostly by London and Paris market-gardeners; tender, brittle, and mild-flavored. Per pkt., 10 40

Green Paris Cos. Considered one of the best of the Cos Lettuce. It has a tender, brittle leaf; some days earlier than the White Cos. Per pkt., 10 . . . 40

Large Spotted, or Tigered. A new and tender variety, with large spotted leaves. Per pkt., 10.

Blood-red. Very tender variety, with red leaves; new. Per pkt., 10 . . . 50

Perpignan. A fine variety, forming large solid heads, with very crisp and tender leaves; new. Per pkt., 10 50

Ne Plus Ultra. Very large, firm head; tender, and keeps well. Per pkt., 10 . . 50

Carter's Giant Brown Cos. Per pkt., 25.

Dunnett's Giant Black-seeded Brown Cos. Per pkt., 25.

The last three are new English varieties, said to be very large, crisp, and good-flavored varieties of Lettuce, with fine broad leaves, which turn in well; all of them are late varieties, coming in some three weeks after the common sorts.

Martynia (MARTYNIA PROBOSCIDIA).

A hardy annual plant, with a strong branching stem two feet and a half high. The leaves are large, heart-shaped, entire, or undulated, downy, viscous, and emit a peculiar musk-like odor when bruised or roughly handled. The young pods are the parts of the plants used. These are produced in great abundance, and should be gathered when about half grown, or while tender and succulent: after the hardening of the flesh, they are worthless. They are used for pickles, and by many are considered superior to the Cucumber, or any other vegetable employed for that purpose.

CULTURE. — The Martynia is of easy culture. As the plants are large and spreading, they should be two and a half feet apart in each direction. The seeds may be sown in April or May, in the open ground, where they are to remain; or the seeds may be sown earlier in a hotbed, and transplanted.

per oz.

Martynia. Per pkt., 10 40

TO THE VEGETABLE GARDEN. 115

WHITE JAPAN MELON.   CITRON-MELON (see p. 114).

Melon, Musk Varieties (CUCUMIS MELO).

German, *Melone.* — French, *Melon.* — Spanish, *Melon.*

The Melon, in some character, is to be found in all tropical countries; but the finest varieties are supposed to have come from Persia and Afghanistan. The delicious flavor and perfume make it very popular in all countries where the climate will admit of its cultivation.

CULTURE. — Plant in hills six feet apart each way, eight or ten seeds in each, and thin out to three or four plants when in a state of forwardness. To grow good melons, the hills should be prepared by digging out the soil from one and a half to two feet deep, and two or three feet broad, according to the richness of the land. Add a very liberal quantity of the best decomposed stable manure, and mix well with the soil, filling up a little above the general level. By this mode, good melons may be raised on almost any soil. Seeds should not be put into the hills until the weather becomes settled and warm.

per oz.
Christiana. This variety originated in Beverly, Mass.; form roundish; size rather small; skin yellowish-green; flesh yellow, sweet, juicy, and of good quality; one of the best; ripens very early. Per pkt., 10 30
Green Citron. Fruit nearly round, but flattened slightly at the ends; medium size; flesh green, quite thick, and of the richest and most sugary flavor; comes in early, and makes a very popular market variety. Per pkt., 5 20
Nutmeg. Fruit oval, good size, thickly netted; flesh light-green, rich, sweet, melting, and highly perfumed; one of the finest. Per pkt., 5 20
Pineapple. Form roundish, inclining to oval; flesh green, melting, sweet, and perfumed; early and productive. Per pkt., 5 20
Skillman's Fine-netted. This variety much resembles the Pineapple; flesh green, sugary, melting, and excellent; the earliest of all the green-fleshed varieties. Per pkt., 5 20
Persian. Long, oval-shaped; skin very thin and delicate; flesh extremely tender, rich, and sweet, and flows copiously, with a cool juice, which renders them very grateful. Per pkt., 10 30
Allen's Superb. A new variety of the Nutmeg; flesh green and sweet. Per pkt., 10 30
Beechwood. Medium-sized; dark-green; flesh very sweet; late; suitable for growing in frames under glass. Per pkt., 25.
Large Yellow Cantelope. An oval variety; good-sized; skin yellow, marbled with green; flesh salmon-colored, sweet, highly perfumed, and of good flavor; early and productive. Per pkt., 5 20
Large Musk. This is a very large, long oval shape; deeply ribbed; flesh very thick, yellow, sweet, and juicy, with musky flavor; very early and productive. Per pkt., 5 20
New White Japan. A new variety from Japan, and decidedly the sweetest thin-skinned of the Musk Melon; color of fruit cream-white; flesh thick; size medium and nearly round. Per pkt., 10 40
Trentham Hall. An English variety; green-fleshed; sweet; suitable for cultivating in frames. Per pkt., 25.
Carter's Excelsior. A new English prize variety, said to be the best green-fleshed variety. Per pkt., 25.
Turner's Scarlet Gem. An English frame variety. Per pkt., 25.

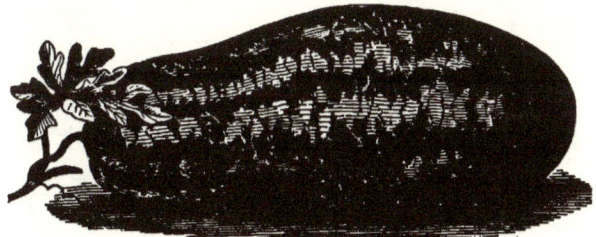

MOUNTAIN-SWEET WATER-MELON.

Water-Melon (CUCURBITA CITRULLUS).

German, *Wassermelone.* — French, *Melon d'Eau.* — Spanish, *Sandia.*

The Water-melon is purely a tropical fruit, greatly appreciated for its refreshing coolness and delicious flavor.

CULTURE. — They require a light sandy soil, not over rich. Plant them in hills, as directed for Melons, giving them more room, as their vines extend much farther. The seeds should be two years old before planting. If they are wanted of a large size, three or four fruit from each plant will be sufficient; and, when one fruit only is taken, they will grow to from twenty to thirty pounds' weight each. It will injure the flavor of the fruit if they are grown near to other varieties of the Melon.

per oz.

Mountain Sweet. A large, long, oval variety; skin striped and marbled with different shades of green; flesh scarlet, and quite solid to the centre; very sweet and delicious. A fine market sort. Per pkt., 5 15
Mountain Sprout, or Long Carolina. Resembling the preceding in most respects. A favorite market sort. Very fine quality, and productive. Per pkt., 5 . . . 20
Black Spanish. Form oblong; size large; skin very dark or blackish green; flesh deep-red, fine-grained, very sugary, and of excellent flavor. Hardy and productive; one of the best for general cultivation. Per pkt., 5 20
Ice-cream. A very large pale-green sort; form nearly round; flesh white, very sweet, tender, and of remarkably fine flavor. Per pkt., 5 15
Orange. Form oval, of medium size; flesh red, not fine grained, but tender, sweet, and of good quality. When in its mature state, the rind separates readily from the flesh, in the manner of the peel from the flesh of an orange. Per pkt., 10 . . . 40
Citron. Employed in making sweetmeats and preserves; form round, medium size; flesh white, very solid. (See engraving on p. 113.) Per pkt., 5 20
Apple-pie Melon. This is a new Japanese variety, said to be an excellent substitute for apples, when stewed, and made into pies: keeps until May. Per pkt., 10 . 20
Apple-seeded. A rather small, nearly round sort; derives its name from its small, peculiar seeds. Flesh bright red to the centre, sweet, tender, and well-flavored; keeps a long time after being gathered. Per pkt., 10 40

Mustard (SINAPIS VAR).

German, *Senf.* — French, *Moutard.* — Spanish, *Mostaza.*

Mustard-seed is too widely known and appreciated to need description. It is useful both in its natural state and manufactured, and is considered wholesome in all its various methods of preparation. It is very refreshing when, in its green state, mixed with salads, and for that purpose alone is worthy of cultivation.

CULTURE. — This salad is cultivated in the same manner as recommended for Cress, — at all times of the year, sowing every week or two either in beds or drills, or, for early use, in hotbeds, or boxes in the windows of a warm room. The seeds should be covered very slightly, and frequently watered, as moisture is indispensable to its growth. A bed three feet wide and twenty feet long, having the plants four or six inches apart, will produce a sufficiency of seed for every domestic purpose.

per pint.
White, or Yellow. Very useful for salads, also for medicinal purposes. Per pkt., 5 . . 30
Brown, or Black. For culinary use. Per pkt., 5 30

Nasturtium, or Indian Cress (TROPÆOLUM).

German, *Kresse Indianische.* — French, *Capucine Grande.* — Spanish, *Capuchina.*

There are many curious varieties of the Cress, though none so beautiful as the common Nasturtium. It has a sharp, warm taste, and is frequently used in salads. The green seeds are frequently pickled in vinegar, and are very palatable.

CULTURE. — Sow the seed thinly, in rows or patches an inch deep, about the end of March or first of April. They will thrive almost anywhere if the ground is rich. They are peculiarly adapted to trellis-work, and form a rich, showy, and enlivening appearance.

TO THE VEGETABLE GARDEN. 117

	per oz.
Tall. Per pkt., 5	30
Dwarf. Per pkt., 10	40

Okra, or Gombo (HIBISCUS ESCULENTUS).

German, *Essbarer Hibiscus.* — French, *Gombo.* — Spanish, *Quibombo.*

This plant is cultivated, to some extent, as a vegetable: served in the same manner as Asparagus. The green seed-pods are used in soups, and deemed a luxury. It is becoming very popular since its introduction to us from the West Indies.

CULTURE. — The seeds are sown thinly, on dry, warm soil, in shallow drills two feet apart, about the same as the Lima Bean. Cover the seeds lightly. After the plants are up, thin them out to nine inches apart; hoe freely, and draw a little earth to the stems as they continue to grow. Gather the pods when quite green and about an inch and a half long.

	per oz.
Long Green. Pods long and ribbed. Per pkt., 5	15
Improved Dwarf Green. Pods small-sized, smooth, green, and round. Per pkt., 5	15

Onion (ALLIUM CEPA).

German, *Zwiebel.* — French, *Ognon.* — *Cebolla.*

No vegetable is more extensively known and cultivated than the Onion. It has been the common seasoning for soups and meats of all nations from the earliest period to the present. In cookery it is indispensable.

CULTURE. — The soil in general cannot be too rich for this vegetable; and, however good it may be, it requires more or less manure for every crop: unlike most vegetables, it succeeds well when cultivated on the same land for successive years, provided it is liberally supplied with nutrition. Previous to sowing, the ground should be thoroughly spaded over, or deeply ploughed, and the surface made smooth and even. The seed should be sown as early in spring as the soil may be in good working condition. Sow in drills fourteen inches apart, and half an inch in depth. When the plants are three or four inches high, thin them out to two inches apart. If the weather is moist, the thinnings may be transplanted into other ground. They, too, will attain full size; but observe, in planting, to put the roots only under ground.

To grow Onions for pickling, sow the seed thinly in March or April. No further culture is required, except hand-weeding, as their thickness in the bed will prevent their growing large, and will cause them to come to maturity sooner. The seed should be thoroughly dried; for when stored in a damp state it is liable to generate heat, and consequently to lose its vitality.

per oz.

Early Red. A sub-variety of the Large Red Wethersfield, and the earliest of the Red Onions. Form and color nearly the same as Large Red; close-grained, mild, and a good keeper. Very productive. Per pkt., 10 50
Large Red Wethersfield. Large-sized, skin deep purplish-red; flesh purplish-white; moderately fine grained, and stronger flavored than that of the yellow and earlier red varieties. Very productive, and one of the best to keep; the variety mostly grown at Wethersfield. Per pkt., 5 50
Danvers Yellow. A very fine variety, originated from South Danvers, Mass. Above the medium size; globular in form; skin yellowish-brown; flesh white, sugary, comparatively mild and well-flavored. Very productive; one of the most popular for general cultivation. Per pkt., 5 50
Yellow Dutch, or Silver-skin. One of the oldest varieties; and, as a market variety, probably better known and more generally grown in this country than any other. Flesh white, fine-grained, mild, sugary, and well-flavored. Per pkt., 5 . . . 50
White Portugal, or Spanish. A very large, flat onion. Skin loose, of a mild flavor, fine early winter use, but decays early. Per pkt., 10 60

per qt.

Top, or Button Onion. Bulbs large, a little flattened; producing, instead of seeds, a number of small bulbs or onions about the size of filberts, which serve as a substitute for seeds in propagation. The bulbs are liable to decay, and should be kept in a cool, dry place, away from frost 50
Potato Onion. Producing a quantity of young bulbs on the parent root, which should be planted in rows, in April, three inches deep (below the surface) and six inches apart: the rows should be eighteen inches apart. Keep them free from weeds, and earth them up like potatoes as they continue to grow; when grown, may be treated as other onions 40

Orache, or Mountain Spinach (ATRIPLEX HORTENSIS).

German, *Garten Melde.* — French, *Aroche.* — Spanish, *Armuelle.*

CULTURE. — This plant flourishes best in rich soil, in open ground. Manure well, and it will reward you for your trouble by its abundant produce. Sow the seed in drills five or six inches asunder; when the plants are sufficiently strong, thin them out to six inches apart. The thinnings may be replanted, and occasionally watered until established. Gather the leaves for use while young and tender.

	per oz.
Orache, or Mountain Spinach. Per pkt., 5	20

Parsley (APIUM PETROSELINUM).

German, *Petersilie.* — French, *Persil.* — Spanish, *Peregil.*

The garden Parsley is a very useful and pleasant vegetable. Its seasoning flavor for soups and stews is very agreeable to many. It may be preserved by drying it till crisp, in summer; then rub it fine between the hands, and put in bottles for winter use.

CULTURE. — Sow it in drills half an inch deep, early in April. These drills may form an edging round any compartment of vegetables, or along the walks. When the plants are three or four inches high, thin them to six inches apart; to keep a young stock constantly for use, cut down about a third part at a time. Root out the plain-leaved, should any appear. Keep it only from severe frost, and it will grow the whole winter. For this object, select a warm spot of ground, light and rich; sow it early in the season; cut them all over in September; surround the bed, early in November, with boards, and cover with mats or shutters; glass is much better, if it can be obtained. By this process, a sufficient supply will be always obtainable.

per oz.

Plain Parsley. The leaves of this sort are plain, or not curled; but it is better flavored than the curled for soups, &c. Requires a slight protection, during the winter, of straw, pine-boughs, or leaves. Per pkt., 5 15
Curled, or Double. A fine dwarf variety, tender; leaves yellowish-green, and beautifully crimped and curled. Fine for garnishing dishes for the table. Per pkt., 5 . . 15
Hamburg, or Rooted. The roots are principally used for flavoring soups. Per pkt., 10 . 30
Dunnett's Selected. A new English variety, superior for garnishing. Per pkt., 10 . . 30
Dickson Extra, or Triple-curled. A new and fine English variety. Per pkt., 25.

Parsnip (PASTINACA SATIVA).

German, *Pastinake.* — French, *Panais.* — Spanish, *Pastinaca.*

The Parsnip is a biennial plant, similar to the Onion, Turnip, and Carrot in duration. It is both wholesome and nourishing, and desirable for winter and spring use.

CULTURE. — It succeeds well in a rich, sandy loam. Sow early in the spring, in drills tolerably deep; scatter the seeds thinly, and cover evenly with the rake. After the appearance of the seed, the soil must be stirred with the hoe frequently, until the leaves cover the ground: they will stand any severity of frost. One ounce of seed is sufficient to supply a family.

per oz.

Long Smooth. Roots long, white, smooth, and regularly tapering to the end; free from side-roots. Tops small, slightly tinged with red at the crown. Very hardy, keeping through the winter where grown without any protection; one of the best for general cultivation. Per pkt., 5 15
Hollow Crown. Roots oblong, ending somewhat abruptly with a small top root; grows mostly below the surface. Best garden variety. Per pkt., 5 15
The Student. A new variety, of delicious flavor, ennobled from the Wild Parsnip by Prof. Buckman, of the Royal Agricultural College, Cirencester, England. A great acquisition. Per pkt., 5 15
Abbott's Improved Crown. A new and superior English variety. Per pkt., 10 . . 25

Peas (PISUM SATIVUM).

German, *Erbse.* — French, *Pois.* — Spanish, *Guisante.*

The Pea is a hardy annual plant, of great antiquity as a culinary vegetable, and is familiar in the domestic cookery of every country. There are numerous varieties; consequently they differ much in flavor and quality.

CULTURE. — Peas, for an early crop, should be sown as soon as the ground is in working condition. The soil for their reception should be light, dry, and well sheltered. Mild manure, such as leaf-mould, has a beneficial effect; but for many of the varieties the soil can hardly be too rich. For general crops, the ground should be well manured the previous year, which causes them to yield more abundantly. They are usually planted in double rows three or four feet apart, and covered to the depth of two and a half or three inches. This is the average depth, though some contend that greater depth prevents the premature decay of the vines. The height of the Pea depends much upon the moisture and richness of the ground. The method of planting Peas in the hills with Potatoes of an early variety has been found successful. In dry weather, soak the Peas a few hours before planting. Pour water into the drills, when the ground is dry, before sowing the seed, which will cause them to grow at once, should the season continue dry. A pint of the small-seeded sorts will sow a row about sixty feet in length; and the same quantity of larger varieties, being sown much thinner, will make a row of nearly a hundred feet. The crop should be gathered as it becomes fit for use. If even a few of the pods begin to ripen, young pods will not only cease to form, but those partly advanced will cease to enlarge. Peas, ordered by mail are subject to an extra charge of 8 cents per pint, for Postage.

per qt.

Early Dan O'Rourke (Pure). One of the earliest varieties in cultivation; pods well filled; of good size and quality; of the finest flavor; grows about three feet high . . 35
Early Emperor. This variety grows somewhat taller, and is a few days earlier, than the Prince Albert. The pods and peas are also somewhat larger. It is an abundant bearer; an excellent variety to come in after the above 30
Carter's First Crop, or Sutton's Ringleader. This is a new English variety, introduced by Carter & Co., of London. It has proved to be the earliest Pea grown; also very prolific; height two and a half feet. 25 cents per half-pint . . . 80
Hovey's Extra Early. Unequalled in earliness; very productive; two and a half feet 40

TO THE VEGETABLE GARDEN. 119

	per qt.
Early Kent. A very popular early Pea; fine pods; two and a half feet	30
Early Dillestone. This is undoubtedly one of the earliest Peas known; seven or eight days earlier than the Dan O'Rourke; fine flavor; good size, and one of the best	50
Drew's New Dwarf. This fine Pea is remarkable for its dwarf and branching growth, forming a bush one foot high and one foot broad; consequently, only about one plant to each foot of row is required. It is medium in earliness, and extremely productive, each plant producing, with good culture, forty or fifty pods of rich, fine-flavored, large Peas	1.00
McLean's Little Gem. A dwarf, prolific, green wrinkled Marrow; habit similar to Beck's Gem or Tom Thumb, and is a first early; a great acquisition; height one foot	90
McLean's Advancer. A dwarf green wrinkled Marrow of fine flavor; long pods, well filled up; very prolific; nearly as early as the Dan O'Rourke; a comparatively new variety	90
McLean's Princess Royal. A very prolific, long-podded, early variety, of fine sugary flavor; one foot high; pods large, well filled; very productive	50
McLean's Prolific. A dwarf early variety, coming in after the Dan O'Rourke; white wrinkled, with the Marrow flavor	50
Early Prince Albert. An old well-known variety; early and productive; three feet	30
Early Washington. A standard sort; very early and prolific; three feet	30
Early Hill. Large full pods; good bearer; three feet	30
Tom Thumb (Beck's Gem). Plants of remarkably low growth, seldom exceeding nine inches in height; stout and branching; pods about two and a half inches in length, containing five or six peas, which are of a creamy-yellow flavor; very productive. It may be cultivated in rows ten inches apart. ~ ~ stick required	75
Bishop's New Dwarf Long-podded. Stems about two feet high; pods nearly straight, almost cylindrical, containing six or seven white peas; very early; an abundant bearer, and of excellent quality	40
Carter's Surprise. A new variety of the Blue Surprise; pods large, very productive, and fine quality; an excellent market variety. Half-pint pkts., 25	50
Alliance, or Eugenie. Plant about three feet in height, with pale-green foliage; pods single or in pairs, three inches long, containing five or six peas. When ripe, the peas are of medium size, cream-colored, and much shrivelled and indented; the earliest white wrinkled Marrow Pea in cultivation	60
Climax, or Napoleon. Plants about three and a half feet high; of robust growth; pods three inches long, containing five or six peas. When ripe, these are of medium size, pale blue or olive, and, like Eugenie, much wrinkled and indented; the earliest of the blue wrinkled Marrow Peas	60
Champion of England. A standard sort, considered by all to be the best grown for general crop; of delicious flavor; very productive, and growing from three to four feet	40
Champion of Scotland. This we consider one of the best for main crop; of rich, buttery flavor; very productive, and of large size	50
Blue Imperial. This is considered by many as a standard sort; very hardy, and yields abundantly; of good quality and size	30
Missouri Marrowfat. This Pea is of American origin; very productive; of good quality, and well deserving of cultivation; about ten days earlier than the common Marrowfat; large pods; an excellent market variety, growing from three to five feet	30
Large White Marrowfat. An excellent and profitable sort; a little later than the preceding; pods large and full; very productive, growing from three to five feet	25
Black Eye Marrowfat. An excellent variety, growing about three feet high; pods large and full; a prolific bearer, and can be recommended as one of the best of the Marrowfat varieties	25
Victoria Marrowfat. A fine late variety; sweet, and of rich marrowfat flavor; very prolific; three to five feet	50
Dwarf Marrowfat. A very early sort, with large full pods; rich flavor; very productive; two feet	30
Veitch's Perfection. A new variety, of superior flavor and sweetness; large pod, and a great bearer; one of the best; five feet	50
Sugar Pea. Eatable pods or string pea; three feet	90

Pepper (CAPSICUM).

German, *Pfeffer.* — French, *Piment.* — Spanish, *Pimiento.*

Capsicum or Pepper is a tender annual, much esteemed for its seasoning qualities. In all the various methods of preparation, it imparts vitality and promotes digestion. It is extensively used for pickling.

CULTURE. — The plants are always propagated from seed. Sow in a hotbed, early in April, in shallow drills six inches apart, and transplant to the open ground when summer weather has commenced. The plants should be set in warm mellow soil, in rows sixteen inches apart, and about the same distance apart in the rows; or, in ordinary seasons, the following simple method may be adopted for a small garden, and will afford an abundant supply of peppers for family use: When all danger from frost is past, and the soil is warm and settled, sow the seeds in the open ground, in drills three-fourths of an inch deep, and fourteen inches apart; and, while growing, thin out the plants to ten inches apart in the rows. Cultivate in the usual manner, and the crop will be fit for use early in September.

AMATEUR CULTIVATOR'S GUIDE

per oz
Cayenne. The pods of this variety are quite small, cone-shaped, coral red when ripe, intensely acrid, and furnish the cayenne pepper of commerce. Per pkt., 10 . . 50
Cherry. The pods or fruit erect, nearly globular or cherry-form, and, at maturity, of a deep rich, glossy, scarlet color, remarkable for its intense piquancy. Per pkt., 10 . . 50
Squash. Fruit compressed, more or less ribbed; skin smooth and glossy; flesh thick, mild, and pleasant to the taste; the best variety for pickling alone. Per pkt., 10 . . 50
Sweet Mountain, or Mammoth. Similar to the preceding in form and color, but much larger; fine for pickling. Per pkt., 10 50
Sweet Spanish. Though one of the largest varieties, it is also one of the earliest; flesh sweet, mild, and pleasant; used for salads and pickling. Per pkt., 10 . . . 50

Potato (SOLANUM TUBEROSUM).

German, *Kartoffel.* — French, *Pomme de Terre.*

CULTURE. — A sandy loam is better calculated for the Potato than a heavy or very clayey soil. Though any soil will do, it must be observed that the roots produced in a light one are more dry and sweeter than those grown in a heavy soil. The finest Potatoes are grown in a new, light, rich loam. If the soil is heavy, the manure used should be composed of well-decayed leaves, horse-manure, and ashes, well blended and mixed together before using. A good crop can seldom be raised if this article is sparingly laid on. Sets for planting should be cut at least one week before planting, and spread out thin on a floor to dry. Another important consideration is, whether small tubers or large ones should be employed for making sets. Large tubers, however, are preferable, for the following reasons: In all plants, large buds tend to produce large shoots; and small or weak buds, the reverse. Now, the eyes of Potatoes are true buds, and in small tubers they are comparatively weak: they consequently produce weak shoots, and the crop from such is inferior to that obtained from plants originating from large tubers furnished with stronger eyes. The part of the Potato planted is not a matter of indifference. It was found, by an experiment made in the garden of the Horticultural Society, that sets taken from the points of the tubers yielded at the rate of upwards of three tons per acre more than was obtained from employing the opposite end of the tubers.

Potatoes are usually planted either in hills or ridges, the former method being the most common in this country. As soon as the plants are fairly started above the surface, hoeing and surface stirring should be commenced. The earth should gradually be drawn about the hills, or along the ridges, at each successive hoeing, and every encouragement given to the side-roots to extend themselves; for, nearly at their extremities, the tubers are formed: so that deeply stirring the ground between the hills or ridges tends to their extension. But this treatment must not be carried beyond a certain stage in the growth of the plant, or after the tubers have reached a considerable size, as the extremities of the roots might be seriously injured. In the preservation of Potatoes, it is of the first importance that they be excluded from light. In a state of complete darkness, they should, therefore, be placed, the day they are taken out of the ground. Drying has a bad effect on the skin of the Potato.

per bush.
Early Handsworth. A new variety lately received from England, which is believed to be the earliest of any in cultivation; superior either for forcing, or culture in the open ground. Dwarf and prolific 6.00
Early Stevens. A variety which originated in Northern Vermont. Very early and productive; tubers of medium size, roundish; flesh white, of excellent flavor. A superior market variety 2.50
Early Sovereign. A favorite early variety, of excellent quality; very productive, and a good keeper 3.00
Extra Early White. An early and well-known variety. Very productive, and of good flavor 2.50
Early Wendall. One of the largest of the early. Very productive, of uniformly good quality; keeps well; one of the best for general cultivation 2.50
Jackson White. Flesh perfectly white when cooked, remarkably dry, mealy, farinaceous, and well-flavored. A good keeper, commands the highest market-price, and, every thing considered, must be classed as one of the best, and recommended for general cultivation 2.00
Dalmahoy. A new variety; from Ireland. A handsome medium-sized Potato, very flowery, and of good flavor. Prolific, good keeper, and, all things considered, one of the best for general cultivation 3.00
Davis's Seedling. For general cultivation, this variety is probably one of the most profitable sorts known, as it yields abundantly, even with ordinary cultivation. It is of good quality and fine flavor; flesh nearly white, slightly tinged with pink when cooked . 2.00
Goodrich's Early. One of the largest and earliest varieties; two weeks earlier than the Jackson White, and one of the most productive, — two hundred and fifty bushels having been grown to the acre. Per pk., 1.50 . . . . 3.00
Goodrich's Garnet Chili. This variety is healthy, yields abundantly, and is greatly superior to many sorts for table use, and might be profitably grown for farm purposes . 2.00
Cuzco. White flesh, good size and flavor. A most abundant bearer; keeps well; good for a general crop 2.00
Calico. A seedling of the Garnet Chili, a little earlier than that variety; has a firm, crisp flesh; cooks white and dry 3.00
New White Peach-blow. A decided improvement upon the well-known Jersey Peach-blow. Flesh white, floury, of most excellent quality. Cannot be too strongly recommended; a first-rate market variety 2.00

Above prices subject to variation.

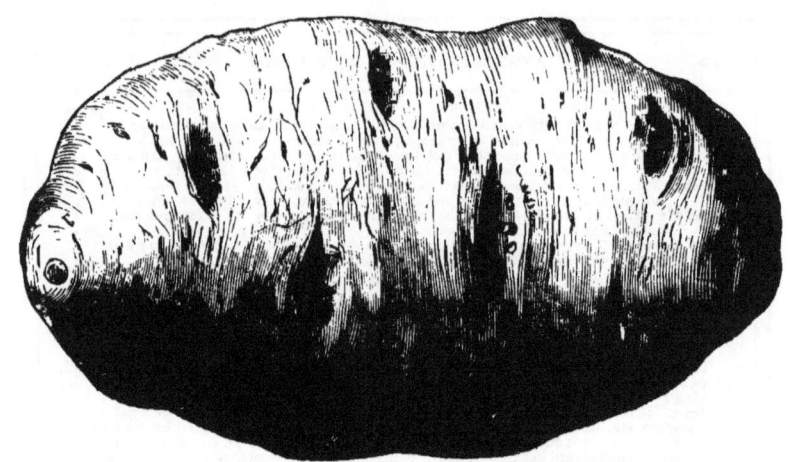

POTATO CLIMAX. See page 142.

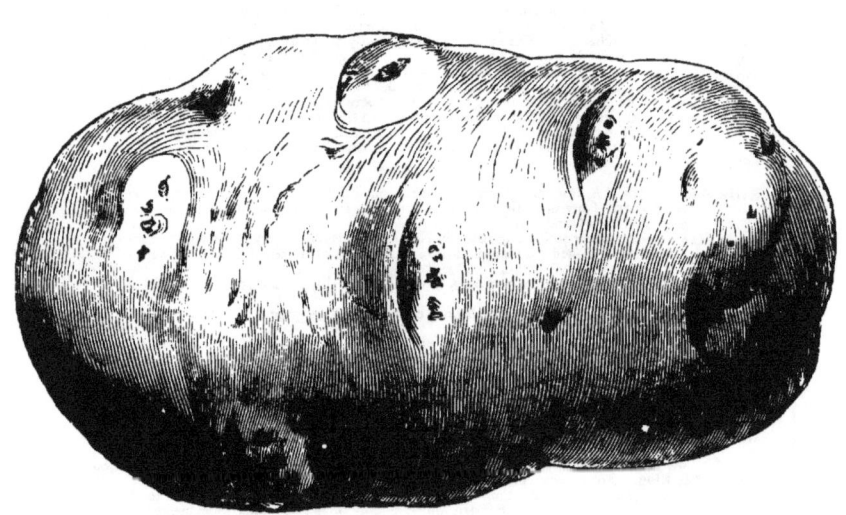

POTATO EARLY ROSE. See page 143.

Pumpkin (CUCURBITA PEPO).

German, *Kurbis.* — French, *Courge.* — Spanish, *Calabasa.*

We cannot think of admitting this vegetable into the precincts of a garden where there are Cucumbers, Melons, and others of similar class. It would mix with and contaminate the quality of the more valuable sorts; besides, they would occupy more space than most could allow, as many of the varieties attain enormous size.

CULTURE. — Pumpkins are not so particular in regard to soil as Melons or Cucumbers, but, in other respects, are cultivated in a similar manner, though on a much larger scale. They are generally raised on cultivated farms, between hills of Indian Corn, and may be planted with success in fields, by themselves.

                                             per oz.

Cheese, Medium-sized. One of the best for cooking purposes. Per pkt., 5 . . . 10
Large Yellow. Grows to a large size; better adapted for feeding purposes than for cooking. Per pkt., 5. Per lb., 40.
Mammoth. A very large, coarse-growing variety. Per pkt., 10 40

Radish (RHAPHANUS SATIVUS).

German, *Rettig Radies.* — French, *Radis, Rave, Petite Rave.* — Spanish, *Rabano.*

The Radish is a hardy annual plant, much esteemed for its grateful relish, and is extensively cultivated for its roots. Its excellence consists in being succulent, mild, crisp, and tender; and the roots should be eaten before they are overgrown, which makes them tough and thready. The seed-pods are excellent for pickling if gathered while young and green.

CULTURE. — For early crops, sow in spring, as soon as the ground can be worked, in light rich soil; for later crops, a deep, moist soil is preferable. Sow the seed thinly in drills, covering them with about a quarter of an inch of fine earth. If space is limited, the seed may be sown with Onions or Lettuce; they are said to be much less affected by the maggot if grown with the former. The plants should be frequently and copiously watered in dry weather, which tends to their rapid growth, thus securing its excellent qualities. For very early use, sow on gentle hotbeds.

                                             per oz.

Early Short-top Long Scarlet. Roots long, growing partly out of the ground, of a beautiful deep pink color; flesh white, transparent, crisp, and of good flavor. Grows quick; standard sort for marketing or private use. Per pkt., 5 . . . 10
Scarlet Turnip. A very early variety, deserving general cultivation on account of its rich color, crisp and tender qualities; should be used while young. Per pkt., 5 . . 15
White Turnip. Bulb similar to the preceding. Skin white; flesh white and semi-transparent. Some days later than the scarlet. Per pkt., 5 15
Scarlet Olive-shaped. In the form of an olive, terminating in a very slim top-root. Skin fine scarlet; neck small; flesh rose-colored, tender, and excellent. Early, and well adapted for forcing or general crop. Per pkt., 5 15
Long Salmon. A fine variety, in size and form similar to the Early Short-top Long Scarlet, but is a paler red; coming in a few days later. Per pkt., 5 15
Black Spanish. One of the latest as well as the the hardiest of the Radishes, and is considered an excellent sort for winter use. Large size; color black; of firm texture. To keep well, should be packed in sand, Per pkt., 5 15
Long White Chinese. Skin white, and of fine texture; flesh fine-grained, crisp, and very good flavored. Its season the same as the preceding. Per pkt., 10 . . . 30
Rose-colored China Winter. Size full medium; skin comparatively fine, and of a bright rose-color; flesh firm, and rather piquant. A very late variety. Per pkt., 10 . 30
New French Breakfast. A new quick-growing variety. Oval form; color scarlet, tipped with white; fine flavored. Very ornamental in appearance: much esteemed by the French. Excellent for forcing. Per pkt., 15 20

Rhubarb (RHEUM HYBRIDUM.)

German, *Rhubarber.* — French, *Rhubarbe.* — Spanish, *Ruibarbo Bastardo.*

CULTURE. — Rhubarb succeeds best in deep, somewhat retentive soil. The richer its condition, and the deeper it is stirred, the better. Sow in drills an inch deep. Thin out to six inches apart. In the fall, trench a piece of ground, and manure it well; then transplant the young plants into it three feet apart each way. Cover with leaves or litter the first winter, and give a dressing of coarse manure every fall. To procure an immediate crop, plant roots which are already grown.

                                             per oz.

Victoria. A large variety; one of the best for general use. Per pkt., 5 . . . 15
Linnæus. Large, tender, and fine-flavored. Per pkt., 5 25
Downing's Mammoth. Extra large, tender and fine. Per pkt., 10 . . . 25
Prince Albert. An early variety; superior quality. Per pkt., 10 25
Champagne. New large scarlet; very tender. Per pkt., 10 25
Cahoon's Mammoth. Very large. Per pkt., 10 25

Salsify, or Oyster Plant (TRAGOPOGON PORRIFOLIUS).

German, *Bocksbart.* — French, *Salsifis.* — Spanish, *Ostra vegetal.*

The Salsify is a hardy biennial plant, and is principally cultivated for its roots, which are long and tapering, and, when grown in good soil, measure twelve or fourteen inches in length. It is considered wholesome and nutritious. When cooked, the flavor resembles that of the oyster, and is a good substitute for it: whence the popular name.

CULTURE. — This plant succeeds best in a light well-enriched soil, which, previous to sowing, should be stirred to the depth of twelve or fourteen inches. Sow the seed in drills half an inch deep, and ten inches apart, early in the spring. Thin them out, when an inch high, to four or six inches apart. Keep the ground clear of weeds, giving them the general culture of carrots. They are perfectly hardy, and may remain out all winter. Store a quantity for winter's use, packed in earth or sand. Those remaining in the ground should be dug before commencing growth in spring.

per oz.
Salsify, or Oyster Plant. Per pkt., 10 25

Scorzonera, or Black Salsify (SCORZONERA HISPANICA).

German, *Schwarzwurzel.* — French, *Scorzonere.* — Spanish, *Escorzonera.*

per oz.
Cultivated like the common Oyster Plant, which it much resembles in its mode of growth. It is also prepared for the table in the same manner. Per pkt., 10 . . . 25

Sea Kale (CRAMBE MARITAMA).

German, *Seekohl Meerkohl.* — French, *Crambe Maritime.* — Spanish, *Breton de mar.*

This plant is found growing on the seacoast of Europe, particularly in England. It is closely related to the Cabbage, and can be obtained with very little trouble. The mode of dressing this vegetable for the table is the same as that for Asparagus, which it much resembles.

CULTURE. — The seeds may be sown in April, in drills an inch and a half deep, and fourteen or sixteen inches asunder. The soil must be previously enriched, and thoroughly trenched. Let the plants remain until the following spring, then transplant them in rows three feet apart, and eighteen inches apart in the rows. The earth should be occasionally stirred when the rains have run the surface together. Late in the fall, cover the crowns of the plants with a few inches of earth, making a ridge over the rows about a foot and a half high. After the cutting is over in the spring, level the earth into trenches, adding a good coat of strong manure.

per oz.
Sea Kale. Per pkt., 10 30

Spinach (SPINACIA OLERACEA).

German, *Spinat.* — French, *Epinard.* — Spanish, *Espinaca.*

Spinach is very hardy, and consequently a very important vegetable for cold climates. It is extremely wholesome and palatable.

CULTURE. — Spinach is best developed and most tender when grown in rich soil. It should be heavily manured and deeply trenched. Sow early in March for summer crop, in drills, which method renders the cultivation and the gathering of the produce more convenient. Encourage the growth with frequent hoeing, which draws the moisture to the roots. For a succession, a few seeds of the summer varieties may be sown, at intervals of a fortnight, from April to August. Sow from the middle of August to the beginning of September, for the winter crop, in a light sandy soil, on raised beds, which enables it better to stand the severe frost. This, too, must be well manured, and deeply trenched. Scatter the seed thinly in drills as for the summer varieties, one to three inches deep, from twelve to eighteen inches apart, and cover them with the finest of the soil. Thin the plants as soon as they are strong enough to draw, leaving them about nine inches apart in the row. Two ounces of seed will plant five drills, each forty feet long.

per oz.
Round or Summer. Leaves large, thick, and fleshy; rounded at the ends; a little crimped; in general use for early planting. Per pkt., 5 10
Fall, or Prick.y. Leaves seven or eight inches long; halbert-shaped; thin in texture, and nearly erect; one of the hardiest, and most generally used for fall planting. Per pkt., 5 10
Lettuce-leaved. Leaves large, thick, dark green, and of superior quality; should be sown in the spring. Per pkt., 10 15
New Zealand. A large-growing variety, requiring a warm rich soil. Its superiority over other varieties consists in the fact that it grows luxuriantly, and produces leaves of the greatest succulency, in the hottest weather. Per pkt., 10 30
Flander's. A very hardy and productive variety, of superior quality. Per pkt., 5 . . 10

Squash (CUCURBITA MELO PEPO).

German, *Kurbiss.* — French, *Courge.* — Spanish, *Calabasa tontanera.*

The several varieties of the Squash are very useful in this and other warm climates, as they can be grown to perfection in the summer. It is in general use from June to August, and the late varieties the whole winter until May. It is extensively cultivated in this vicinity for the market.

CULTURE. — Any good enriched soil is adapted to the growth of the Squash. They only thrive well in a warm temperature, as all the varieties are tender annuals; and the seed should not be sown in spring until all danger from frost is past, and the ground is warm and thoroughly settled. The hills should be made from eight to ten inches in depth, manured well, and covered about three-fourths of an inch deep. Keep the earth about the plants loose and clean, removing the surplus vines from time to time, allowing not more than three plants to a hill. The custom of cutting or nipping off the leading shoots of the running varieties is now practised to some extent, with the impression that it both facilitates the formation of fruitful laterals and the early maturing of the fruit. Whether the amount of product is increased by the process, is not yet determined.

TO THE VEGETABLE GARDEN.

 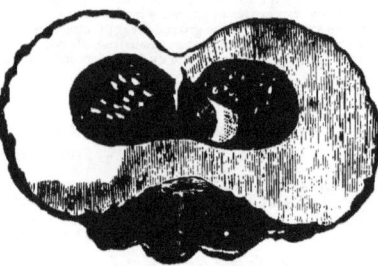

TURBAN SQUASH.   YOKOHAMA SQUASH.

	per oz.
Early Egg, or Apple. Skin yellowish-white; thin; flesh dry and well-flavored in its green state; fruit small. Per pkt., 5	20
Early Yellow Bush Scolloped. An early, flat, scollop-shaped sort; color yellow; flesh pale yellow, tolerably fine-grained and well-flavored; very productive. Per pkt., 5,	15
Early White Bush Scollopsk. This is a sub-variety of the Early Yellow Bush. The plant has the same dwarf habit, and the fruit is nearly of the same size and form. Per pkt., 5	15
Early Summer Bush Crookneck. This is generally esteemed as one of the finest of the summer varieties; color bright yellow; skin very warty, thin, and easily broken; flesh dry and well-flavored; should be used while young. Per pkt., 5 . .	15
Boston Marrow. Form ovate; skin thin; when ripe, bright orange; flesh rich salmon-yellow, very dry, fine-grained, and for sweetness and excellence unsurpassed; a very popular variety in the Boston market; a fall and winter variety. Per pkt., 5,	20

HUBBARD SQUASH.

Hubbard. This is a superior variety, and the best winter Squash known; flesh bright orange-yellow, fine-grained, very dry, sweet, and rich-flavored; keeps throughout the winter. Per pkt., 10	25
Fall or Winter Crookneck. The kind most generally cultivated in New England for fall and winter use; flesh salmon-red, very close-grained, dry, sweet, and fine-flavored; keeps well. Per pkt., 5	15
Canada Crookneck. A smaller variety of the preceding; ripens early, and, all things considered, is one of the best of the Crooknecks for general cultivation; very prolific. Per pkt., 5	15
Honolulu Nectarine. Productive, and of good quality; keeps well. Per pkt., 10 .	25
Valparaiso, or Lima Cocoanut. A large-growing winter variety; a good variety for fall and winter use. Per pkt., 5	20
Custard. Skin or shell creamy-white; flesh pale yellow, not remarkable for solidity or fineness of texture; one of the hardiest and most productive. Per pkt., 5 . .	20
Mammoth. This is the largest variety known, and, under favorable conditions of climate, and in rich soil, it often grows to the weight of from a hundred to a hundred and forty pounds. Per pkt., 25.	

Moore's Vegetable Cream. A new English variety of the Vegetable Marrow, introduced by Thomas Moore, Esq., Secretary of the Royal Horticultural Society, and recommended as a most valuable acquisition. Per pkt., 25.
Turban, or Turk's Cap. A superior late-growing variety. At the blossom-end, the fruit suddenly contracts to an irregular, cone-like point or termination; of a greenish color, striped with white, and thus in form and color somewhat resembling a turban; whence the name; flesh orange-yellow, thick, fine-grained, sugary, and well-flavored. (See engraving, p. 121.) Per pkt., 10 40
Yokohoma. A new variety from Japan; finest-grained of all the Squashes, with a rich Marrow flavor. (See engraving, p. 121.) Per pkt., 15 40

Tomato (Solanum Lycopersicum).

German, *Liebesapfel.* — French, *Tomate.* — Spanish, *Tomate.*

There is no vegetable on the catalogue that has obtained such popularity in so short a time as the one now under consideration. It may be served in various ways, and, in nearly every form, is highly esteemed.

Culture. — The Tomato is raised from seeds, which should be sown in a hotbed in March, or in pots in a warm window. They should be started as early and forwarded as rapidly as possible, whether by hotbed or open-air culture. When about two inches high, they should be transplanted, in single plants, to warm, light, rich soil. Water freely at the time of transplanting. Shelter from the sun for a few days, or until they are well established. If sown in the open ground, select a sheltered situation, pulverize the soil finely, and sow in drills. This may be done the last of March or first of April. When the plants are three or four inches high, transplant to where they are to remain, as before directed.

per oz.
Early Apple-shaped. A very early and productive variety; round, smooth, and of medium size. Per pkt., 10 30
Large Smooth Red. Fruit somewhat flattened, inclining to globular in its general outline; medium size; skin deep rich crimson; flesh bright pink or rose color; one of the best for general cultivation. Per pkt., 5 25
Lester's Perfected. Of recent introduction; regular form; large size; flesh firm and well-flavored. Per pkt., 10 40
Large Red. A very early variety, of large size; skin bright red; flesh pink or rose color. Per pkt., 5 25
Pear-shaped. A small, red, pyriform or pear-shaped variety; fine for preserving. Per pkt., 10 35
Large Yellow. A sub-variety of the Red Pear-shaped, with a clear, semi-transparent, yellow skin and yellow flesh; little used except for preserving and pickles. Per pkt., 5, 30
Red Plum. Remarkable for its symmetry, and for its uniform size. It is hardy and productive; used principally for preserving and pickles. Per pkt., 10 35
Yellow Plum. Similar to above, except in color, which is bright yellow. Per pkt., 10 . 40
Cherry. A small variety, growing in clusters. Per pkt., 10 40
Grape. A quite small red variety, growing in long clusters, like grapes, and useful for preserves; a new variety. Per pkt., 10 50
French Tree (*Tomato de Laye*). A new French variety, growing erect, in tree form; very ornamental, as well as large, and one of the best flavored. Per pkt., 10 . . . 1.50
Fejee Island. Fruit large, bright red, sometimes ribbed; often smooth and well-filled to the centre. Per pkt., 10 30
White Tomato. Similar to the Large Red, except in color. Per pkt., 10.
Early York. One of the very earliest varieties; of good size, productive, and excellent flavor. Per pkt., 10 40
Cook's Favorite. A comparatively new variety; medium size, oval form, fair skin, deep crimson, very productive, and excellent flavor; one of the best for general cultivation. Per pkt., 10 40
Tilden's New Seedling. This new and valuable variety was originated by Mr. Tilden, of Iowa. It is rather dwarf in its habit, and has distinct and peculiar foliage. The fruit is large, roundish, or roundish-oval, in shape; skin smooth, glossy, and of a bright-red color; flesh remarkably solid. It ripens early, bears abundantly, keeps a longer time after being gathered, and bears carriage better, than any other variety. Five hundred bushels were produced on an acre by Mr. Tilden. Per pkt., 10 50
Strawberry, or Ground Cherry (*Physalis Alkekengi*). This, though called a Tomato, is a distinct species; excellent for preserves, having a peculiar delicate strawberry flavor. Per pkt., 10 50

Turnip (Brassica Rapa).

German, *Steckrübe.* — French, *Navet.* — Spanish, *Nabo comun.*

This is a wholesome and useful plant both for man and beast, and highly deserving of cultivation. It has become in some countries an extensive field-crop.

Culture. — All the sorts are propagated by seeds, which should be sown where the plants are to remain, as they do not generally succeed well when transplanted. Sow as early as the ground will allow, in drills fourteen inches apart and half an inch in depth. The young plants should be thinned to five or six inches asunder. When the bottoms begin to enlarge, remove the earth gently to the depth of an inch and a half, and apply wood-ashes. The sowing for the winter's supply is made in August. One thing must be observed, — to have the ground always fresh dug before sow-

TO THE VEGETABLE GARDEN. 125

ing. Turnips must be harvested before severe freezing weather; for, though comparatively very hardy, few of the varieties will survive the winters of the Northern States in the open ground. Cut the leaves off to about half an inch from the bulb; collect the latter and put them in a dry pit or cellar; cover with straw and earth over all. Thus protected, they will keep fresh till February. The seed will retain its vitality for three years if kept in a dry place. If it is two years old, soak it in water twenty-four hours before sowing.

per oz.

Early White Flat Dutch, or Spring Turnip. Size medium; of quick growth, juicy, and of excellent quality; may be used either in spring or fall. Per pkt., 5 . . . 10
Early Snowball. Round; white; a fine early variety. Per pkt., 5 10
White-top, Strap Leaf. This is an early variety, which is fast taking the place of the old early Dutch; considered one of the best for market, or table use. Per pkt., 5 . 10
Purple-top, Strap Leaf. This variety has the form and character of the White-top, Strap Leaf, except in color. These two kinds are the best for spring or fall sowing, and for all garden culture, where they may be grown fair and free from worms, if not sown too early in the fall; flesh fine-grained, and rich and buttery flavored. Per pkt., 5 10
Yellow Malta. A beautiful, very symmetrical, small-bulbed, early variety; skin very smooth, bright orange-yellow; flesh pale yellow, fine-grained, and well-flavored. Per pkt., 5 10
Yellow Aberdeen. A hardy and productive variety; flesh pale yellow, tender, and sugary; keeps well. Per pkt., 5 10
Early Yellow Dutch. A variety similar to the preceding, and is a good garden variety. Per pkt., 5 10
Orange Jelly. A superior variety, of quick growth and fine flavor; flesh bright yellow. Per pkt., 5 10
Robertson's Golden Stone. Smooth and symmetrical; skin bright yellow; flesh firm, sweet, and well-flavored; remarkably hardy, and keeps well; one of the best for winter use. Per pkt., 5 10
Large White Norfolk. A sub-variety of the Common Flat Turnip; grows to a large size; flesh white and coarse-grained, but sweet. Per pkt., 5 10
Long White Tankard. This variety is recommended for its earliness and productiveness, but must be considered a field rather than a table variety. Per pkt., 5 . . . 10
Red Top Tankard. Similar to above, except in color. Per pkt., 5 . . . 10
Long White, or Cow Horn. An excellent variety; grows quickly to a good size; flesh white, fine-grained, and sweet. It keeps well, and is esteemed by many the best of all for culinary purposes; to have it keep well, gather before severe frosts. Per pkt., 5 10
Long White French, or Sweet German. One of the very best for winter or spring use, either for the table or for feeding stock. The flesh is firm, sweet, and of excellent flavor; none better for keeping; should be sown in June. Per pkt., 5 . . 10

RUTA-BAGA, OR SWEDE TURNIP.

Skirving's Purple-top. This is a superior variety, hardy and productive; flesh yellow, of solid texture, sweet and well-flavored. It is a good keeper. Per pkt., 5 . . . 10
Early Stubble Swede. This is recommended for its quick growth, and is well adapted for late sowing. Flesh firm, and well-flavored; very productive. Per pkt., 5 . . 10
White's Eclipse, or Hybrid. A comparatively new variety, and excellent for early feeding purposes. Large size, and well-flavored. Per pkt., 5 10
Laing's Improved Purple-top. A superior variety, hardy and productive. Flesh yellow, solid, and well-flavored; one of the best. Per pkt., 5 10

AROMATIC, POT, AND SWEET HERBS.

The generality of Aromatic, Pot, and Sweet Herbs, may be raised from seed sown early in spring. As only a small quantity of these are necessary for family use, they may occupy a corner by themselves. They thrive best in a mellow, free soil, and care should be exercised to harvest them at the proper time. The greater part of the following-named Herbs are perennial, and will multiply from the seed they drop, or from partings from the roots. The offsets, roots, or young plants, thus raised, should be planted at suitable distances from each other. The beds should be kept free from weeds; and, as the herbs come into flower, cut them on a dry day, and spread them in a shady place to dry for use. The best method for preserving them is to rub them through a sieve when thoroughly dry, and pack them in tin boxes. Be careful to put them in a dry place. Price, per pkt., 10; by the ounce on application.

Angelica.	Coriander.	Pennyroyal.
Anise.	Corn Salad.	Pot Marigold.
Balm, Lemon.	Cumin.	Rosemary.
Basil, Sweet.	Camelina.	Rue.
Borage.	Dandelion.	Sage.
Bene Plant.	Dill.	Saffron.
Burnet.	French Sorrel.	Summer Savory.
Cardoon.	Hyssop.	Sweet Marjoram.
Caraway.	Horehound.	Sweet Fennel.
Chervil.	Lavender.	Thyme.
Chiccory.		

VEGETABLE & AGRICULTURAL SEEDS, &c.

PRICES OF SOME LEADING ARTICLES BY THE POUND OR BUSHEL.

	per bush.
Beans.	
Early Mohawk	$8.00
Early China	7.00
Early Yellow Six-weeks	8.00
Early Valentine	9.00
White Marrow	6.00
Horticultural Pole	9.00
Indian Chief	14.00
Large Lima	4.00
Case-knife	12.00
Dutch Runners	12.00
Beets.	per lb.
Early Bassano	2.00
Early Blood Turnip	1.50
Long Blood	1.50
White Sugar	.75
Mangel Wurzel	.75
Mangel Wurzel, Yellow Globe	.75
Cabbage.	per lb.
Early York	2.50
Early Oxheart	3.00
Early Wakefield	5.00
Mason's Early Drumhead	6.00
Stone Mason Drumhead	6.00
Winningstadt	5.00
Large Drumhead (American)	4.00
Large Drumhead (imported)	2.00
Premium Flat Dutch (American)	5.00
Green Globe Savoy (American)	4.00
Red Dutch	4.00
Carrot.	per lb.
Early Horn	1.50
Long Orange	1.50
Large White Field	1.00
Long Yellow Altringham	1.25
Cauliflower.	
Half-early Paris	per lb. 30.00
Le Normand	per oz. 2.50
Large White French	per lb. 8.00
Walcheren	" 14.00
Celery.	
White Solid	per lb. 4.00
Red Solid	" 4.00
Boston Market	per oz. .50
	per lb.
Chiccory (for coffee)	1.25
	per lb.
Chinese Sugar-cane	.50
Corn.	per one hundred ears.
Darling's Early. Shelled, 6.00 bush.	4.00
Red-cob Sweet. Shelled, 5.00	4.00
Assylum Sweet. Shelled, 8.00	5.00
Stowell's Evergreen. Shelled, 6.00	5.00
Burr's Improved Sweet. Shelled, 6.00	5.00
Cucumber.	per lb.
Early Cluster	1.50
Early Short Prickly	1.50
Early White-spined	2.00
Long Green	2.00
Kohl Rabi.	per lb.
Early White	4.00
Purple	3.00
Lettuce.	per lb.
Early Silesia	3.00
Drumhead	3.00
White Cabbage	4.00
Large India	5.00
Butter	4.00

	per lb.
Melon (Water).	
Mountain Sweet	$1.50
Black Spanish	2.00
Mountain Sprout	2.00
Melon (Musk).	per lb.
Nutmeg	1.50
Jenny Lind Early	2.00
Green Citron	1.50
Large Yellow Musk	1.50
Christiana	3.00
Large Cantelope	1.50
Onion.	per lb.
Large Yellow	6.00
Yellow Danvers	6.00
White Portugal	7.00
Large Red	6.00
Parsnip.	per lb.
White Dutch	.80
Parsley.	per lb.
Extra Curled	1.50
Peas.	per bush.
Early Dan O'Rourke	7.50
Early Emperor	6.00
Early Kent	7.00
Blue Imperial	6.50
Champion of England	10.00
Missouri Marrowfat	5.00
White Marrowfat	4.50
Black-eyed Marrowfat	4.50
Victoria Marrowfat	9.00
Pumpkin.	per lb.
Large Cheese	.75
Large Yellow Field	.40
Radish.	per lb.
Scarlet Turnip	1.25
Early Olive-shaped	1.25
Long Scarlet	1.00
Spinach.	per lb.
Summer	.75
Winter, Prickly	.75
Salsify.	per lb.
Salsify	2.00
Squash.	per lb.
Early White Bush	1.25
Summer Crookneck	1.25
Winter Crookneck	1.50
Boston Marrow	2.00
Hubbard	2.00
Tomato.	per lb.
Early Red, or Apple	4.00
Large Smooth Red	3.00
Lester's Perfected	4.00
Large Yellow	4.00
Pear shaped	4.00
Turnip.	per lb.
Early White Dutch	1.00
Extra Early White-top	1.00
Red-top, Strap-leaf	1.00
White-top	1.00
Long White French	1.00
Long Yellow French	1.00
Golden Ball	1.00
Yellow Aberdeen	1.00
Yellow Swedish, or Ruta-baga	.75
Purple-top Ruta-baga	1.00
Laing's Improved Ruta-baga	1.00
White Sweet German	1.00
Fine American Ruta-baga	1.00

TOBACCO SEED.

Connecticut Seed-leaf. Extra. Per oz., 35	per lb.	$3.50
Havana True (imported). Per pkt., 20	per oz.	1.00
Maryland. Per pkt., 10	"	.50
Virginia. Per pkt., 5	"	.50

COMPLETE ASSORTMENTS OF VEGETABLE SEEDS,

FOR ONE YEAR'S SUPPLY,

Selected by us with particular regard to the wants of every purchaser, and containing only the most popular and approved sorts, such as we can confidently recommend, and such as we are sure will give the most perfect satisfaction.

These Collections are always on hand, and can be sent by express, or No. 5 by mail, at the shortest notice, upon receipt of the price named.

ARTICLES.	No. 1, for $20, contains	No. 2, for $10, contains	No. 3, for $5, contains	No. 4, for $3, contains	No. 5, for $2, contains
Peas. Early Dan O'Rourke	3 quarts	3 pints	1 pint	½ pint	packet
Dwarf Blue Imperial	2 quarts	1 quart	1 pint	½ pint	
Champion of England	2 quarts	1 quart	1 pint	½ pint	packet
Dwarf Marrowfat	2 quarts	1 quart	1 pint	½ pint	
Beans. Large Lima (pole)	1 quart	1 pint	½ pint	packet	
Horticultural (pole)	1 quart	1 pint	½ pint		
Early Long Yellow Six-weeks	1 quart	1 pint	½ pint	packet	
Early China	2 quarts	1 quart	½ pint	packet	
Beets. Early Blood Turnip	2 ounces	1 ounce	½ ounce	packet	packet
Long Blood	4 ounces	2 ounces	½ ounce	½ ounce	
Early Bassano	2 ounces	1 ounce	½ ounce	packet	packet
Brussels Sprouts	1 ounce	½ ounce	packet	packet	
Broccoli. Early Purple Cape	½ ounce	packet	packet	packet	
Carrots. Early Horn	2 ounces	1 ounce	½ ounce	packet	
Long Orange	4 ounces	2 ounces	1 ounce	packet	packet
Cauliflower. Half-early Paris	¼ ounce	packet	packet	packet	packet
Cabbage. Early York	1½ ounces	½ ounce	¼ ounce	packet	packet
Winningstadt	1½ ounces	½ ounce	packet	packet	
Premium Flat Dutch	1½ ounces	½ ounce	¼ ounce	packet	packet
Red Dutch	½ ounce	packet	packet	packet	
Celery. Seymour's White Solid	1 ounce	½ ounce	packet	packet	packet
Corn. Darling's Early	1 quart	1 pint	½ pint	packet	
Large Twelve-rowed Sugar	2 quarts	1 quart	1 pint	packet	
Stowell's Evergreen	1 quart	1 pint	½ pint	packet	
Cress. Fine Curled	2 ounces	1 ounce	½ ounce	½ ounce	packet
Cucumber. Extra Early Russian	1 ounce	½ ounce	¼ ounce	packet	
Early White Spine	2 ounces	1 ounce	½ ounce	packet	packet
Leek. London Flag	1 ounce	½ ounce	¼ ounce	packet	
Endive. Green Curled	1 ounce	½ ounce	¼ ounce	packet	
Lettuce. Early Curled Silesia	1 ounce	½ ounce	¼ ounce	packet	packet
Early Tennisball	1 ounce	½ ounce	packet	packet	packet
Large India	½ ounce	¼ ounce	packet		
Musk-melon. Nutmeg	1 ounce	½ ounce	¼ ounce	¼ ounce	packet
Green Citron	2 ounces	1 ounce	½ ounce	¼ ounce	packet
White Japan	packet	packet	packet		
Water-melon. Mountain Sweet	2 ounces	1 ounce	½ ounce	¼ ounce	packet
Citron (for preserves)	½ ounce	packet	packet		
Onion. Yellow Danvers	2 ounces	1 ounce	½ ounce	packet	packet
Large Red Wethersfield	2 ounces	1 ounce	½ ounce	¼ ounce	packet
Okra. Long Green	2 ounces	1 ounce	½ ounce	packet	
Parsley. Double Curled Extra	1 ounce	½ ounce	¼ ounce	packet	packet
Parsnip. Large Dutch	4 ounces	2 ounces	1 ounce	½ ounce	packet
Student	packet	packet	packet		
Pepper. Large Squash	½ ounces	¼ ounce	packet	packet	packet
Radish. Long Scarlet Short-top	3 ounces	1½ ounces	1 ounce	½ ounce	packet
Olive-shaped	3 ounces	1½ ounces	½ ounce	¼ ounce	packet
Salsify	3 ounces	1½ ounces	½ ounce	¼ ounce	packet
Spinach. Round, or Summer	6 ounces	3 ounces	1 ounce	½ ounce	packet
Prickly, or Winter	6 ounces	3 ounces	1 ounce	½ ounce	
Squash. Early Bush, or Scollop	1 ounce	½ ounce	packet	packet	packet
Hubbard	2 ounces	1 ounce	½ ounce	packet	packet
Boston Marrow	2 ounces	1 ounce	½ ounce	packet	
Winter Crookneck	1 ounce	½ ounce	packet	packet	
Tomato. Early Red	1 ounce	½ ounce	¼ ounce	packet	packet
Large Red Smooth	1 ounce	½ ounce	¼ ounce	packet	packet
Erect, or Tree	packet	packet	packet		
Turnip. Red Top Strap-leaved	4 ounces	2 ounces	1 ounce	½ ounce	packet
Long White French	2 ounces	1 ounce	½ ounce		
Sweet German	2 ounces	1 ounce	½ ounce	¼ ounce	packet
Egg-plant. Large Round Purple	½ ounce	¼ ounce	packet	packet	packet
Sweet and Pot Herbs.					
Sweet Marjoram	packet	packet	packet	packet	packet
Caraway	packet	packet	packet	packet	
Summer Savory	packet	packet	packet		
Sage	packet	packet	packet	packet	packet
Thyme	packet	packet			
Rosemary	packet	packet			

GRASS SEEDS.

Agrostis Stolonifera. (Creeping Bent Grass.) This variety is well adapted for moist places, which sometimes overflow; fine for lawns or permanent pastures on account of its growing earlier and later than other varieties . . . . . per bushel, $6.00
— **Vulgaris.** (Red Top.) This valuable grass is well known throughout the Northern and Middle States, generally sown with clover and Timothy. Market price. .
per lb.
Alopecurus Pratensis. (Meadow Fox-tail.) A very useful variety for pastures; closely resembling Timothy, but may be distinguished from it as having one palea only; grows quickly and very early, succeeding best in meadow land 80
Anthoxanthum Odoratum. (Sweet-Scented Vernal Grass.) This is one of the earliest spring, as well as one of the latest in the autumn, and is almost the only grass that is fragrant. It yields but a moderate crop, yet it should be planted freely on account of its quality for feeding green, or cut for hay 1.10
Avena Flavescens. (Yellow Oat Grass.) Suitable for dry meadows and pastures; should be cultivated with other grass: Sweet Vernal and Crested Dog's-tail are best adapted; useful for fodder 75
Bromus Schraderi. (Rescue Grass) A very valuable variety for general cultivation, especially for dry grounds, yielding two crops each season; is much liked by cattle in green state. Native of Australia 1.25
Cynosurus Cristatus. (Crested Dog's-tail.) A fine variety for permanent pastures or lawns; forms a close turf, rather fine foliage; succeeding best on dry and gravelly soils; the seed-stocks are dry and wiry, but the foliage is much liked by cattle . . .80
Dactylis Glomerata. (Orchard Grass.) This is one of the most valuable and widely-known of all the pasture-grasses. Its rapidity of growth, the luxuriance of its aftermath, and its power of enduring the cropping of cattle, commend it highly. It should be fed close to prevent it running to seed, when it loses a large proportion of its nutritive matter. All kinds of stock eat it greedily when green; well adapted for growing under trees . . . . per bushel 3.50
per lb.
Festuca Duriuscula. (Hard Fescue.) A fine variety, suitable for lawns and pastures; growing well in most any kind of soil, particularly dry soils; fine foliage, adapted for sheep-grazing; should be planted with Festuca Pratensis and Poa Trivialis. . .50
— **Pratensis.** (Meadow Fescue.) One of the most common of the Fescue grasses, said to be the Randall grass of Virginia. An excellent pasture-grass, forming a very considerable portion of the turf of old pastures and fields. In addition to its qualities as a pasture-grass, it is said to make a very good quality of hay; much relished by cattle. Thriving in any soil 60
— **Ovina.** (Sheep Fescue) This is much used by the English for sheep-pastures; yields but a moderate crop, and is only recommended for sheep-pastures, as they are very fond of it. It improves the flavor of mutton very much 60
— **Loliacea.** (Darnel Spike Fescue.) This variety is nearly allied to the tall Fescue, and possesses much the same qualities. It grows naturally in moist rich meadows, forming a good permanent pasture-grass 80
Holcus Lanatus. (Meadow Soft Grass.) This beautiful grass grows best in moist fields and peaty soil; productive, and of easy cultivation, but cattle are not very fond of it; only recommended for planting on poor peaty soil, where other grasses will not succeed. .75
Lolium Perenne. (English Rye Grass.) A very valuable variety for permanent pasture; best adapted for moist land. Very nutritious . . . . per bushel, 5.00
— **Italicum.** (Italian Rye Grass.) This variety has been lately introduced. Said to be superior to the perennial Rye Grass; excellent for early sheep-feeding. per bushel, 5.00
Phleum Pratense. (Timothy or Herds-grass.) This well-known variety is highly recommended for hay-crops. Thriving best on moist peaty or loamy soils of medium tenacity. It grows very readily, and yields large crops. It should be cut in the blossom, or directly after: it is much relished by horses and cattle, while it possesses a large amount of nutritive matter in comparison with other grasses. Market price.
Poa Trivialis. (Rough-stalked Meadow Grass.) This is a valuable grass to cultivate in moist, sheltered soils, possessing very considerable nutritive qualities; exceedingly relished by cattle, horses, and sheep; when sown with other varieties, it yields more than an average crop . . . . per lb .80
— **Nemoralis.** (Wood Meadow Grass.) This is certainly to be classed among the good shaded pasture-grasses, furnishing a fine succulent and very nutritive herbage which cattle are very fond of; much recommended for pleasure-grounds, particularly under trees . . . . per lb. .75
— **Pratensis.** (Kentucky Blue Grass, or June Grass.) This is an early grass, very common in the soils of New England and the West, and highly recommended for lawns; grows well in dry gravelly soils; very nutritive for all kinds of grazing-stock. Per bushel, from $4.00 to $8.00.

GRASS SEED FOR LAWNS.

One of the most pleasing features connected with a garden is a well-kept lawn; but, to secure this most desirable object, much depends upon the selection of such grasses as will present a fresh and luxuriant verdure throughout the season. For this purpose, a mixture of several kinds of the finer grasses is most suitable. These we can supply ready mixed, of the best sorts, and proper proportions of each. The quantity usually sown is two bushels per acre. Per bushel, $6.00; 30 cents per qt. Extra fine French, best adapted for dry soil, 30 cents per qt.

GRAIN AND GRASS SEEDS.

The prices of these are variable; but purchasers may depend on having them at the lowest market rates and of the best quality.

Barley.	Hungarian Grass.	Fowl Meadow Grass.
Bedford Oats.	Chinese Sugar Cane.	Orchard Grass.
Buckwheat.	Canada Corn.	Perennial Rye Grass.
Spring Wheat.	Dutton "	Meadow Foxtail Grass.
Winter Wheat.	King Philip Corn.	Sweet Vernal Grass.
Spring Rye.	Herds Grass, or Timothy.	Italian Rye Grass.
Winter Rye.	Northern Red-top Grass.	Northern Red Clover.
Broom Corn.	Southern Red-top Grass.	Southern Red Clover.
Field Peas.	Rhode-Island Bent Grass.	White Dutch Clover.
Spring Vetches.	Fine-top, or Dew-grass.	Lucerne, or French Clover.
Flax-seed.	Millet.	Kentucky Blue Grass, ext. clean.

FRUIT SEEDS.

Apple Seed	lb. $0.50	Peach Pits	bush.	$2.00
Cherry Pits	" .50	Plum Pits	lb.	.50
Currant Seed	oz. .75	Pear Seed	"	3.00
Gooseberry Seeds	" 1.25	Quince Seed	"	4.00
Grape (Hothouse)	" 1.00	Raspberry Seed	oz.	.75

STRAWBERRY SEED.

Saved from our large collection of over forty varieties, embracing all the best European and American kinds in cultivation. Mixed seed. Per pkt., $0.25.

ORNAMENTAL TREE SEEDS.

Norway Spruce (*Abies Excelsa*)		lb. $1.50	oz.	$0.20
European Silver Fir (*Abies Pectinata*)		" 1.50	"	.20
Norway Maple (*Acer Platanoides*)		" 1.50	"	.20
Sugar Maple (*Acer Saccharinum*)		" 1.50	"	.25
Tree of Heaven (*Ailanthus Glandulosa*)		" 2.50	"	.30
Shelbark (*Carya Alba*)			qt.	.25
Ornamental Thorn (*Cratægus Coccineus*)		lb. 1.25	oz.	.25
Burning Bush (*Euonymus Americana*)		" 3.00	"	.50
Salisburia (*Ginko Biloba*)			100 seeds,	5.00
European Mountain Ash (*Fraxinus Excelsior*)		lb. 1.25	oz.	.25
Red Cedar (*Juniperus Virginiana*)			" .75	.15
Scotch Larch (*Larix Europa*)			" 2.50	.25
Tulip Tree (*Liriodendron Tulipifera*)			" 2.00	.30
Magnolia (*Magnolia Acuminata*)			" 4.00	.40
Scotch Pine (*Pinus Sylvestris*)			" 2.00	.25
Austrian Pine (*Pinus Austriaca*)			" 3.00	.25
White Pine (*Pinus Strobos*)			" 4.00	.40
Yellow Locust (*Robinia Pseudo Acacia*)			" 1.00	.15
American Arbor Vitæ, clean seed (*Thuja Occidentalis*)			" 7.00	.60
American Elm (*Ulmus Americana*)			" 4.00	.40
Yellow Wood (*Virgilia Lutea*)			"	2.00

Many other varieties of Tree and Shrub Seeds can be supplied on seasonable application.

SEEDS FOR HEDGES.

Honey Locust, or Three-thorned Acacia (*Gleditschia Triacanthus*)	lb.	$0.75
Buckthorn (*Rhamnus Catharticus*)	"	1.25
Osage Orange (*Maclura Aurantiaca*)	"	1.25
American Arbor Vitæ (*Thuja Occidentalis*)	oz.	.50

CULINARY ROOTS, PLANTS, &c.

Asparagus Roots, Giant. One year old	hund.	$1.00
—— —— Two years old	"	1.50
Garlic	lb.	.40
Shallots. A species of onion, esteemed for its fine flavor	"	.40
Potato Onions. Early, and mild flavor	bush.	3.00
Top or Tree Onions. Valuable for pickling	"	6.00
Rhubarb. Myatt's Victoria. Very large; a popular variety	doz.	2.00
—— Myatt's Linnæus. Large, very tender, and excellent	"	2.00
—— Prince Albert. Early and fine	"	3.00
—— Downing's Mammoth. Extra large and tender	"	3.00
—— Cahoon's Mammoth. One of the largest; very tender	"	2.00
—— Champagne. Large; tender; fine flavor	"	3.00
Chinese Potato	"	1.00

Tomato, Cabbage, Cauliflower, Celery, Pepper, Sweet Potato, and Egg-Plants, &c., of different varieties, supplied, in their season by the hundred or thousand, at reasonable prices.

NOVELTIES AND SPECIALITIES

FOR 1867 AND 1868.

VEGETABLE SEEDS.

Bean.

per pkt.

Giant Wax. Recently introduced, and differing essentially from the old GERMAN WAX BEAN, being of a more robust growth and more productive. The pods are from six to nine inches in length, and from three-fourths to one inch in breadth; the beans, when ripe, are of a reddish color. Mr. A. L. FELTON, a highly successful vegetable-grower near Philadelphia, who has grown them for several seasons, estimates the yield at about one-half peck of pods to the pole, of three plants. The pods, when fit for use, are of a clear, waxy color, perfectly stringless, and, when cooked, are as tender as marrow, and truly delicious. . 25

Brussell Sprouts.

Dwarf Cabbage. A variety with a shorter stem, sprouts somewhat larger and closer set than the old variety 10

Beet.

Simon's Early. An improvement on other early kinds; and is now superseding the Bassano, being quite as early, and of a blood-red color; smooth and turnip-shaped. Considered a most valuable variety for the market . . . 10

Carter's Champion Mangel: This improved variety of Orange Globes is believed to be superior to any other sort, and to produce a greater weight per acre. Price, per oz., 10; per lb., 75.

Broccoli.

Carter's Summer. A new variety, with enormous, close, white heads, coming at a time when it will be most valuable, — between the late Broccoli, and the Cauliflower. This variety is very distinct from all other sorts in seeds, foliage, and heads . 25

Borecole, or Kale.

Abergeldie. A dwarf-curled Kale, of extreme beauty, good color, delicate mellow flavor, and as double as a fine curled Parsley. This is a valuable winter green, and will be found a very useful and extremely handsome garnish 25

Cabbage.

Foltler's Improved Brunswick. *The Earliest, Shortest-stemmed, and very best Drumhead yet offered.* The Boston market-gardeners all use it in preference to any other; and, to show how highly it is esteemed in this market, we will state that it sold readily at $5.00 per ounce the past season, and all were well satisfied that it is the best variety for either early or late planting. Every plant produces a good head, — when fully grown, weighing from twenty to thirty pounds, — and requiring only ordinary cultivation. The quality is excellent. Mr. JOHN STONE, of Marblehead, Mass., the originator of the well-known Stone-mason Drumhead, allows us to state that he considers it far superior to any Drumhead he has ever seen. He has raised good-sized heads the past season in eighty-five days from planting the seed. We warrant our stock the purest in the country. Five for $1.00 25

Early Schweinfurth. A very remarkable and valuable variety, both for earliness and large size; adapted chiefly for summer and autumn use. (See cut.) Per oz.. 50. 10

Early Pancalier Joulin Savoy. A very good variety, with a head of medium size, and very early; indeed, the earliest of all Savoys 10

per pkt.

Marblehead Mammoth Drumhead. The largest Cabbage in the world.
This (the Mammoth) is, without doubt, the largest variety of the Cabbage family in the world, being the result of the extreme of high culture. In form this variety differs, the head being sometimes nearly hemispherical, at other times nearly flat. Under high culture it is compact and hard. Its size is indeed *mammoth*, ranging from that of a half-bushel measure up to that of a two-bushel basket, and even larger. They have been grown, and, when stripped of all waste leaves, could not be got into a two-bushel basket, having a greater diameter by two inches! Mr. ALLEY, the originator of this Cabbage, has grown them measuring seventy inches, or nearly six feet in circumference, when measured around the solid head! The weight of these Cabbages is proportional to their size, *averaging, by the acre*, under the high culture of our Marblehead farmers, about thirty pounds a plant. The Cabbage that, for size, took the first premium of the Massachusetts Horticultural Society at the exhibition of 1860, was of this variety, weighing over forty pounds. Of the famous crop of Mr. SETH HATHAWAY, grown in 1856, the largest Cabbage weighed sixty-two pounds.
Cultivate in rows four feet apart, and allow about four feet between the plants. For early marketing, start in a hotbed: for winter use, plant in latitude of Boston by the 23d of May. Price, Mammoth Marblehead, $1.00 per oz. . 25
Cannon Ball. An early variety; round, and the hardest headed of all cabbages . . 25

Cauliflower.

Lemaitre. A fine variety of the half-early Paris Cauliflower, producing a large, firm head, very white, and of superior quality; much esteemed by the Paris market-gardeners; stem short 15
Boston Market. The seed of this celebrated Cauliflower was saved by one of the successful Boston market-gardeners, and can be relied upon as the best, in every respect, for family or market purposes 15

Carrot.

Improved White Green-Top Orthe. An improved variety of the white Belgium Carrot, with shorter and much larger roots; perfectly smooth, cylindrical, and tapering to a rather blunt point. It is easily pulled out, and yields very large crops . 10

Celery.

Boston Market. A favorite variety in the Boston market; remarkable for its tender, crisp, and succulent stems, and its peculiarly mild flavor. It is extensively cultivated by the market-gardeners around Boston, and surpasses any other variety for its great excellence 15

Cucumber.

General Grant. One of the newest and best varieties. It is perfect in form, solid, crisp, and most agreeable flavor; grows from twenty to thirty inches long; very hardy, and succeeds well in the open ground. It is a most desirable variety for exhibition or for the table 25
Bedfordshire Surprise. One of the most popular English varieties; black spine; growing from sixteen to twenty inches long; fine form; good flavor, and very solid; succeeds well in the open ground 25

Corn.

Crosby's Early Twelve-Rowed. The earliest variety of twelve-rowed sweet corn brought into Boston market, full kernelled, sweet, and delicious. Received the premium of the Massachusetts Horticultural Society, in 1867, as the best early corn. Cultivated almost exclusively by Boston market-gardeners 15
Early Dwarf Sugar. A very valuable sort for early use, and also for planting in succession. The kernel is sweet and tender, and white before maturity; dull yellowish-white, when ripe 10
Red Sweet. This is a new variety, produced by crossing the old red with the white. The producer says that it is superior to any other variety for the table, so tender that a person without teeth can eat it. It is also of large size, sweet, and mellow or fat. When in eating order it is pink, but turns to a bright red when dry. Should not be cooked until the ears are well filled. We have secured the entire stock of this rare novelty. 25

Corn Salad.

Striped-Leaved. A striped-leaved variety, quite a novelty for the kitchen-garden . . 15

Cotton.

Sea Island (Long Staple). A very showy plant, with handsome althea-like flowers, yellow, with maroon centre. Small pkts. 10

Egg Plant.

Pekin New Black. An entirely new and distinct kind, from China. The plant grows erect and handsome, attaining the height of two to three feet; with rich, dark, bronzy-purple foliage, very ornamental. The fruits are round, or globular, of a deep purple, almost black, weighing four to eight pounds each; skin, smooth and glossy. Exceedingly prolific, and as early as the long purple. The flesh is white, fine grained, and more delicate flavored than the old varieties. Specimens exhibited by us at the annual exhibition of the Massachusetts Horticultural Society, September, 1867, attracted great attention, and were awarded a prize . . . . 25 per pkt.

Lettuce.

Bossin. Said to be the best Cabbage Lettuce in cultivation; in shape, color, and quality, it resembles the Batavian Lettuce 25

Melons.

Aehapesnorricher. A handsome green-fleshed variety from Ionian Islands, of very fine flavor 25
Carter's Excelsior. An English variety, said to be one of the best green-fleshed sorts . 25
Turner's Scarlet Gem. A fine scarlet-fleshed variety, highly esteemed for growing in frames 25
Princess Alexandra. Another English variety. A new hybrid, of globular shape, very evenly quartered and netted; pale-green colored flesh, with very little pulp in the centre, delicate pine-apple flavor, highly recommended 25
Trentham Hall. An English variety, green-fleshed, sweet, suitable for cultivating in frames 25

Peas.

per qt.
Drew's New Dwarf. This is the greatest acquisition yet made, and has proved one of the most valuable introductions to the numerous variety of Peas. It grows only one foot high, branching profusely, and forming an erect, dense bush. The pea is of the largest size, of a bluish tinge, slightly shrivelled, and as sweet and delicious as the Champion of England, without the tough skin of that variety; medium early. It is very productive, and a most valuable and extra fine pea. A single row, planted one foot apart, will fill the row a foot wide and one foot high . . 1.00
Sutton's Ringleader. A new, extra early pea, imported from London, and introduced by Messrs. Sutton & Son as the earliest pea in England, and also as a very prolific variety 80
McLean's Little Gem. A dwarf, prolific, green, wrinkled marrow; habit similar to the very early Tom-Thumb Pea, and is a first early. This pea is a great acquisition. The chief fault hitherto in early peas has been want of flavor; but this valuable variety has all the sugary flavor of the late wrinkled peas, coupled with a first early pea. Height, one foot 90
McLean's Epicureans. A second early wrinkled marrow, of delicious flavor; fine large peas, in well-filled pods, and plenty of them; marked by the Royal Horticultural Society as being a very profuse bearer 1.00
McLean's Wonderful. This is recommended as the best dwarf late pea in cultivation, remarkable for its large, well-filled pods, fine, sugary flavor, and great productiveness. Height, two feet 80
Laxton's Prolific Early Long Pod. This valuable variety was raised by Thomas Laxton, of Stamford, England. Some pods (in a green state) were exhibited at Mark Lane, London, last June, averaging eleven and twelve peas in a pod; and they were pronounced by several eminent members of the London seed-trade to be an exceedingly fine variety. For a second early pea, there is no pea of a similar class in cultivation to equal it; and we feel every confidence that it will be in general cultivation in a very few years. The pea has the same habit and character as Dickson's favorite, excepting that the pods are nearly double the size. Price, per pkt., containing ½ pint, 50 cents 1.50

The following are extracts from some English testimonials:—
"I have also personally tested, and can confidently recommend, the new pea as a first-class second early variety." (Signed) M. MATHESON,
Gardener to Marquis of Exeter.

"I consider it decidedly an improvement upon all other early peas."
(Signed) GEO. ABBOTT,
One of the Committee of the Stamford Horticultural Society.

"I grow a great number of peas, but have seen none to be compared to Mr. Laxton's."
(Signed) C. CLARK.
Superintendent Stamford Horticultural Society Exhibitions.

The Peabody. A very dwarf, prolific, branching, late variety; of the Tom-Thumb habit; height, fifteen inches; good flavor, and very productive. The Peabody is a later variety than the Dwarf Waterloo, to which it forms a good succession. Per pkt., containing ½ pint, 50 cents 1.50

TO THE VEGETABLE GARDEN. 133

per qt.
Dwarf Waterloo, Late Branching Marrow. A dwarf variety of tall Royal Victoria or Waterloo Marrow; of Tom-Thumb habit; height, fifteen inches; the most valuable dwarf pea for general and late cropping ever offered; very dwarf, good flavor, and very productive. Per pkt., containing ½ pint, 50 cents 1.50
Carter's First Crop. This early variety is imported direct from Messrs. Carter & Co., London, who say it is the earliest pea in cultivation, an excellent bearer, and can be recommended for cultivation without sticks 80
Dickson's First and Best. A new English variety, remarkably productive, and recommended as one of the very earliest peas in England 1.00
Waite's Caractacus. A very early sort, carefully selected from the well-known Dan O'Rourke. It has a very strong constitution, and is represented to be several days earlier 80

Peppers.

per pkt.
Long Red Arabian. Very pretty; new variety of the Long Red Capsicum; fruits upright, a little smaller than the ancient varieties, but produced in greater quantity, and of a more pleasing shape. 15
Monstruosus or Grossum. A new, remarkably fine variety, growing to very large size; highly recommended for stuffing 10

Potatoes.

The following English varieties, some of them never before offered in this country, having become very popular in Europe, we have imported a few of the following sorts, which we shall offer to our patrons, with their descriptions, as received from England : —

per peck.
Confederate. The tubers are of a large oval or oblong form; eyes numerous, but not deeply set; skin, yellowish-white and very smooth; flesh, white when cooked; good quality; very prolific. Mr. C. N. Bracket, Chairman of the Vegetable Committee Massachusetts Horticultural Society, raised, last season, from eight medium-sized tubers, five and a half pecks of good sound potatoes . . 1.50
Ash Top Fluke. Recommended as a second early sort. Very handsome tubers, and, when boiled, is very mealy and of most excellent flavor. Keeps well; wherever shown in England, always considered the best 2.00
King of Potatoes. Large, prolific, and hardy; not liable to disease; said to be the best Kidney Potatoes yet introduced for main crop 1.50
Pheasant Eye. A very early sort; highly recommended as being very prolific; floury and fine flavored 1.50
Wheeler's Milky White. A very fine seedling, coming in after the early varieties; of delicious flavor; color, as white as milk; very highly recommended . . 1.50
Sutton's Early Race-Horse. Another English variety, but a few days later than the preceding; productive, and of extra fine quality, excellent for forcing. A trial the past season authorizes us to recommend this with the greatest confidence. Our stock of this variety is quite limited. 1.50
Carter's Champion Early Forcing. Said to be the earliest frame potato in cultivation, of exceeding fine flavor, with scarcely any haum, and therefore very suitable for forcing 1.50
Prince of Wales, or Red Regent. From the original stock, which took the first prize at the Birmingham show, and also several distinguished prizes in other parts of the country, including the first prize at the Worcestershire Agricultural Show, as the best seed potato for general and field culture. It is one of the finest and most productive 1.50

The following popular American varieties we can supply from the original stocks, prices subject to variation : —

per bush.
Goodrich's Early. A very early and prolific variety, often yielding a crop of three hundred bushels per acre. Skin and flesh, white; eyes, smooth; solid and sound to the core, keeping well. Price, 50 cts. per peck $2.00
The Harrison. A winter variety, large, smooth, with full eyes, white skin, and flesh sound and healthy; an admirable keeper; always solid to the heart, of first quality, and enormously productive. Average yield, on good rich soil, 400 bushels per acre. Per pk., 75 . . . . 2.00
Gleason. A fine late winter variety, very hardy and productive; slightly coppery color, oval, very smooth and handsome; flesh, white; table qualities, superior. Under Dr. Gray's cultivation, it is said to yield at the rate of 400 bushels to the acre, being more productive than its parent, the Rusty Coat. Per pk., 75 . . 2.00
Heffron. A long, smooth tuber of flesh color, with full eyes and white flesh, ripening in early autumn; has proved entirely free from disease, and is equalled in productiveness only by the Harrison. For table-use it has few equals. Per pk., $1.00. 3.00
Early Sebec, or Boston Market. A large and superior early variety; flesh white, nearly smooth; white skin, fine grained, and keeps late; quality good, as an early or late variety; lately introduced from Maine, preferred by Boston market-gardeners to any other variety. Per pk., 75 cents 2.00
Colebrook Seedling. A large purple or light-red variety; very productive and of fine quality; keeping late in the season; highly recommended. Per pk., 75 cents. 2.00

per bush.

The Calico is a kidney-shaped white variety, with splushes of red near the stem, white fleshed, very handsome and prolific, entirely hardy, and is a very fine sort for early winter use. It is a seedling of the Garnet Chili Cooks white and dry for a new seedling, and promises well; very productive, yielding at the rate of 400 bushels to the acre. Per pk., $1.00 . . . . 3.00

POTATOES BY MAIL.—To Parties residing at a distance from Railroads and Express Offices, we will send a package containing four pounds of either the above varieties by mail, postpaid, for one dollar; six packages for five dollars. No less than one dollar's worth, or more than one kind in a package, will be sent by mail.

"Raphanus Caudatus,"

per pkt.

Or Edible Podded Raddish. This valuable new vegetable belongs to the Radish tribe; but, unlike that esculent, the seed-pods (not the root) are eaten: these are very curious, attaining an immense size in a wonderfully short time, sometimes growing as much as three inches in a night. It is a native of Java, where it is known under the name of *Mougri*, and is much used in some parts of India, for salading, &c. It can be sown in the open air, or in pots, and then transferred to the ground; and will grow in almost any soil, care being taken that the plants stand two to three feet apart, to allow room for the growth of the pods. This vegetable can be used in various ways; indeed, it may be regarded as one of the most useful that have been introduced for many years. The seed, when sown, easily vegetates, and in about eight weeks the plants flower profusely, and then produce extraordinary siliquas (pods), which are very remarkable from their attaining the enormous length of about two feet. These pods have a most agreeable flavor, and when about half grown can be eaten in the same way as roots of the common Radish, which they greatly resemble in taste, but are far superior in delicacy of flavor. In salads they will be highly estimated; for, added to their other merits, they possess the excellent advantage of being easily digested; they also make a good pickle, for which purpose they are well adapted. It is, however, when the pods are boiled that they are most delicious, eating like marrow, and having a most delicate flavor; they should be served on toast, and will form a most agreeable addition and novelty for the table 25

Radish.

White-Tipped Scarlet Turnip. This is a new variety, which will prove more acceptable than our white-tipped Scarlet Olive-shaped Radish, on account of its round root; and we have no doubt it will soon be a great favorite with all market and vegetable gardeners 15
New French Breakfast. A new, quick-growing variety. Oval form; color scarlet, tipped with white; fine flavored. Very ornamental in appearance; much esteemed by the French. Excellent for forcing 15

Squash.

Mammoth Prize. This is a far superior variety to any hitherto introduced, surpassing all competitors at the Massachusetts Horticultural Exhibition, and to which the Prize Silver Medal was awarded for 1866-67. Weight, 165 lbs.; described by Mr. Meehan in "Gardener's Monthly," p. 378, as a perfect monster in size. (See illustration.) 25
Danna's Selected. This is an improved variety of the Canada Crookneck, the very best of its class 10

Sunflower.

New Mammoth Russian. This is a new variety; and, under ordinary cultivation, the heads grow to the enormous size of twenty inches in diameter. The seeds are large, exhibited at the Massachusetts Horticultural Exhibition, and highly commended by the Committee for ornamental purposes. For planting in shrubberies, it is a desirable acquisition. Salad oil of superior quality is extracted from it. To poultry-keepers it is invaluable for its extraordinary productiveness. Price, to the trade, on application 10

Tomato.

Keyes's Early Prolific. Leaves large, long, and quite entire, not lobed as in other kinds; and the growth is dwarf, compact, vigorous, and strong. The Tomatoes are of medium size, round, of brilliant color, quite smooth, and free from wrinkles of any kind, perfectly solid, and of excellent flavor. They are borne in large compact clusters from ten to twenty each, and from seven to twenty clusters on each vine. The introducers claim that it possesses the peculiar and valuable quality of ripening thirty days earlier than any other variety. (See illustration.) . . 10
Maupay's Superior. The fruit is of a beautiful *deep-red* color. In form it is round, slightly flattened, and without a crease or wrinkle. Smoothness of the surface is not only one of its most remarkable, but one of its most desirable characteristics. This freedom from creases or wrinkles prevents the great waste usual with almost every other variety. It is of a medium size, and the flesh almost

TILDEN'S TOMATO. See page 135.

	per pkt.
as solid as a beefsteak. In proof of their solidity, it is not improper to state, that, although not of extraordinary size, the average weight is from nine to twelve ounces each. It has very few seeds, and, from the solidity of its flesh, comparatively little water. One bushel will make as much catsup, or fill as many cans, as two bushels of the ordinary kind, besides being possessed of a flavor that is unapproachable. For marketing purposes, they possess the great advantage of not only being solid, but of having a thick skin, or rind, which protects them from bruising and mashing in transportation. Another great advantage of this thick skin is, that it admits of their being peeled or skinned for the table without scalding, which is always troublesome, and, at the same time, takes away the desired freshness and flavor, when desired for slicing cold. It can be peeled in half the time usually required for the common varieties. As an evidence of the superiority of these Tomatoes for marketing purposes, they commanded ready sale at $2.00 per bushel, when others were offered at $1.00; and this without any care having been taken to select them. 50 cents per ounce	10
Tilden's. This new and fine variety we have now cultivated two years, and have exhibited specimens before the Massachusetts Horticultural Society, which have attracted much attention. Our seeds have been raised by ourselves, and selected from the largest, smoothest, and handsomest specimens, taken from plants raised from seeds received direct from Mr. Tilden, the originator.	
The plants are rather dwarfer in habit than the common Tomato, and the fruit sets nearer the root; and it is the earliest of all the large-growing Tomatoes, and continues in bearing until the vines are killed by frost. The fruit varies from round to roundish-oval, which is the general form of the main crop, and is free from the warty protuberances which disfigure ordinary sorts. Color, light brilliant scarlet, with a glossy skin. Flesh solid, light red, less watery than other kinds, and of good flavor. But its greatest excellence consists in its remarkable keeping qualities, and the ease with which it may be handled without injury, rendering it altogether the most valuable variety for the market. Per oz., 50 cents	10
Eureka. A new and fine variety, from Mr. Perriam, of Chicago, who alludes to it as follows: "I consider it superior to any thing I have ever tried; dwarf, early, bush-shape, and prolific	15
Tree, or Erect. This remarkable and excellent variety, introduced three years ago, is still one of the best, — the fruit being very large and smooth; and the plants, from their erect, compact growth, highly ornamental	10
The Foard. This variety originated with a market gardener, of the same name, in the vicinity of Philadelphia. It is stated to be, without exception, the most beautiful variety; is of a bright-scarlet color, cuts as solid as a well-ripened apple, and almost entirely free from seeds, which are deposited mostly on one side of the fruit. It is quite early, and a good cropper. Recommended as being the most perfect and the most desirable of the whole class	15
New Californian Whortleberry. A remarkable and curious acquisition, with fruits, in size and color, exactly like the whortleberry	50
Sims's Early Cluster. A new English variety, introduced the past season, described as follows: Mammoth variety of the Cherry Tomato, *very early, of extremely robust habit,* requiring little support; fruit, very large and smooth, in grape-like bunches, averaging from four to twenty fruits. This variety was raised by Mr. Sims, gardener to —— Weddowson, Esq., Dulwich Common, and is much recommended.	15
Cedar Hill Early. A new American variety, in high repute among the New-York market-gardeners; said to be very early; large size, solid, and productive.	15

Turnip.

	per lb.
Carter's Imperial Hardy Swede. The very best Swede in Cultivation. Price, per oz., 10 cents	1.00

MUSHROOM SPAWN.

DIRECTIONS FOR GROWING MUSHROOMS. — The only conditions required for the healthy growth of Mushrooms are a mass of short dung, heated to from fifty-five to sixty degrees, and lumps of Spawn about the size of walnuts, six inches apart, just beneath the surface; the whole covered with an inch thickness of good light friable earth, and three or four inches of straw, or litter of any kind, to keep in the very moderate warmth. This can be managed in any dark cupboard or cellar; and the size of the bed is immaterial.

Take of horse-droppings from the stable, without the straw, as much as will make the bed the size you want it, a foot thick: put this anywhere out of the weather, away from the light and draught. Let this be pressed, but not hard; and in a few days, when it is nice and warm on thrusting the hand in, get the Spawn, and break the cakes in small pieces and put them in all over the dung, even with the surface: upon this being patted down smooth, but not hard, it will require from half an inch to an inch of earth all over it. Pat it down to keep it in its place, and put some loose hay or straw over it. When it approaches dryness, it must be sprinkled with water with the chill off, enough to wet the earth, but not the dung. Sooner or later, according to the attention paid to these several points, you will have Mushrooms, and plenty of them.

Best Mill-track Mushroom Spawn, per pound, 15 cents; 8 pounds for $1.00

RARE FLOWERS
AND
NOVELTIES FOR 1868.

Particular care has been taken that the selection should be of the purest character. We cannot affirm the accuracy of the various descriptions, having tested but few of them; but the reputation of the growers, from whom we import, is to us the best assurance that satisfaction will surely follow. Our patrons, wishing novelties, will please send their orders early, as our stock of some of the varieties is limited.
For cultural direction, see respective headings in body of the Guide.

NO.		PRICE
1891	**Antirrhinum Multiflorum.** Hybrid of A. Rupestris and A. Majus, with rose and white flowers, which are not so large as those of the latter, but in such a quantity that the plant, ½ foot in height, is entirely covered with them. Very hardy, and always in bloom	.25
1892	**Aphanostephus Ramosissimus.** A half-hardy annual; from Texas; four inches in height; much branched; the flower-head with a yellow disk, and violet-blue ray florets; of a close, carpet-like growth; blooms profusely throughout the summer.	.25
1893	**Artemisia spec. ex St. Petersburgh.** Ornamental plant of exceedingly rapid growth, reaching in the first months of summer the height of four or five feet; of pyramidal habit, and with light-green, needle-like foliage, by which the plant receives the gracious appearance of an elegant Conifer. Like A. Annua, introduced to the trade some years ago, this sort is as proper for beds as for being isolated on grass-plots, and will prove a very valuable acquisition for every garden	.25
1894	**Artemisia Japonica.** Very large plant; of the same habit as the common Artemisia, which it resembles in many respects, but is more fragrant. It is rather a plant for the lawn than the flower garden, and succeeds in the poorest and stoniest of soils.	.25
1895	**Ablopappus Rubiginosus (Haplopappus).** A Compositæ from Mexico; annual; from 3 to 3½ feet high; well branched from the middle of its height, with small, dentated leaves, and bearing a large truss of bright-yellow or orange flowers, producing together a fine effect. This plant reminds us, by its habit and growth, of the Aster (Michaelmas Daisy), with which it will form a nice contrast, flowering, as it does, about the same time (August and September). In fact, a fine plant for borders	.25
1896	**Bidens Warscewicziana var. Pinnata.** Herbaceous Compositæ from the mountains of South America, 3½ to 4½ feet high. The stems, which are very much branched, terminate in flowers with an orange disc, and white petals. Being a very free flowerer, and of rather tall habit, it will be a desirable plant for large flower-gardens, especially for public parks, &c.	.25
1897	**Briza Compacta.** Very correct and compact-growing; variety of the Quaking Grass; and will be found very ornamental for winter decoration and for bouquets	.25
1898	**Calceolaria Extra Choice Hybridised.** Saved from the finest-formed and most beautifully marked flowers from Mr. W. Bull's collection	.50

1899 **Celosia. Coccinea Pyramidalis.** Magnificent, free-flowering, graceful-growing plants, producing in the greatest profusion spikes of the most beautiful feathery-

NO.		PRICE
	looking flowers; and, if gathered when young, they are valuable for winter bouquets. Plants of the Celosia flower freely if planted out in June in a warm, sheltered situation. Grown in pots, they are the most elegant of greenhouse and conservatory plants, where, with a little management, they may be had in flower the whole winter, growing freely in rich loamy soil. Half-hardy annuals	.25
1900	**Collinsia Verna.** This is a most elegant plant, which, for freshness of its fine, half pure-white, and half tender-blue flowers, and the earliness of its blooming, deserves to become a general favorite. Fine for pot-culture	.25
1901	**Centaurea Moschata Atropurpurea.** It agrees, in almost every point, with the variety hitherto cultivated; but its tint is a deep purple, closely verging on crimson. "The Gardener's Chronicle," Oct. 12, 1867, says, "A very fine variety, and quite distinct in color from any we have previously seen Instead of the pale purple of the ordinary kind, this is of a deep, rich, port-wine color, rather paler in the centre when fully blown. It is quite an acquisition among ornamental annuals."	.25
1902	**Centaurea Pseudo-Depressa.** This plant is scarcely more than half the height of C. Depressa, and has much smaller seeds. The ray-florets are of a fine blue, the central ones being of a reddish-purple	.25
1903	—— **Species de Teneriffe.** Herbaceous Compositæ of 1½ feet in height, with thick leaves, the edges of which are slightly spinous; the flowers resemble those of C. Cyanus, but are much larger, and of a fine azure-blue	.25
1904	**Cineraria Extra Choice Hybridised.** Saved from Mr. W. Bull's superb collection of the best varieties in cultivation	.50
1905	**Cerinthe Aspera.** The finest species of Honeywort; produces an abundance of snowy, yellow flowers, the tube of which is black at its base. In general habit, it closely agrees with the other species of the genus, but the seed is somewhat larger	.25
1906	**Cedronella Mexicana.** A hardy, herbaceous plant, from Mexico, with a large, violet flower-spike, highly recommended for its sweet scent	.25
1907	**Chrysanthemum Carinatum Hybridum fl. pl.** The Chrysanthemum New Golden Double and Dunnettii fl. pl., offered to the trade last year, are completed by the new varieties above. The flowers of the greater part of them are very double, and will prove a fine acquisition; the different shades of the flowers in orange, scarlet, rose, and red-brown, are very pretty	.25
1908	**Chenopodium Scoparium.** A fine annual; very useful for edgings, on account of its dwarf, compact habit	.25
1909	**Cucurbita Florida.** A very useful gourd, on account of its curiously-shaped seeds and handsome fruit	.50
1910	**Clarkia Elegans Alba Pura.** The nearest approach to white in this section of Clarkias has heretofore been only a pale pink; the variety now offered is a pure white, and from its habit and color will be found a desirable novelty for mixed borders and back-grounds	.25
1911	—— **Integripetala Carnea, Tom Thumb.** A delicate, flesh-colored variety of the whole-petalled section of Clarkias, with compact, Tom-Thumb habit	.25
1912	—— **Pulchella Marginata, Double.** The most elegant Clarkia ever yet brought before the public; the flowers are very double; color, bright magenta; the extremity of each petal marked with a beautiful, broad, white margin. We offer this with the greatest confidence, fully believing it will supersede all other varieties of Clarkia, beautiful though they are, both as border-flowers, and also for making bouquets. This variety will not produce single or semi-double flowers	.25
1913	**Dianthus Heddewegii lilacins.** Recommended for borders and little beds, and is to be highly recommended for its long continuance in bloom. The flowers produce a fine effect by their pure lilac color	.25
1914	**Delphinium Cardinale.** A beautiful scarlet Delphinium	1.00
1915	**Desmodium Gyrans.** This very curious sensitive plant attains, out of seeds, its maturity in the first season; the small side leaflets move up and down all along. It is a very interesting plant for the close spectator of vegetable life	.50
1916	**Eschscholtzia Dentata Sulphurea.**	.25
1917	—— —— **Aurantiaca.** This and the preceding are two new varieties of Eschscholtzias, which are of great curiosity and importance; they may be justly ranked as a new section of Eschscholtzias. The flowers take the form of a Maltese cross, each petal having its edges lapped upon itself, and is intersected by a mark of deeper color running up the centre; the edges are very curiously jagged or toothed. From the peculiar construction of the petals, the blossoms of these varieties (unlike all other Eschscholtzias) are always open	.25
1918	—— **Crocea Striata.** A striped Eschscholtzia is a great novelty. The color of the flower is composed of alternate stripes of deep orange and sulphur, from the base to the circumference of the petals, which produces a very elegant appearance	.25
1919	**Echinocistis Lobata.** Of all the "Cucurbitacea," one of the best, beautiful, white, scented flowers, standing well out in clusters	.50
1920	**Egg Plant, Green.** Introduced by Mr. Bourret, from Thibet. A very fine fruit, often growing a foot in length	.25
1921	—— **Ribformed.** A strong-growing variety, fine foliage, with a dark violet tint, about two inches in diameter; the fruit, violet color, often attains the weight from flowers 4 to 6 lbs., ribbed-formed after the style of some kinds of melons	.25
1922	**Eryngium Bromeliæfolium.** Fine herbaceous plant, of which seed has been obtained for the first time	.50

138   AMATEUR CULTIVATOR'S GUIDE

NO.		PRICE

1923 **Felicia Angustifolia.** From New Holland, and one of the best acquisitions horticulture has made lately; it is a low shrub from two to three feet high, narrow foliage, the branches terminating in flowers of a yellow disc, and petals of a beautiful purple-violet. As to the habit, it is almost an Aster; and in color it resembles the beautiful Cinerarias. This lovely shrub flowers in spring, and will be appreciated highly in the North, where it will take a place in every greenhouse collection 50
1924 **Geranium Anemonifolium.** A very useful variety, very dwarf habit . . .50
1925 **Gloxinia, Extra Choice Hybridised.** This seed has been saved from the splendid new varieties offered by Mr. W. Bull 50
1926 **Gomphrena Globosa, Aurantiaca Isabellina.** Yellowish-white flowers, constant . .25
1927 **Helianthus Grandiflorus Plenissimus.** Compositæ, annual, 4 to 5 feet high, much resembling H. Californicus, but a quite new variety, distinct from its gigantic growth. The flowers are twice as large as those of H. Californica and as double. When perfectly grown, they have the appearance of a globe 25
1928 —— **Texanus Hybridus.** Annual Compositæ, height 10 to 12 feet, surpassing in beauty *H. Argophyllus;* excellent plant, recommended for the abundance of its flowers 25
1929 —— **Maximiliani.** Herbaceous Compositæ, from Mexico, from 4 to 5 feet high, with orange-yellow flowers, and narrow lanceolated leaves; picturesque and interesting plant, which will be more effective if planted in groups than singly 25
1930 —— **Rigidus, or Harpalium Rigidum.** Herbaceous Compositæ, from North America; in strong bushes, from 6 feet to 9 feet and more in height, with oval, coarse leaves, flowering at the end of each branch; blooms of the same shape as the Sunflower, but only averaging 4 inches in size; a picturesque plant of some value for public parks, which succeeds in any soil 25
1931 **Hypericum Calycinum Repens.** This is a very useful plant for growing in exposed situations, as well as deep shady places, under evergreens 25
1932 **Heracleum Platzænium.** This fine plant will prove a valuable acquisition for ornamenting lawns and the garden; leaves, of large size, and elegantly lobate. The seed germinates very slowly, sometimes requiring a year 25
1933 **Heartsease, Large-Flowering, Stained.** These may be considered as an extra fine selection of the popular, large-flowering Pansies; the inferior petals of which are spotted with very large and showy stains; said to be remarkable 50
1934 **Impatiens Balsamina Abrosanguinea Plenissima.** A new and fine dark-red, very double variety of the Balsam 50
1935 —— **Solferino.** A splendid new variety; the finest; white-striped, and blotched with lilac and scarlet, like carnations; very double 50

New Ipomœas (with self-colored foliage).

1936 **Hederacea Alba Grandiflora Intus Rosea.** Handsome white flower, with dark-rose throat. Single seed 50
1937 —— **Alba Grandiflora Intus Rosea Semi-Plena.** Of the same form and color as the foregoing ; a few petals, tongue-shaped, which appear from the corolla to transform the flower into a semi-double one, which is seldom seen in this family. Single seed 50
1938 —— **Atrocarminea Grandiflora Alba Marginata.** Handsome variety, with brilliant carmine flowers, edged pure white. Single seed 50
1939 —— **Atrocarminea Grandiflora Azurea Marginata.** With brilliant carmine flowers, edged with clear azure-blue. Single seed 50
1940 —— **Atrolilacea Grandiflora Azurea Marginata.** With dark-lilac flowers, edged with bright azure-blue. Single seed 50

New Ipomœas (with variegated foliage).

We attach much importance to this new section, and find them worthy of recommendation. We beg to state that we have tried them carefully, and found them to come true from seed. For this reason, as well as the curious combination and richness of color of their flowers, we have no hesitation to place them in the first rank of novelties for this season.

1941 **Grandiflora Alba Picta Carminea (with silver-marbled leaves).** Heart-shaped leaves, largely marbled with silver-gray; flowers white, dotted with brilliant carmine. Single seed .50
1942 —— **Alba Picta Lilacina (with golden-marbled leaves).** Heart-shaped leaves, largely marbled with silver-gray; white flowers, spotted with clear lilac. Single seed 50
1943 —— **Hederacea Grandiflora Atrocarminea Intus Alba (with silver-marbled leaves).** Tri-lobed leaves, largely marbled, silver-gray; flowers dark carmine, with large, white throat. Single seed 50
1944 **Ixodia Alata.** Soft-wooded shrub from New Holland, with everlasting flower; five feet high; short, dark-green leaves; flowers resembling those of *Ammobium Alatum* 25
1945 **Leavenworthia Aurea.** Pretty, cruciferous annual; from Arkansas; of very dwarf habit; single flowers, about half an inch across, with white petals, stained at the base with deep yellow. It has been treated as a half-hardy annual, and blooms in May and June 25

NO.		PRICE
1946	**Lobelia, New Herbaceous, Choice Mixed.** A beautiful class of perennials, becoming very popular, containing several new colors, among which are carmine, rose, magenta, ruby; great acquisition	.50
1947	**Marigold, Dwarf French, New Golden.** A pure golden, dwarf, French Marigold; very double and constant. The habit is dwarf and compact, and the flowers are so double as to have the appearance of miniature African Marigolds. This variety is a suitable companion and contrast to *Dunnett's New Orange French Marigold*	.25
1948	**Myosotis Azorica var. Cœlestina.** A new variety of the well-known general favorite, M. Azorica. The flowers are sky-blue, nearly turquoise-blue; very constant, and of the same habit as the type. This variety, offered here for the first time, will be welcome in every flower-garden	.25
1949	**Melothria Cucumerina.** A small Cucurbitaceæ, from China; fine glossy foliage, flowers yellow, the fruit sometimes used in vinegar for pickles	.25
1950	**Mimulus Duplex Flowering, Choice Mixed.** Saved from the best and most distinct varieties; which received a first-class certificate, when exhibited before the Floral Committee of the Royal Horticultural Society	.50
1951	**Nemophila Discoidalis Argentea.** A charming little variety, with silvery-white blossoms spotted with chocolate; particularly adapted for rockeries or pots	.25
1952	—— **Discoidalis Nigra.** A perfectly black blossom in any flower must be a great novelty; the blossom of this Nemophila, when young, is a pure jet black from centre to circumference	.25
1953	**Nierembergia Frutescens.** Soft-wooded shrub, a native of the mountainous districts of Chili; 2½ feet high, stem straight, well branched, same foliage as *N Gracilis*, but of a more elegant habit; the flowers also are of the same color, but a little larger and more open; worthy of recommendation	.25
1954	**Œnothera Drummondii Lacinæfolia.** This Œnothera distinguishes itself by the vigorous growth, and by the strongly laciniated leaves, which are linear and somewhat elongated. Constant	.25
1955	**Pelargonium, Fancy.** Saved from the newest and best varieties in cultivation	.50
1956	—— **Ivy-Leaved.** These Ivy-leaved Pelargoniums are extremely useful, from their graceful, drooping growth, for vases, rustic, or suspending baskets; their rich, waxlike foliage alone is ornamental; but, added to that, they have pretty flowers, and the different varieties present a contrast and charm attained by few other plants	.50
1957	—— **Nosegay.** The varieties in this class, from their giving huge trusses, and in the greatest profusion, are admirably adapted for bedding purposes	.50
1958	—— **Spotted.** This strain of Pelargonium seeds has been obtained by hybridising the attractive French kinds with the best varieties of the most eminent English growers. It is believed that this will produce finely-formed flowers of good substance, rich and varied colors, clearly and purely defined spots, and free blooming.	.50
1959	—— **Tricolor Varieties.** The seed now offered was saved from distinctly-marked varieties; which, having been carefully hybridised, may be expected to yield a good proportion of this deservedly popular section	.50
1960	—— **White Variegated Section.** As with the preceding, this may be expected to produce plants of the variegated class, which for decorative purposes are considered superior to any other class	.50
1961	—— **Zonal.** The seeds may be expected to produce the following colors: scarlet, white, pink, cérise, rose carmine, blush, salmon, rose-pink, orange, scarlet, &c., &c.	.25

The above Pelargoniums are Mr. W. Bull's growing (imported direct from him), all extra choice hybridised; and are believed to be superior, in every respect, to any e er before offered in this country.

1962	**Pelargonium Lateripes Grandiflorum.** Leaves of this variety have a brown margin; flower large, salmon color. A fine plant, in flower from May to October. Very useful for ribbons and borders, said to surpass all others of this class	.50
1963	**Pentstemon Glabrum.** Flowers large, in clusters; bright blue, shaded to the centre, with lilac	.50
1964	—— **Extra Choice Hybridised.** This seed was saved by Mr. W. Bull from his celebrated collection, and is believed to be superior	.50
1965	**Phalacraea Wendlandi.** For bedding purposes this surpasses the old Ageratum, better color and sweet scented	.25
1966	**Phyllanthus Spec. Nova.** A very pretty plant for decoration, flowering in five or six weeks from planting, foliage very ornamental, flowers freely from the axels of the leaves	.25
1967	**Primula Chinensis Erecta Alba.** A very strong-growing variety, throwing the flowers well out from the fine foliage. Flowers beautifully fringed. White	1.00
1968	—— —— **Fimbriata Marginata Lilacina.** A new variety of this family; flowers, fine imbricated white and lilac shaded; the leaflets are narrow, bordered with white	1.00
1969	—— —— **Erecta Flore Pleno Alba.** A beautiful variety of the double white Chinese Primrose, very choice	1.00
1970	**Saxifraga Fortunei.** This is an exceedingly handsome Japanese plant; it produces fine corymbs of white flowers, at a season when flowers are very scarce, viz., September, October, and November; being an easily cultivated plant, it is an exceedingly desirable introduction	.50
1971	**Salvia Lupuliniflora.** A splendid new variety; flowers blue, with white centre	.25

NO.		PRICE
1972	**Sphenogyne Speciosa Aurea**	.25
1973	—— —— **Sulphurea.** Two beautiful varieties of *S. Speciosa*, one a fine golden orange, the other a bright sulphur. The colors are pure and well contrasted, and will prove far more effective than the original *S. Speciosa*, from which they are quite distinct	.25
1974	**Silene Orientalis.** A very showy and effective annual; compact habit, and every stem crowned with a corymb of very large, delicate pink flowers, forming a mass of bloom of great elegance	.10
1975	**Siphocampylus Fulgens.** This free-flowering, effective plant, from South America, is a great acquisition. Compact habit, foliage dark green, ovate, acuminate, the blossoms rich orange-scarlet, with yellow throat; remaining in flower a long time; very useful for bouquets, requires greenhouse culture, rare	1.00
1976	**Stock, Florist Variety, White.** This is a new variety, and is superior to any thing ever before offered; very strong-growing, flowers large, well-branched; growing and flowering a long time; fragrant; will produce 90 per cent of double flowers. We can recommend this variety with confidence to parties growing for market, either for plants or cut flowers	.25
1977	—— —— —— **Scarlet.** Same as the preceding; scarce	.50
1978	**Tagetes Palula Aurea Nana fl. pl.** Marigold Dwarf, French; new; pure golden; very double, and constant	.25
1979	**Thladiantha Dubia.** The male plant only of this elegant hardy perennial climber, which produces clusters of fine yellow flowers, was known until lately; but the female plant, of recent introduction, which bears abundantly fruit the shape and size of an egg, will allow all amateurs of fine climbers to cultivate. The fruit, when ripe, takes a deep scarlet shade, giving a fine effect to the whole plant	.50
1980	**Tropæolum Tom Thumb Cæruleo Roses.** The greatest novelty of the season. A Nasturtion, with the free-blooming, compact habit of all the Tom-Thumb Nasturtions; the flowers, which are thrown well above the foliage, are of brilliant rose, shaded, underlaid with a peach-blue, a color never before seen in Nasturtions. This variety has been very much admired by the many visitors to our seed-farms during the past season, in consequence of the decided novelty of color; and we consider this the first step towards a perfectly blue Nasturtion, in the same manner as *Beaton's Indian Yellow Geranium* is towards a perfectly Yellow Geranium. This splendid novelty is quite distinct from, and infinitely superior to, the *Rose Tom-Thumb Nasturtion*, introduced by us last season	.50
1981	—— **Lilli Schmidt, Tom Thumb.** A Tom-Thumb variety of *T. Lilli Schmidt*; a very profuse bloomer, with intensely-bright scarlet flowers; flowers, very large, the petals overlapping each other so as to form very perfect flowers. The formation of the flowers of the *Lilli-Schmidt* section of Tropæolums is quite distinct from the ordinary *Tom-Thumb* Nasturtion, the flowers being smaller and more perfect in form. The present novelty partakes of the good qualities of both sections, having the beautiful form and intense color of the former, with the compact and free-blooming habit of the latter	.50
1982	—— **Pyramidalis.** An annual Tropæolum, growing in the form of a dwarf pyramid, or sugar-loaf, which is covered with a quantity of bright scarlet flowers; this variety is quite constant, and the habit very novel	.50
1983	**Trichosanthes Coccinea.** The whole class is very curious and interesting; but this, with its bright scarlet flowers and fine foliage, surpasses them all. The seeds are larger and strongly marked. It is very striking and prominent among other plants	.25
1984	**Veronica Imperialis.** A great improvement in this class; flowers fine purple, very large; fine, glossy foliage	.25
1985	**Viscaria Elegans Picta.** The gem of the season, and certainly the most elegant Viscaria ever offered to the public. The centre of the flower is dark crimson, gradually merging into a bright scarlet, belted with a pure-white margin; from the neat habit, profusion of flowers, and brilliant appearance, this Viscaria will become a great favorite, both as a border flower, and also for pots or beds	.25
1986	**Viola Tricolor Maxima Inimitable.** A very large, fine flower; fancy margin; raised by an amateur, who has devoted many years to the Pansy; very highly recommended	.50
1987	—— **Cornuta Mauve Queen.** One of the most attractive bedding and border plants in cultivation, continuing in one mass of bloom throughout the early spring, summer, and autumn months; no plant can be more welcome or valuable for bedding purposes	.25
1988	—— **Lutea.** A perfect gem; invaluable for dwarf beds or edgings; bright yellow; compact habit; dark-green, glossy foliage; blooms profusely throughout the season	.50
1989	—— **The Czar.** A new and very large and beautiful variety of the violet; with single flowers of the deepest blue, and possessing unusual vigor and hardiness; the leaves are large, and the flowers are borne on very long footstalks (five to six inches in length), and are nearly twice as large and much sweeter than the old Russian violet. It is so hardy that it commences blooming in September, and continues flowering until May, even during the frost and under the snow	.50

NOVELTIES AND SPECIALTIES
FOR 1869.
VEGETABLE SEEDS.

Asparagus.
Per pkt.

Conover's Colossal. A European variety, introduced several years since, which, by a careful selection of seeds from the most vigorous shoots, has been wonderfully improved both in size and quality, in point of which it surpasses all other varieties in cultivation. Specimens were exibited the past season by Mr. Conover, which were grown alongside the best "Oyster Bay" varieties, and received the same care and treatment, which attained four times the size of that popular variety. Though but two years from the seed, many of the plants produced twenty to thirty sprouts, averaging from two to four inches in circumference, and were ready for cutting one year in advance of the ordinary varieties. Packets containing ¼ ounce each. See cut 50

Beans.

Carter's Champion Runner. A gigantic variety of Scarlet Runners, having pods nearly double the size of the old variety: it is more robust in growth and is an extraordinary cropper 25

Cabbage.

Early Wyman. This is the best and most profitable early-market cabbage grown. It originated with Mr. John Wyman of Arlington, about ten years since, and has not been disseminated to any extent. It heads early in the season, is of large size, and first quality, and brings the highest price of any early cabbage brought into the Boston market, selling readily last season by the thousand, at $18 per hundred; but a limited quantity of seed can be procured 50
This cabbage took the first prize on the 11th of July last, at the exhibition of the Massachusetts Horticultural Society, as it has on several previous occasions.

Corn.

Bates's Early Bronze Field. Mr. C. Bates of Kingston, Mass., has spent twenty years of labor and care in producing this valuable variety of corn, obtaining the following results: —

It is a cross between the Whitman, or Smutty White, and Early Canada. A rapid-growing and early-maturing corn, of low growth, small stalk, throwing its strength into the corn; ears growing very near the ground; cob small; corn large and well-filled; color bronze, or a blending of yellow and white with a slight trace of red; very productive, yielding large crops even on poor soil; dwarf, averaging from root to top of spindle, from four to five feet.

By years of labor we now obtain
   A corn with fodder small, but large in grain;
   Long, slim cob, with eight full rows around;
   Top very low, earing near the ground;
   Thus filling the crib and not the mow;
   Having more corn for horse than tops for cow.

This corn is highly recommended for all latitudes, particularly Northern, on account of the above-mentioned qualities, — early maturity, large yield of grain, and small amount of stalk. The favorable reports, together with the good impressions received on visiting Mr. Bates's corn-crib, has induced us to secure the entire stock; and we now offer it, in large or small quantities, at the following prices: — (see cut.)

One Quart, by mail, postpaid, $1.00. One Bushel (express to be paid by the purchaser), $12.00; Five Bushels, $50.00.

Per pkt.

Farmers' Club Sweet. Comes to table in seventy to seventy-five days; ears of the best table size, with eight regular rows; kernels large, and of a pearly-white at all times; *delightfully tender, sweet, and of unsurpassed creamy flavor*, and retains those qualities longer than any other variety; should be boiled no more than twenty minutes. The stalk and leaves are of medium size, and heavily marked with purple. It is a very noticeable and distinct variety. Highly recommended by Solon Robinson, Thos. Mecham, M. C. Weld, Donald G. Mitchell, and Chas. L. Flint 50

Dandelion.

Large-leaved (*improved*). Improvement of the common Dandelion: its leaves are larger erect, almost entire, or at least much less denticulated 25

Thick-leaved (*improved*). This is also an improved variety of the common Dandelion, its leaves are smaller and more denticulated, but more numerous than in the preceding variety, more thickly set, and forming in the centre almost a bunch . .25
 . These two varieties will, we have no doubt, soon supersede everywhere the old one, which has become in the last ten years one of our best and most-asked-for winter and spring salads. . . . .

Gourd.

Bonnet or Dish-Cloth (Luffa Acutangula). One of the most interesting and probably useful members of the family of Cucurbitaceæ, and one but little known, is the Bonnet Gourd; and so new that it is worthy of a place in every garden, whether cultivated for its graceful and handsome foliage, its rich-colored flower, or its curious fruit. The principal use of this Gourd is for the curious membrane of fibrous material, which has been used in the South during the rebellion to manufacture a kind of bonnet (whence its name); and from its snowy-white color, and curious appearance, is quite a novelty: for any washing purposes, it cannot be excelled, as it is soft and pliable in water like a sponge; as a substitute for hair-gloves, for frictional purposes, it has no equal; requires about the same treatment as the melon. 25

Melon.

Persian Water. New Watermelon, introduced by the celebrated traveller Bayard Taylor, brought by him from the Caspian Sea, and heretofore entirely unknown in this country. It is globular and elliptical in form, of pale green color, with dark stripes; flesh crimson, and remarkably firm texture, with only half an inch of rind; a peculiarity of this melon is, that it can be taken off the vine to ripen, and will keep till winter. It grows to a very large size 25

The Alton Large Nutmeg. This melon is said to combine more desirable qualities than any other now before the public.
Its great productiveness, beauty, size, and firmness of flesh, made it unequalled as a shipping variety; while its delicious flavor and long-bearing season render it worthy a place in every garden. Melons of this variety sold the past season in the Chicago market for double any other variety 25

Onion.

Red Sallon. In shape and size this new variety resembles the Maderia Onion; but its color is of a darker red, it has a stronger onion-flavor, and keeps much better. Very fine variety. 25

Pea.

Laxton's Supreme. A variety raised from LAXTON'S PROLIFIC crossed with LITTLE GEM. The plant grows about 3½ ft. in height, and is quite as early as DANIEL O'ROURKE, a great advantage in a Pea of such high-class quality.
The editor of "The Gardener's Chronicle" says it is "a grand Pea: the sample sent exhibited remarkably fine large full pods." The Royal Horticultural Society of England describe this as "a grand Pea, a Green Marrow of excellent quality, with very long well-filled curved pods." It has received a first-class certificate from the Royal Horticultural Society, also at every other place that it has been exhibited 50

Imperial Wonder Pea (Carter's). A fine large wrinkled variety, habit resembling VEITCH'S PERFECTION, but coming in three weeks later 50

Potatoes.

Climax. The Climax is a seedling of the Early Goodrich, and originated with Mr. D. S. Heffron in 1864, and is thus described by him:—
"It has a stout, erect stalk; large leaves; tuber about medium size; smooth, cylindrical form, swelled out at centre; eyes shallow, but strongly defined; skin considerably netted or russet, tough, white; flesh entirely white, solid, heavy, brittle, and never hollow; boils through quickly, with no hard core at centre; is mealy, of floury whiteness, and of superior table-quality. It is equally productive with the Early Rose, but a few days later; earlier than the Early Goodrich; while its keeping qualities are as good as the Peachblow's."
We have made arrangements for a portion of the stock, which we offer to our patrons, fully confident of its good quality. Price $3.00 per pound, by mail, postpaid.

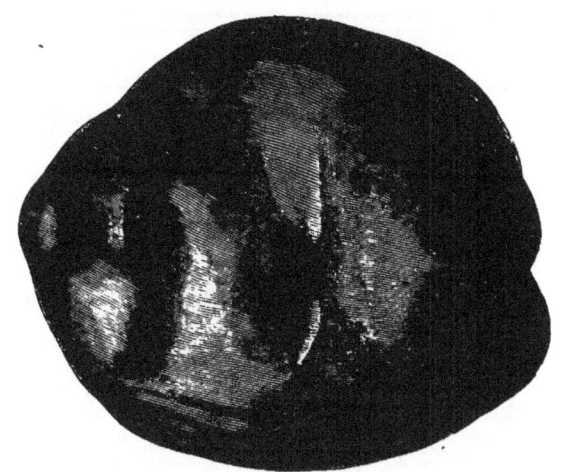

WORCESTER OR RIELLY POTATO. See page 143.

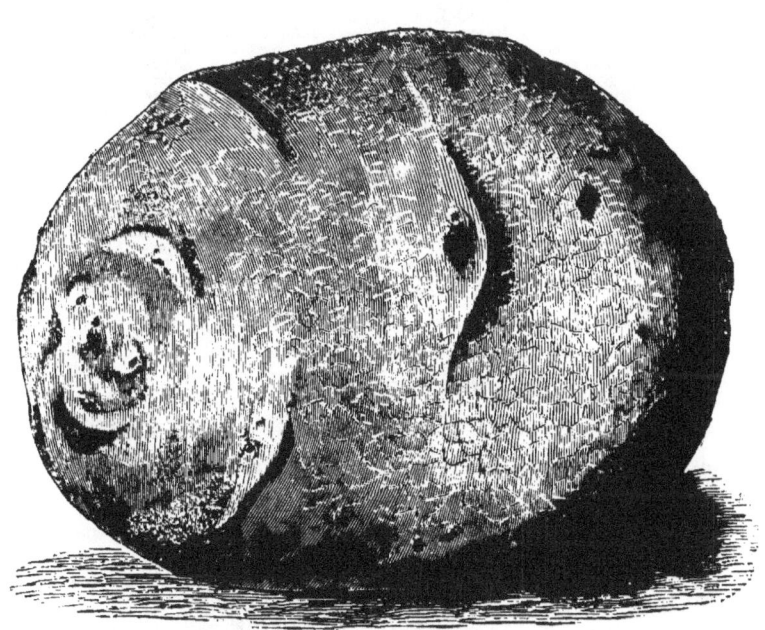

BRESEE PROLIFIC, or No. 2. See page 143.

Bresee's Prolific (or No. 2). This remarkable variety originated with Albert Bresee, Esq., of Hubbardston, Vt., who was also the originator of the justly-celebrated *Early Rose*; *both varieties being produced from the same seed-ball* of the Garnet Chili.

The vines of *Bresee's Prolific* are of medium height, quite bushy, somewhat spreading; large leaves; have produced no seed-balls; tubers large, regular in shape, and very smooth, slightly oblong, somewhat flattened; skin dull white, inclined to be russeted; eyes but little depressed, and slightly pinkish; flesh white; cooks quickly, is very mealy, and of excellent quality; yield very large, often exceeding *a hundred-fold;* matures about three weeks later than the Early Rose, and will prove a most valuable variety for field-culture. A silver medal was awarded to this variety at the annual exhibition of the Massachusetts Horticultural Society last September. Price $2.00 per pound by mail, postpaid.

Early Rose. This new and popular potato has proved all that was claimed for it when offered for the first time the past spring. It is very productive, yielding from fifty to ninety fold with common culture; two weeks earlier than the Goodrich, and a very strong grower. Tubers quite smooth, nearly cylindrical, varying to flattish, largest at the centre, tapering gradually towards each end. Skin a dull rose color, flesh white, and one of the best-flavored varieties in cultivation; highly recommended for early marketing on account of its large and uniform size and productiveness. It has been awarded special prizes at the Massachusetts Horticultural and the New-York State Agricultural Societies. On account of the popularity of this potato, there are many being offered as the Early Rose which are worthless in comparison: therefore, only purchase of reliable parties that have a reputation at stake.

A large and fine stock of this popular Potato, grown from the original stock, and warranted genuine.

One pound, $1.00; three pounds, $2.00, by mail, postpaid. One peck (15 lbs.), $5.00; ½ bush., $8.00; 1 bush (60 lbs.), $15.00; 1 bbl. (165 lbs.), $40.00. Prices to the trade, in larger quantities, will be given upon application. The freight on all packages by express, boat, or railroad, to be paid by the purchaser. No charge for packages or cartage.

Worcester, or Rielly. This valuable variety has not been well-known until the past season, when Mr. B. HARRINGTON of Lexington (who had grown it for a number of years), induced by his high opinion of its value, and the united testimony of all who had ever grown or eaten it, challenged a trial in quality with any seedling, old or new, from any State in the Union. Last September, at the Annual Dinner of the Committee of the Massachusetts Horticultural Society, a trial took place at the Parker House, Boston. There were present many distinguished horticulturists: among them Col. M. P. Wilder, Charles Downing, Esq., Hovey Breck, President Hyde, B. K. Bliss, Albert Bresee (originator of the famous Early Rose), besides all the various Committee, numbering about forty present. Among those offered for trial was the Early Rose and several other varieties, considered by their respective friends the best. But it was the unanimous decision that the Worcester was the best table-potato offered. It proved to be very mealy, dry, and of the most delicate flavor; free from any earthy taste; fair size; form inclined to roundish; color light pink; flesh very white; skin thin; eyes deep; and of superior baking quality. Another characteristic of this variety is, that it will be found dry and mealy when but two-thirds grown. For twenty years it has stood the test of disease much better than other varieties. They mature in ninety days from planting. Yield varies according to the season.

The Potato from which the cut was taken was one of a lot dug Nov. 1, from a meadow soil, all of which were sound and healthy, while other varieties growing near were more or less attacked with disease.

Below are a few of the many testimonials received:—

From Hon. Marshall P. Wilder.

BOSTON, Nov. 20, 1868.

DEAR SIR,—Please receive my thanks for the Worcester Seedling Potatoes. As a table-potato, it is certainly of first quality. MARSHALL P. WILDER.

From the Editor of the Hartford Times, November, 1868.

"We have received the Worcester Seedling Potatoes from you. We have found them to be superior to any we have tried for several years; and we have tested about all of the best sorts."

From H. S. Goodale, Editor of the Berkshire Courier, Nov. 12, 1868.

"We tried the quality of the Worcester Seedling with the Rose and many other famous seedlings, and found it so decidedly the best, that nearly all others seemed coarse and earthy, and inferior in delicacy of flavor and fineness in grain,—a little to my disappointment, as I have quite a little stock of Rose in store. A gentleman from New York visiting with me claimed he could tell the Worcester from any other variety by smell. He was blindfolded, and, to my surprise, I found that he invariably could; also others, without confusion."

After much care, we have succeeded in securing a stock of this Potato, which we shall offer at the following prices : —

Four Pounds, by mail, postpaid, $1.00. One peck (express to be paid by purchaser), $3.00 ; One Bushel, $10.00 ; One Barrel, $20.00.

Upon receipt of $5.00, we will mail, postpaid, to any address in the United States or British Provinces, ONE POUND EACH of the CLIMAX, BRESEE'S PROLIFIC, WORCESTER, and the EARLY ROSE. Orders will be booked in the order in which they are received, and the potatoes forwarded on and after April 1, when they will be free from danger of frost. They can be forwarded earlier if desired, at the risk of the purchaser. No orders will be accepted unless accompanied with the cash.

The prices of above Potatoes variable according to the market.

Squash. Per pkt.

Lungren. The plants of this new variety attain a length of twelve or fifteen feet, and are remarkably healthy and vigorous. The leaves are singularly variegated with yellow, the depths of color varying in different plants from pale yellow to bright orange, and differing also in the amount of variegations as the season progresses. The color is most profuse at the base of the leaf, and is distributed thence in serrated stripes, towards, but not reaching, the borders.

The fruit is bottle-formed, much resembling the " Puritan ; " entirely white, about one foot in length, eight inches in its greatest diameter, and weighs from eight to ten pounds. The stem is thick, short, and fleshy. The flesh is pale yellowish-white, thick, fine-grained, dry and sweet, and peculiarly free from the strong flavor common to many varieties. It cooks well, early or late in the season, and even before it has attained its full size, and is also a good keeper.

Among the numerous kinds now cultivated, there are few superior to it for pies, and there are certainly few more mild and delicate.

In a trial-growth last season, the plants suffered little, if any, from bugs, and they entirely escaped the attacks of the borer 50

Strawberries.

Alpine, FOR TABLE-DECORATION. Berry-bearing plants have been very much sought after of late years for table-decoration ; and, in our anxiety to procure novelties, we may perhaps sometimes have overlooked really useful materials already in our possession. I think this may be truly said with regard to the Alpine Strawberry ; for what can be more interesting and pretty for the table, during December and the two following months, than a few pots of these, nicely fruited, placed in vases or otherwise, according to the taste of the decorator? For this purpose, I select in May or June nice little plants of last year's runners, and plant them in seventy-twos. I then plunge them in an open border, exposed to the sun, but never allow them to suffer for want of water. They have an occasional watering with liquid-manure. The flowers are cut off as they appear, until it is thought necessary to allow them to fruit. They are transferred to the fruiting-pots (forty-eights) in August, and placed with the general stock for forcing. The Alpine forces better than any other strawberry we have, requiring but little heat to bring it into fruit. An early vinery just started is a capital place for it. — *W. Robbins, in Florist and Pomologist.*

—— Red 25
—— White 25

Tomato.

The Unrivalled Prize, " General Grant." We take great pleasure in announcing to the public that we have secured the entire stock of this justly celebrated Tomato. It originated in the garden of an amateur, who, after growing it for a number of years in connection with all the leading sorts, became convinced that it was far superior to any other, and that it should be widely disseminated ; and for this purpose it was put into our hands. In consideration of the many disappointments experienced in the introduction of new varieties, we have given it a thorough trial of two years ; and it has far exceeded our expectations, ever attracting great attention wherever exhibited, taking the first prize above all others at the Massachusetts Horticultural Society's Exhibitions the past two years. We feel the fullest confidence that too much cannot be said in its praise. We believe it the nearest approach to perfection of any thing of the kind yet offered, combining more superior qualities.

Size above the medium, three to four inches in diameter, growing in clusters ; form round, slightly flattened, very regular, symmetrical, and rarely ribbed or wrinkled ; color brilliant glossy crimson ; flesh unusually firm, solid, and free from water, weighing from ten to twenty pounds more per bushel than other varieties ; skin remarkably fine, smooth, and shining, coloring well up to the stem, — a quality very desirable to those preparing them for the table ; very productive, and of the finest flavor : bears carriage well, and keeps in good condition a long time after being gathered, retaining its goodness, and free from wilting. It will be found to ripen uniformly, and as early as, if not earlier than, other varieties. Our whole stock of seed has been grown for us by Mr. C. N. Brackett, Chairman of the Vegetable Committee of the Massachusetts Horticultural Society, and saved only from the most perfect fruit ; and we are warranted in saying that it cannot fail to give satisfaction in every instance.

ASPARAGUS. Conover's Colossal.
See page 141.

CORN.
Bates' Early Bronze Field.
See page 141.

TOMATO HOOP TRAINING.

TO THE VEGETABLE GARDEN.

We offer the following testimonials from practical parties, — gentlemen whose judgment in such matters is fully reliable.

From Andrew S. Fuller, Author of Small-Fruit Culturist.

We have had an opportunity of testing this tomato the past season, and believe it will prove to be one of the very best varieties in cultivation.

From J. F. C. Hyde, President of Massachusetts Horticultural Society.

I have known the General Grant Tomato now for two years, and last season raised a few tomatoes of this variety. I think it is the smoothest and every way the handsomest variety I have ever seen: it is quite solid, equal in this respect to any other variety. I have regarded it as a great acquisition to our list of tomatoes.

From C. N. Brackett, Chairman of the Vegetable Committee, Mass. Horticultural Society.

Gents. — I have given the new tomato, "General Grant," a fair trial of two seasons, in connection with a dozen or more of the new varieties recently introduced, such as the Cook's Favorite, Tilden, Valentia Cluster, Keyes, Eureka, Maupay, Foard, Cedar Hill, &c., and find it surpasses them all in earliness, productiveness, and all the qualities which I consider requisite in a first-class market variety; and can heartily recommend it. No person, I think, who makes any of the above-named varieties his standard of excellence, will, after giving this variety one season's trial, grow any other. Its extraordinary beauty, and singular richness of color, command the attention of the most careless observer.

From C. Bates of Kingston, Originator of Bates's Early Tomato.

The General Grant Tomato I have tried with several other varieties; viz., Cedar Hill Foard, Tilden, Keyes, Bates's Early. The General Grant beat all in earliness except Bates's Early: with that it was about "neck and neck." But for beauty of form, color, and compact flesh, it stands head and shoulders above all the rest. Planted the 15th of May; fruit ripe 6th of August.

From George Hill, Esq., Arlington, Mass.

Have grown the General Grant Tomato the past year, and consider it one of the very best in every respect. It ripens with me earlier than the Cedar Hill, Keyes, and Boston Market; of fair size, very solid and heavy, uniform, and fine flavored.

CAUTION.

On account of the immense popularity of this variety, we find that parties are offering for sale a spurious seed, desiring to obtain large prices for the common sorts. We would therefore recommend parties purchasing only those sealed packets bearing our name, as none other can be genuine.

Price per packet, 25 cts.; 5 packets, $1.00. Prices to the trade on application.

Alsike Clover.

This variety is a native of Alsike, Sweden; perfectly hardy; does not heave in winter or spring from frost; stands drouth well; and is in every respect superior to the common red variety; highly recommended for sheep . . . . Per lb. .75

Latakia Tobacco. Per pkt.

The Best Smoking Tobacco in the World. Introduced by Baynard Taylor, the well-known traveller, from the East, where it is esteemed the most delicate-flavored tobacco known. It is quite distinct from the American tobacco, having a soft glossy-surfaced leaf, quite unlike the coarse foliage of the Virginia tobacco. Cultivated precisely like the American, in rich soil 25

Rare Tree-Seeds.

Among which are the Palma Regia, or Royal Palm; Pithecolobium Montanum; Umbrella Tree; Algerba (beautiful tree, delicate foliage); Kukui (Candlenut); Acacia; Braziliana (seed-pods three feet long); Carthartocarpus; Fistula; Seligua Dulce (St. John's Bread) 50

California Evergreens or Conifera.

Pinus Coulteri, Pinus Insignis, Pinus Lambertiana, Pinus Ponderosa, Muricata, Fremontiana, Picea Grandis, Cupressus Marcrocarpus, Sequoi Gigantea (Big Tree of California) 50

NOVELTIES AND SPECIALTIES

FOR 1869.

RARE FLOWERS.

Per pkt.
1990 Antirrhinum Majus Dwarf. Purplish red and yellow. This is one of those new, fine dwarf varieties of Antirrhinum Majus, producing a large, bushy plant, with numerous large spikes of very showy flowers, from 10 to 12 inches high, very valuable for borders, &c. 25

ANTIRRHINUM MAJUS DWARF.

1991 Aster Schiller. This variety of new form is splendid in its formation ; each individual plant will make a show for itself; pyramidal ; the leaves round, the stock regular and ornamental, the flowers splendid, double, and well set 1¼ feet in height ; mixed colors 50
1992 Giant Pæony Perfection. This new and fine variety was produced from the New Giant Emperor and Pæony Perfection. The flowers not only reach, but surpass, the enormous dimensions of the Giant Emperor Aster. They are, however, dissimilar to the preceding ; flowers perfectly double, like the Pæony-flowered ; color brilliant dark rose. 50
1993 Balsam double Solferino. This is one of the best varieties of double Balsams, with fine white flowers, striped, stained, and spotted with crimson ; very showy . .50
1994 Begonia Semperflorens. Very fine variety ; one of the best for out-door cultivation ; flowers very abundant ; white leaves, rather small, fleshy, of a brilliant green, making a fine contrast with the flowers. Plant, bushy, compact, about 12 inches high ; in bloom during the whole summer ; very valuable for borders in the open ground, as well as a pot-plant. The leaves have the flavor of sorrel, and are often eaten 25
1995 Calandrinia speciosa alba. Too much cannot be said in praise of this novelty, which is a pure white variety of the popular C. Speciosa. The very dwarf habit of this variety, in conjunction with the pure white of the flowers, must necessarily make it very useful for the edgings of beds, rockeries, and also as a pot-plant. .25
1996 Campanula celtidifolia. This new variety, introduced from the Caucasus by Mr. Balansa, has, sown early in spring, produced, after three or four months vegetation, a very fine bushy plant, the ramifications of which bear pretty large five-dented flowers of a tender blue ; very fine aspect. 25
1997 Candytuft dwarf lilac. Dwarf variety of the old lilac Candytuft, interesting for its small bushy size ; very good plant 25

ROSE BALSAM. (Natural Size). See page 21.

CHAMÆROPS EXCELSA. See page 147.

CANDYTUFT, VERY DWARF WHITE.

Per pkt.
1998 **Candytuft very dwarf white.** Iberis offinnis (Vilmorins). First-class novelty (annual and biennial) ; from 4 to 7 inches high, producing large compact bushes, 7 to 9 inches large ; finely-cut leaves, which are, when the plant is in bloom, almost completely covered with a multitude of brilliant white flowers, slightly sweet-scented, very valuable for borders 25
1999 **Chamærops Excelsa.** This fine palm, which has attracted so much attention in the south of France, where it stands the winter without protection, is considered a valuable addition to this class of plants. See cut 50
2000 **Convolvulus Minor Unicaulus.** This variety is the result of at least ten years' careful selection. It has a single upright stem without a branch ; the strength of the whole plant is directed to one point ; and the result is a compact head of flower-buds in great profusion, which expand into blossoms of immense size, of a very rich purplish-blue color, and continues in bloom through the whole season 25
2001 **Dianthus Heddewegii diadematus fl. pl.** (Double Diadem-Pink). Lorenz. This is a striking novelty of wonderful beauty. It differs from the D. Heddewegii, being more luxuriant, compact, and dwarfish : its flowers have a diameter of each, 2 to 4 inches. They are regular densely double, and have all tints, from lilac, crimson, and purple, to the deepest black purple, having very often a velvet-like tint 50
2002 **Eschscholtzia alba rosea.** Splendid new variety of this general favorite, which merits the greatest attention. Its tender blossoms are tinged at the exterior of a rosy pink color, verging sometimes to crimson lake. From the disposition of the flowers to remain closed during the greater part of the day, this color is a very striking one ; but the effect of the rose-colored buds half open is also most charming. There is great hope that this variety will become later a quite red Eschscholtzia 25
2003 **Godetia Versicolor Grandiflora.** A charming rock-plant received from Texas, producing a profusion of flowers in great variety of color, and as large in size as G. The Bride. This annual appears to be identical with G. reptans, excepting that the flowers are three times as large, and the habit is more procumbent : altogether we can strongly recommend this showy annual for rockwork, and all purposes of a similar nature 25
2004 **Helichrysum apicult t m.** This very neat everlasting resembles the plant sold under the name of H. stritum, but has broader foliage and much larger flowers. Native from Australia 25
2005 **Lobelia erecta biro!or.** A lovely new variety of the upright Lobelias, its pretty flowers tinged half white, half blue 25
2006 **Lupinus spec. ex. Texas litesinus** (supranosus, subcarnosus.) New variety of this favorite Lupin, with lilac flowers 25
2007 **Mimulus repens.** Distinct species, with slender trailing stems with ovate foliage ; flowers of pale lilac-purple color, the lower lip prettily spotted with orange on yellow ground. Best suited for pot-culture, blooming during the summer months 25
2008 **Myosotis azorica alba.** The sky-blue variety of the popular M. azorica was introduced the past season. We now offer the pure white one, a delicious middle, between the deep dark-blue and sky-blue varieties 50
2009 **Myosotis oblongata.** This Forget me-not, highly to recommend, is in all its portions larger and more vigorous than M. alpestris, but has its flowers of the same fine blue tint. Blooming already the first year if care is taken to sow it early . . .25
2010 **Nasturtion Golden King of Tom Thumbs.** This varietv is similar in habit to the well-known scarlet King of Tom Thumbs, introduced some years since, and which has given the greatest satisfaction. The variety now offered for the first time has deep golden flowers, thrown well above the dark-colored foliage, and will form a suitable companion and contrast to its predecessor : it will, without

| Per pkt.
doubt, prove a very valuable bedding-plant, as it stood the late dry summer
remarkably well 25
2011 Oxalis Valdiviana. A showy hardy Oxalis, introduced by the late Mr. R. Pearce.
Quite hardy, of compact growth, throwing its bloomspikes well above the foliage. The flowers are sweet-scented, of a bright yellow color, produced in bunches of large size, and continuing a long time to bloom. Contrasts admirably when bedded out with other plants. . . . . ,25
2012 Palava flexuosa. Highly recommended, newly introduced from Bolivia by Mr. R. Pearce. 15 to 18 inches high, branching freely, it produces its charming flowers, of an inch in diameter, in the greatest profusion. Its leaves are very neat and graceful. The color of the flowers is of a bright rosy pink; the base of the sepals and petals is almost black, producing a dark eye, contrasting most beautifully with the other portions of the flower. For open-air and pot-culture, producing its numerous flowers throughout the greater portion of the summer and early autumn. Received the first prize at the Great International Horticultural Exhibition at London, 1866 50
2013 Petunia Hybrid striped large flowering. Mixed. First-class novelty, with large red, violet, purple, or crimson flowers, covered with large stains, spots or striped, of a pure white, often star-shaped 25

POTENTILLA HYBRVDA FLORE PLENO.

2014 Potentilla Hybrida flore pleno. This fine perennial is a great improvement on the old varieties, producing a large proportion of double and semi-double flowers .25
2015 Phlox Drummondii Heynholdi. The New True Scarlet Phlox (Benary). There is already in our gardens a bright variety of much value, known under the name of P. scarlet (coccinea); but its flowers, though of a very brilliant color, are far of being the true scarlet, and only of a radiant, bright dark-crimson tint. The flowers of this new variety offered here are of the pure true scarlet, with a slight tinge of copper-color. The Phloxes, among which we have a good portion of distinct tender and bright tints, belong to our best and most useful Annuals; but this new variety will have the first place everywhere, between the most striking of them; and for composing whole true scarlet groups of it, it will be highly welcome. It is quite constant, of dwarf, compact habitus, one of the best acquisitions of modern horticulture, and the very completement of Phloxes . $1.00
2016 Rodanthe Manglesi major. A very great improvement of the old and much-admired R. Manglesi, having the giant and robust habit of R. maculata 25
2017 Viscaria oculata perfection dwarf (Vilmorins). This is a remarkably fine novelty, very dwarf (6 to 8 inches high), very bushy and compact; exceedingly floriferous; flowers rosy white, slightly shaded lilac with a purplish stain in the centre. Variety of Viscaria oculata Dunnettii 25
2018 Zinnia elegans pumila fl. pl. varietates (Benary). This new variety differs in nothing from the other double Zinnias on account of the brilliant tints and doubleness of its flowers. It is of great value, attaining only a height of 1 to 1½ foot, and being a precious acquisition for ribbon borders and low groups by this exceedingly agreeable height in comparison of the older varieties having a height of 2 to 2½ feet. Of compact growth 25
2019 Zinnia elegans alba semi-pleno. Ever since the introduction of the double varieties, which proved such acquisition to our numerous effective annuals, the want of a white variety has been much regretted by all lovers of this popular flower: we have therefore much pleasure in offering this novelty, being the first step towards obtaining a perfect double flower 25
2020 Zinnia tagetiflora fl. pl. varietates. Of neat and gracious habitus, as fine colored as Z. elegans fl. pl., being pompon-like, double, as Asters and Chrysanthemums, and of particular beauty 25
2021 Zinnia Ghresbreghti; or, Zinnia Haageans Hybrida. A charming acquisition, dwarf in habit, similar to Zinnia Mexicana, of various colors, useful for bedding in groups, borders, &c. 25

GLADIOLUS.

Splendid French and Belgian Hybrids of Gandavensis.

The new hybrid productions of the Gladiolus Gandavensis are, without doubt, the most superb flowering-bulbs in cultivation, producing their magnificent, long, and densely-flowered spikes of bloom, varying from white to rich salmon, and brilliant carmine, to the most intense scarlet or crimson. A single bulb will often give two or three stems of bloom, and a succession of flowers will be produced for two months. These splendid flowering-bulbs are now considered unsurpassable ornaments, and one of the finest features of the flower-garden. Having made large additions to our stock from the most extensive growers in Europe and the United States, we are enabled to offer to our patrons the largest and best-selected collection ever offered in America.

General Treatment. — The bulbs should be planted as soon as the ground is fairly dried in the spring, and all danger of frost is over; planting may be made every two weeks until the middle of June to secure a succession of bloom. Plant the bulbs from two to four inches deep, according to their size: the soil should be enriched with well-decomposed manure, and well pulverized. The Gladiolus show to the best advantage when planted in beds four feet wide, setting the bulbs three-fourths of a foot apart each way. The plants should be well staked, and the bloom will be magnificent. When the frost has killed the leaves, or before, if the leaves, by turning yellow, show the ripening of the bulb, the bulb should be taken up, dried rapidly in full sunlight, the new bulbs separated from the old, and the flowering bulbs (the stocks being cut off about an inch from the crown of the bulb) put up in paper bags, carefully labelled. Should be kept during the winter in a dry, cool cellar, free from frost.

A discount of five per cent from catalogue prices will be made when one dozen varieties are ordered, ten per cent on two dozen varieties, and fifteen per cent on fifty varieties. The whole collection 20 per cent.

Purchasers will please state whether we may substitute, in the event of our being out of the varieties ordered.

Forwarded by mail to any address in the Union, post-paid, at catalogue prices.

NEW VARIETIES FOR 1869.

Offered for the First Time in this Country.

PRICE.

Antonius. Fine spike of large, well-opened, perfect flowers, cherry colored, slightly tinged with orange, blazed with carminate-red; very fine pure white stains; charming little plant $1.00

Argus. Long spike of large, well-opened flowers, glittering fire-red; centre and lower divisions very pure white; admirable, brilliant plant 3.50

Circe. Fine spike of large, well-opened perfect flowers, of a fine rose slightly tinged with lilac, largely blazed with bright carmine; centre well lighted; very fine plant . 1.75

Cornelie. Handsome spike of large light-cherry-colored flowers; centre very transparent, bright-cherry-colored, darkening towards the border 1.75

Fenelon. Tall plant, with long and large spikes of large well-opened flowers of a tender rose tinged with violet and blazed with bright carmine; very fine, vigorous variety 2.50

Homer. Vigorous plant; very long spikes of very large, perfect flowers, of a light amaranth, blazed with very bright purple; magnificent plant (perfection) . . . 4.00

Jenny Lind. Fine long spike of handsome flowers of a tender rose, blazed with bright carminate-cherry color; centre transparent; charming variety 2.00

Mme. Desportes Very vigorous plant; very large and wide spike; flowers very large, well-opened, of a very pure white; the inferior divisions slightly striped with violet; splendid variety 4.00

Mme. Dombrain Small, vigorous plant; very long spike of large, perfect, well-inserted flowers of a carminate violet, blazed with bright purple; well-lighted in the centre; charming little variety 3.50

Mary Stuart. Very vigorous plant; very long spike of large, well-opened, and well-inserted flowers, white, very slightly tinged with rose, and blazed with very bright, carminate, cherry color; first-rate variety (perfection) 4.00

Michel-Ange. Vigorous; long spike of large well-opened flowers; dark crimson, slightly blazed with brownish purple on the superior divisions; centre well lighted; white stains; first-rate variety, as well for its peculiar color, as for the elegant insertion of the flowers on the spike, which makes them resemble Lilies . . . 8.00

Mr. Legouve. Vigorous plant; very long and wide spike; flowers very large, perfect, very bright fire-red; the superior divisions divided by a white line; on the inferior divisions a pure white stain; plant of a grand effect. 4.00

150   AMATEUR CULTIVATOR'S GUIDE

        PRICE.
Picciola. Very handsome, vigorous plant; fine spike; flowers of a fine rose, glazed and blazed with very bright carminate rose; centre well lighted; stains very large, pure white, covering, completely the inferior divisions 2.00
Racine. Very fine, tall plant; very long spike of cherry-colored flowers, tinged with violet; centre white, well-lighted, striped with pure white. 3.50
Romulus. Long spike of pretty large flowers, very brilliant brownish red; large pure white stain; large white lines on the inferior divisions; very showy variety. . . . 1.50
Thomas Methwen. Flowers large, well-shaped, violet tinged with rose; centre very well-lighted, transparent, the extremity of the divisions carminate dark violet; very fine variety 4.00
Van Dyck. Amaranth-red, striped with white; very fine shade; vigorous, medium-sized plant 1.00

GENERAL COLLECTION.

        PRICE.   PRICE.

Anais. Middle-sized flower; good shape, white, slightly tinged with lilac; very large sulphur-white stains, broadly striped with lilac-carmine; very striking plant (*dwarf*) $1.75
Apollon. Large flower of a perfect shape; rosy-lilac, with a large stain of light-rose, finely striped with white in the centre 1.00
Alexander. Flower large, well shaped, very fine bright red 1.00
Amabilis. Bright vermilion, stained with yellow 20
Adonis. Light-cherry, yellow throat, with light-yellow spots 20
Aglae. Rose-colored salmon, beautifully mottled 25
Aristote. Light-rose, with purplish crimson stripes. 25
Achille. Bright-red, striped with white . .75
Archimede. Large, rich, flamed salmon-red, opening carmine 20
Belle Gabrielle. Very fine lilac-rose, slightly marked with bright-rose; perfect form; large flowers 1.00
Berenice. Beautiful rose, striped with red, with purple-carmine colored-spots . .30
Bertha Habourdin. Pure white, with beautiful large carmine stain 75
Brenchleyensis. Deep scarlet; fine . . .20
Bernard de Jussieu. Flower large, wide, perfect ground violet, shaded and tinted with cherry-color and purple'; stains purple on white ground; new and almost indescribable color 3.50
Brilliant. Large flower, good shape; purple-red, very fine color 1.50
Cherubini. Large flower, perfect shape; white ground, largely blazed with carminate-violet 1.50
Calendulaceus. Bright-nankeen 35
Calypso. Rose-striped, blotched with carmine 35
Canari. Light-yellow, striped with rose . .50
Ceres. Pure white, blotched with purplish-rose; large flower 80
Charles Dickens. Beautiful rose, tinted with chamois; blazed and striped with carmine 1.00
Charles Michel. Bright-vermilion, spotted with purplish-violet 40
Chateaubriand. Clear cherry; a magnificent spike 30
Clemence. Satin-like rose, with large bright-carmine stains; very large flower. .35
Comte de Morny. Dark cherry-red, blotched with white, and striped with purple 50

Comtesse de Bresson. Deep blush-pink in centre, shaded with crimson; outside petals veined with white; two lower petals striped with purple . . .25
Couranti fulgens. Bright-crimson; fine. .20
De Candolle. Cherry, flamed with scarlet, and blotched with violet 1.00
Diomade. Large, fine form; white, flamed with carmine, and blotched with dark-violet 1.50
Daphne. Light-cherry, with darker stripes, and stained with bright-carmine .30
Diana. Light-salmon, variegated with rose, and blotched with light-carmine, on white ground. 50
Duc de Malakoff. Orange-red, on yellowish-white ground; fine 80
Dana. Delicate straw-color, with violet spots 60
Doctor Andry. Very bright orange; fine. .25
Don Juan. Vivid blush-pink; petals beautifully mottled with deep crimson, and veined with pure white 20
Edulia. Upper petals white, spotted with violet; lower striped with white . . 1.00
Edith. Large flower; carnation-rose, deeply striped with same 30
Egerie. Orange-rose; petals slightly marked with carmine. 30
Emma. Clear carmine; dwarf 20
Emile. Scarlet, flamed with crimson and white, and spotted scarlet and white . 2.00
Endymion. Rose; beautiful 30
Erato. Delicate rose; with dark stripes and carmine blotches. 50
Eldorado. Fine clear yellow, striped with red 75
Eugene Scribe. Flower very large and wide, perfect, tender-rose, blazed with carminate-red 3.50
Etendard. Flower very large and wide, perfect, white, slightly blazed with lilac or bluish-violet, spike very long . . 3.00
Emilie. White, blazed with rose, with a dark-brown stain 2.00
Flavia. Very bright red, a color little darker than Napoleon III. 1.00
Fulton Vermilion. Velvet; very bright, spotted with purple; magnificent . . 1.25
Fanny Houget. Rosy-flesh color, striped with rosy carmine 20
Florian. Cherry-rose, with large violet spots, the centre petals lined with white .35
Fulgens. Deep rich fiery scarlet 25
Galathee. White, beautifully spotted with carmine 30
Goliath. Light-red, striped and spotted with carmine; large flower 25

TO THE VEGETABLE GARDEN.

Variety	PRICE
Greuze. Cherry-red, blazed with purple; growing very strong; very fine	.80
Hebe. Very tender flesh-color, beautifully striped with fine lake	.35
Helene. White, slightly tinged with lilac, spotted and striped with violet	.35
Hector. Delicate rose, sometimes striped	.20
Henrietta. Large, well-shaped flower, white-tinted and blazed with lilac; very nice *dwarf* plant	1.00
Imperatrice. White, slightly suffused with pink, spotted with bright-carmine	.20
Imperatrice Eugenie. White, flamed with rose, violet in the centre	1.50
Isoline. Blush, spotted with carmine violet	.30
Isabella. Middle-sized flower, very fine spike, pure white, with large, very dark carminate-violet stains	1.50
Jean d'Arc. White, very slightly tinged with rose; striped and stained with purple	.50
Lord Byron. Very brilliant scarlet, stained and ribboned with pure white; very showy plant	1.50
Le Titien. Large flower; perfect shape; disposed in a very showy spike, light-red and very brilliant; very fine plant	1.75
La Favorite. Flower large, rose, blazed with carmine; lower divisions light yellow	1.75
La Fiancee. Flower large, perfect, very pure white, small, bluish-violet stains; very fine variety	3.00
Leonora. Flower large, perfect, cherry-colored red, slightly tinted with orange	1.00
Lord Granville. Straw-color, stained with deep yellow, and striped with red	.50
La Quintinie. Beautiful light-orange	.60
Lady Franklin. Large flower, good shape, white slightly tinged with rose, finely striated with carmine, and very largely blazed with carminate-rose (*dwarf*)	2.00
Louis Van Houtte. Brilliant red, blotched with violet	.20
Le Poussin. Light-red, white ground, very large white blotch on lower petals	.80
Laelia. Peach-pink, stained with lilac	.30
Madame Basseville. Large cherry-colored flower, with purple blotches on a yellowish-white ground, striped with white	.80
Madame de Vatry. Yellowish-white, stained with carmine; very large flower	.75
Madame Binder. Pure white; long carminate-rose stripes on the lower petals	.75
Madame Coudere. Bright-carmine, shaded with fine rose in the throat	.20
Madame Herincq. Yellow white, changing to a dull white, with large marbled veins of lilac	.20
Madame Leseble. Pure white, blotched with rose	.80
Madame Domage. Rose, spotted with amaranth, and striped with violet	1.75
Madame Furtado. Rose, changing to pink, flamed with carmine	2.00
Madame Paillett. Cinnamon, with white stripes and violet spots	.40
Madame Pereire. Pure white, large purple stains, white centre	1.00
Madame Habourdin. Rose, flamed with carmine and white, striped in the centre of each petal	1.50
Madame Vilmorin. (Souchet.) Bright-rose, with white throat shaded with deep-rose, and striped with carmine and white	1.00
Maria Dumortier. White, slightly streaked with rose, violetish-purple stains on a streaked ground	.80
Mars. Beautiful; fine deep scarlet	.30
Marie. Pure white, blotched with dark carmine	.75
Meyerbeer. Very brilliant red, flamed with vermilion, and blotched with amaranth. Superb	2.00
Mazeppa. Orange-rose, blotched with yellow and striped with red	.30
Mons. Blouet. Tender-rose, shaded with carmine; large flower	.20
Mons. Gorgeon. Rose, with salmon-colored tint	.20
Moliere. Flower very large and wide, perfect, cherry-colored red, with very large, pure-white stains	2.00
Mozart. Flower large, very wide, spike spreading, bright rose, slightly tinted with violet, very largely blazed with very dark carmine; very large, pure-white stains; very beautiful plant	3.00
Milton. White slightly tinted with rose, largely blazed with red; large flower, and perfect form	2.00
Napoleon III. Brilliant scarlet, streaked with white	.40
Neptune. Beautiful red, with carmine spots and stripes	.25
Nemesis. Vivid-rose, with white lines and carmine stains on yellow ground	.35
Norma. Middle-sized flower, spike spreading, pure white, very slender, and very slightly blazed with very tender lilac	3.00
Noemi. Flower large, light lilac-rose, spike very long	1.00
Oscar. Flower large, well shaped, very bril'nt, bright cherry-color, stains white	2.50
Osiris. Brilliant cherry-rose; fine	.30
Ophir. Yellow, blotched with purple	.80
Othello. Light red; dwarf, very showy	.20
Oracle. Brilliant cherry-rose; fine	.50
Pallas. Bright rose, with stripes of a darker shade; spots of a violet-carmine on a slight orange-tinted ground	.30
Penelope. White, slightly tinged with pink; lower petals yellow tinted, and striped with carmine	.35
Pegasus. Carnation, flaked with rose; lower petals shaded with maroon	.20
Pellonia. Rose, spotted with crimson	.20
Princesse Marie de Cambridge. Very large and well-opened flower, unexceptionable shape and upright habit; white, with very large light-carmine stains (*extra*)	3.50
Princess Alice. Flower very large and wide, perfect, tender lilac, slightly tinted with rose, very large white stains; new and charming shade; first-rate *dwarf* plant	4.00
Princess Clothilde. Beautiful salmon-rose; very large	1.00
Prince Imperial. Blush-white, blotched with carmine	.40
Premices de Montrouge. Brilliant red; dwarf	.30
Rossini. Flower large, perfect, very long spike, dark amaranth-red, lined and stained with white; very good variety	3.50
Reverend Berkeley. Large flowers, of a good shape, disposed in a large spike; light rose, tinged with violet and carminate striped on white ground	1.50
Reine Victoria. Pure white, stained with violet carmine; very large	1.00
Raphael. Deep and vermilion	.35
Rebecca. White, shaded with lilac	.35
Rembrandt. Very bright deep scarlet	.30
Shakspeare. White, very slightly blazed with carminate, rose, large rosy stain; fine form, large flower	2.00

AMATEUR CULTIVATOR'S GUIDE.

	PRICE.		PRICE.
Sulphureus. Sulphur-yellow	.50	shape; red slightly tinged with light orange color, finely striated with carminate-red on white ground; very brilliant color	2.00
Solfateree. Rich Jonquil-yellow; large	1.00		
Stephenson. Large; fine form; superb spikes, cherry-carmine, lined with white	1.00		
Sir William Hooker. Very large and well-opened flower; perfect shape, light-cherry color, rose-carmine stain on pure white ground; plant of a great effect	2.00	**Triomphe d'Enghein.** Rich-flamed crimson	.20
		Velleda. Soft rose, blotched with lilac	.50
Stolzi. Flower large, well shaped; ground white, slightly tinted with yellow and rose, and blazed with carminate-red.	2.50	**Vesta.** Pure white, with violet-carmine spots on yellow ground	.35
		Vulcain. Very rich velvety scarlet-purple, with violet shades in the centre	.50
Thalia. Flower large, perfect, white, blazed with white striated with carmine; very fine, vigorous plant	1.00	**OTHER SORTS OF GLADIOLUS.**	
Thunberg. Flower very large, perfect, lightly orange-colored cherry-red; stains pure white, very large	1.75	**Gandavensis** (the original variety). Vermillion, shaded with yellow	$0.10
		Ramosus (original variety). Rose and white	.20
Thos. Moore. Large flower, good shape; very fine carminate-rose on white ground, blazed and stained with light carmine	3.00	**Pisittacinus.** Yellow and brown	.10
		Floribundas. White, with rosy stripe along the centre of each petal	.20
Thos. Paxton. Large flower; perfect			

CHOICE MIXED VARIETIES.

We have a fine collection of mixed varieties, saved from seedlings, and others where the names have been lost, which we offer at $2.00 per doz., by mail, postpaid. By the hundred, prices on application.

Gladiolus Lyonii.

Cardinalis habit. Flowers large spreading petals of good form: color pure white, vividly flaked with bright scarlet; very free bloomer, and altogether a most exquisite variety. Spikes of bloom were exhibited at the Rose show at the Massachusetts Horticultural Society last June, attracting great attention; highly recommended for pot culture. Price $1.50 each.

Tigridias.

A genus of Mexican bulbs, grows about one and a half feet high, producing flowers of the most exquisite beauty: the flowers large, about four inches across, of singularly curious shape, and the color of each variety gorgeous, and purely contrasted. No flower can exceed it in beauty. In bloom from July to the first of October. In autumn, take up the bulbs, and keep them in a dry place, away from frost, until the time of planting in the spring.

Conchiflora. Orange and golden-yellow, spotted with black. 12½ cents each; $1.25 per doz.
Pavonia. Riches; scarlet, tinged and spotted with pure yellow. 12½ cents each; $1.25 per doz.
Tigridias by mail, postpaid, at the above prices.

Double Tuberoses.

The Tuberose is one of the most delightfully fragrant and beautiful of summer-flowering bulbs, throwing up small spikes of double white flowers, two to three feet high, which remain in bloom a long period. The bulbs may be planted from February to May. When they are needed very early, they may be planted in the greenhouse or hot-bed in February or March; and, for a succession of flowers, in April and May. In planting, remove the useless, small offsets around the main root, and place a single tuber in a pot four or five inches wide. Use good loam and leaf mould, with good drainage. Start them slowly, upon a temperate heat, in the hot-bed or forcing-pit, cr later in the season in a frame. Water slightly at first; and, when the bulbs begin to grow, increase the quantity. Those started early should be supplied with a good bottom heat till May, when they may be shifted into pots six or seven inches wide. By the first of June, all may be plunged out in a warm border, staking each plant to prevent their being broken by the wind. On the approach of cool weather, in September, those remaining in bloom should be removed to the conservatory or parlor, where they will continue in flower for a long period.
Fine bulbs, $1.50 to $2.00 per dozen; bulbs started in pots in May, $3.00 per dozen.

Vallota.

A splendid bulbous-rooted plant, allied to the Amaryllis. It blooms in August, throwing up its strong stems about one foot high, with from five to eight brilliant, scarlet, lily-like flowers; very ornamental for bedding out in summer, or cultivation in pots and vases.
Purpurea, each $0.75.

Tritoma.

Splendid, half-hardy, evergreen, herbaceous plants, forming large, robust, stemless, leaf-crowns, from the centre of which their tall flower-stems, three to five feet in height, are produced in summer and autumn, in large, dense-flowered terminal racemes of rich pendent, orange-red and scarlet tubulous flowers; each raceme a foot or more in length.
They are admirably adapted for bedding out; and the numerous terminal, flame-colored blossoms form a stately distant or mediate effect. They thrive in any rich light garden-soil. On approach of winter, they should be taken up, and placed in the greenhouse or cellar for replanting out again in spring.

Uvaria glaucescens . . . . $0.50 **Uvaria Rooperi** $1.00
" **grandiflora** . . . . 1.00 " **scrotina** 25

LILIUM AURATUM. (One-half its natural size.)

Lilium Auratum, Golden-Striped Lily. This new and magnificent species of Lily, lately introduced from Japan, is spoken of by Dr. Lindley as follows: "If ever a flower merited the name of 'glorious,' it is this, which stands far above all other Lilies, whether we regard its size, sweetness, or its exquisite arrangement of color. Imagine upon the end of a purple stem, not thicker than a ramrod, and not above two feet high, a saucer-shaped flower at least ten inches in diameter, composed of six spreading, somewhat crisp parts, rolled back at their points, and having an ivory-white skin, thinly strewn with purple points or studs, and oval, or roundish, prominent purple stains. To this add, in the middle of each of the six parts, a broad stripe of light satin-yellow, losing itself gradually in the ivory skin. Place the flower in a situation where side-light is cut off, and no direct light can reach it, except from above, when the stripes acquire the appearance of gentle streamlets of Australian gold, and the reader who has not seen it may form some feeble notion of what it is."

We have the pleasure to inform our friends that we have secured a very fine stock of this beautiful plant, which we shall offer at greatly reduced prices.

Very strong flowering bulbs, ... $1.50 each, . . $12.00 per dozen.
Second size bulbs, ... 1.00 " . . 9.00 " "
Third " " . . . . .75 " . . 6.00 " "

www.ingramcontent.com/pod-product-compliance
Lightning Source LLC
Chambersburg PA
CBHW031442160426
43195CB00010BB/822

John Aspinwall Hodge

Recognition after Death